Can We Laugh at That?

The publisher and the University of California Press Foundation gratefully acknowledge the generous support of the Ahmanson Foundation Endowment Fund in Humanities.

Can We Laugh at That?

COMEDY IN A CONFLICTED AGE

Jacques Berlinerblau

UNIVERSITY OF CALIFORNIA PRESS

University of California Press
Oakland, California

Library of Congress Cataloging-in-Publication Data

Names: Berlinerblau, Jacques author
Title: Can we laugh at that? : comedy in a conflicted age / Jacques Berlinerblau.
Description: Oakland, California : University of California Press, [2026] | Includes bibliographical references and index.
Identifiers: LCCN 2025032316 (print) | LCCN 2025032317 (ebook) | ISBN 9780520403024 cloth | ISBN 9780520403031 paperback | ISBN 9780520403048 ebook
Subjects: LCSH: Comedy—Political aspects—United States | Comedians—United States—Social conditions | Freedom of speech—United States | Social media and society—United States
Classification: LCC PN1929.P65 B47 2026 (print) | LCC PN1929.P65 (ebook)
LC record available at https://lccn.loc.gov/2025032316
LC ebook record available at https://lccn.loc.gov/2025032317

Manufactured in the United States of America

GPSR Authorized Representative: Easy Access System Europe, Mustamäe tee 50, 10621 Tallinn, Estonia, gpsr.requests@easproject.com

35 34 33 32 31 30 29 28 27 26
10 9 8 7 6 5 4 3 2 1

To Laurette Berlinerblau

PUBLISHER'S NOTE

This book contains quotes from comedians and performers that use racial, ethnic, and homophobic slurs and other offensive and derogatory terms. We acknowledge that encountering these may be disturbing or triggering for readers. In consultation with the author, we chose to retain this language to accurately document these jokes in their tellers' own words.

CONTENTS

Acknowledgments ix

Introduction: The Slap to the Consensus 1

PART ONE
COMEDIC CONTROVERSIES IN THE UNITED STATES: ARTISTS GET "CANCELED" BUT THE CONSENSUS HOLDS (FOR THE MOST PART)

1 · Dave Chappelle: Audience Participation 17

2 · Sarah Silverman: Un-canceled, Self-canceled, Un-cancelable 30

3 · Is "Cancellation" Gendered? Kathy Griffin and Shane Gillis 44

PART TWO
COMEDIC CONTROVERSIES IN OTHER LIBERAL DEMOCRACIES: THE CONSENSUS UNDER SIEGE

4 · The Ab/uses of an Audience: Vir Das 61

5 · *Charlie Hebdo*: The Terrorist's Veto 75

6 · Dieudonné M'bala M'bala: Postcolonial Provocateur, Consensus Destroyer 93

PART THREE
NO CONSENSUS: JOKES IN
NON-DEMOCRATIC SPACES

7 · "I'm Just a Satirist": Politainment and Bassem Youssef 113

8 · Premeditated Provocation and Zimbabwe's Pseudo-Consensus 128

9 · *The Interview:* Comedic War Games 142

Conclusion: Troll Your Own 157

Notes 171
Index 237

ACKNOWLEDGMENTS

Aside from thanking everyone on earth who crossed my path over the past five years and left me unchagrined and unmolested, I do wish to express gratitude to a few standout souls.

I started conceiving of this book roughly around the year 2020—a joyous time. Along the way many student research assistants helped me with the preparation for this manuscript and the classes on which it was based, "Comedy, Blasphemy, and International Relations" and "Writing Comedic Fiction." These hard-working and talented young people included Zoe Winburn, Carolina Wesley, Raghuv Chutani, Kriti Edala, Connor Lannaman, Lecholas Njomin, Leo Ledlow, Annie Stegall, Jillian Proshan, and Jonathan Bar-On.

An immense debt of gratitude is owed to the person I referred to as the "Project Manager," Lainey Lyle, who wrangled all of the aforementioned talents, as well as myself.

The good people at University of California Press, including editor Raina Polivka, publicity director Emily Grandstaff, and Sam Warren, have been a delight to work with. Anne Canright performed a lovely line edit. My agent, Michael Mungiello, was always there—as always. All honor to the library staff at Georgetown University and Jeff Popovich.

To my family, friends, and all the dogs I love—you know who you are, no need to thank you by name (there are not many of you).

Finally, I dedicate this book to my mother, who taught me how to read and how to laugh (at myself).

Introduction

THE SLAP TO THE CONSENSUS

HALFWAY THROUGH THE 2022 OSCARS ceremony actor Will Smith administered what in pop culture parlance has become known as "The Slap."[1] Inflicted upon the face of comedian Chris Rock, The Slap was triggered by a mean-spirited quip. Rock had just poked fun at the physical appearance of Smith's wife, Jada Pinkett Smith. Understandably upset, the star of *King Richard* bore down on his target—a target that was stationary, tuxedoed, and exceedingly well lit. In front of a live global audience, Smith delivered not only a fateful blow, but an iconic image that memorializes a disturbing truth about comedy today.

The disturbing truth is that humorists the world over are being assailed in all sorts of ways. They are called out and harassed online. They are boycotted and subjected to "cancellation." They are hounded in the courts through civil suits and federal investigations. They are menaced by vigilantes, religious fundamentalists, paramilitaries, and terrorist cells. Sometimes they are cracked across the brow like Chris Rock. In extreme cases, comedians are forced into exile, kidnapped, imprisoned, or even murdered.[2] For good measure, their comedy clubs may be razed to the ground by irate mobs.[3]

This is a book about "comedic controversies," a type of cultural flashpoint that will no doubt be with us for years to come. I define a comedic controversy as follows: *an ongoing public disagreement triggered by a humorist whose jokes ignite outrage in certain audiences.* These audiences then express their dissatisfaction through: (1) *various forms of media*, (2) *the legal system*, and/or (3) *acts of intimidation and violence*. Hundreds of these incidents occur across the world every year, and their number appears to be mounting. In order to understand comedic controversies, we will carefully examine twelve signal cases that have occurred in eight different countries since 2000. Unlike the Smith-Rock encounter, these episodes feature outraged groups, as opposed to a solitary outraged individual.

Collective or individual outrage directed at a wag is, of course, not a recent development; jesters, political satirists, cartoonists, and assorted acid-tongued wits have enraged certain auditors for centuries. In the 1970s, sitcoms like *All in The Family, Maude*, and *Bridget Loves Bernie* incensed television viewers.[4] In the 1830s, King Louis Philippe of France placed caricaturists on trial for drawing him as a pear. After Voltaire published his satiric masterpiece *Candide* in 1759, police in Paris confiscated all copies.[5]

Comedic controversies, then, are not new. What is new is the internet and its ability to instantly blast gags across the earth. "The capacity for information to be spread on social media," it has been observed, "likely exceeds the capacity of any other medium in history."[6] What is also new—and not unrelated to the internet—is comedy's rise to a position of unprecedented global visibility. Aside from being wildly lucrative for select entertainers and media companies, this art form (which synergizes with digital technology in profitable ways that serious fiction, jazz, and glassblowing do not) can legitimately be said to have conquered culture.[7] Comedy is everywhere. It follows that people everywhere are taking exception to it.

After The Slap, *New York Magazine* released its "Complete Guide to Will Smith Slap Takes."[8] That the compilation appeared mere hours after the altercation testifies to the superpowers of social media. Never before could so many opinions be publicly expressed, disseminated, memed, curated, and re-disseminated so quickly and so far afield; jokes and responses to jokes have suddenly acquired digital wings.

In every comedic controversy we will examine, the internet is an accelerator and force multiplier of discord. Social media's omnipresence is central to the themes we explore in this book. It forces us to rethink old assumptions not only about the art of making jokes, but also about the free speech laws which make that art possible.

THE PRE-DIGITAL LIBERAL FREE SPEECH CONSENSUS

Why *shouldn't* one slap a comedian? Or at the very least, why shouldn't a person, group, or government have the right to censor offensive jokes or punish those who make them? Although the answers may seem obvious to some, they are not obvious to the many aggrieved audiences we will encounter throughout this book.

My own answer to this deceptively complicated question is as follows: In advanced democracies, most of us don't slap comedians because we adhere to what I call the Pre-Digital Liberal Free Speech Consensus. This refers to the ways that we conceptualize, legislate, and often sentimentalize expressive liberty. The Consensus (for short) is not necessarily identical with the law, though a given country's Consensus might overlap with some of its constitutional pronouncements and judicial rulings.

Centuries, perhaps millennia, in the making, The Consensus has had countless architects. Its unwitting authors have ranged from the ancient Greeks and Romans, to medieval Muslim philosophers, to Protestant reformers, to Enlightenment intellectuals, to Victorian thinkers like John Stuart Mill, to First Amendment icons like Lenny Bruce.[9] Their diverse contributions slowly summated across centuries to endow us today with a most majestic insight: *The suppression of human political, intellectual, and artistic expression, either by the government or by citizens, should be avoided to the greatest extent possible.*

The Consensus makes an exacting ethical demand on citizens, not to mention their rulers. It asks all of us to tolerate (with a few exceptions to be noted in what follows) speech that drives us to distraction. This act of civic forbearance has benefits for us all. The French sociologist Émile Durkheim reminded us that while Socrates was indeed a criminal, his "independence of thought . . . was useful not only for humanity but for his country."[10] John Stuart Mill famously affirmed that silencing one person is akin to "silencing mankind."[11] If you mix Durkheim and Mill together you affirm that a state-backed guarantee of robust expressive freedom is a social good and therefore must be accorded to *each* and *every* individual citizen.

Free speech, argues The Consensus, injects novel and fresh ideas into the body politic—ideas that might in fact benefit a government disinclined to hear them. This enables citizens to think for themselves. They can reflect without being unduly influenced by their rulers, bosses, religious leaders, kinfolk, etc. The open exchange of ideas lets them learn what their compatriots think, thereby enriching democracy.

The Consensus, which hit its stride in the United States in the decades after World War II, has many noble virtues. All things considered, it is probably the best framework to think about free speech in large diverse democracies. It is imperfect, yes, but far less imperfect than alternative ways of thinking about—and restricting—expressive freedom.

As will become clear in the coming chapters, The Consensus has legions of critics. At their worst, what they are really saying is "free speech for me, but not for thee."[12] At their best, these critics, be they religious conservatives or left-wing academicians, raise valid concerns about its imperfections. The result is that The Consensus is under siege in the digital era; like secularism, like liberalism, like liberal democracy itself, standard assumptions about free speech are being widely challenged and disrupted.

THE CONSENSUS AND COMEDY

Comedy is a subset of free speech. The Consensus, however, came into existence across the centuries not because of comedy, but because of *blasphemy*. Historically, figures who defended free speech were usually defending the right of someone to say something that insulted someone else's religious sensibilities (and whether the sacrilege was funny or not is neither here nor there). This book focuses on humorous free speech in the twenty-first century. For this reason we need to extrapolate a bit. We need to ask how The Consensus and its lofty precepts can be applied to the specific case of jokes made by professional comedians—which is, I repeat, not precisely what The Consensus was built for.

The Comedic Consensus, I would conjecture, holds that humorists should be allowed to "speak their truth" and "do their thing." The blasphemous or obscene contents of a joke are thus not a valid reason for suppressing humor, as they were in previous centuries when religion monitored all speech acts.[13] In fact, there are precious few justifications for ever stifling comedy.

What types of jokes are beyond the pale? What types of jokes will The Consensus not permit? Such arguments parallel those we see in general free speech law. The American Consensus holds that speech that triggers "imminent lawless action," to quote the Supreme Court of the United States, provides one possible justification for censorship. "Hate speech" and "threats to public order" provide two more. But even there, The Consensus urges maximal restraint when it comes to muzzling "harmless little jokes."[14]

As for those offended by jokes, The Consensus urges them to just relax. After all, no one in a democracy has a right "not to be insulted or offended."[15] If some people don't like what they're hearing, they don't need to listen. Of course, if they did listen, maybe they'd learn something new.

The Consensus therefore holds that censoring a comedic voice, no matter how hair-raisingly obnoxious it may be, is counterproductive and the option of last resort. This approach draws on the so-called counter-speech doctrine. Its author, Justice Louis Brandeis, reasoned that when it comes to hateful, dangerous speech, "the remedy to be applied is more speech, not enforced silence."[16] Reasoning by analogy, I assume that a better way to respond to an offensive joke is not by censoring it, but by making sure more jokes can be cracked.

The Consensus has had defenders in high places. In 2014, President Barack Obama somberly articulated its precepts as he reflected on North Korea's response to the film *The Interview* (see chapter 9). When a group calling itself the Guardians of Peace threatened to attack America in retaliation for the film's mockery of Kim Jong-Un, Obama did not flinch.[17] Instead he delivered a majestic defense of political satire, reminding us "that some people's sensibilities probably need to be offended."[18]

So we don't slap comedians because of a commitment to the civic value of free speech. When an expletive-spewing stand-up can riff on a politician's vaginal discharge or a cleric's death by autoerotic asphyxiation without fear of censorship, The Consensus breathes a sigh of relief. Tyranny is subdued. Liberty is expanded. One's humanity is actualized. Wisdom is imparted. In sum: democracy prospers and comedy plays its part.

THE CONSENSUS: A SUICIDE PACT?

But comedians, as we shall soon see, *are* being slapped, and far worse than that. Those who wish to censor humorous speech are certainly to blame. But in order to understand why comedic controversies are happening with increased frequency, we must take other factors into consideration. Let's start with the internet.

The Pre-Digital Liberal Free Speech Consensus was forged in the nineteenth and twentieth centuries—before the advent of social media. Digital technology, I suggest in what follows, is today so radically changing the free speech status quo that we might need to consider rethinking our arcane laws. Politically extremist forms of comedy help us grasp this insight.

In their excellent study *That's Not Funny: How the Right Makes Comedy Work for Them*, communication scholars Matt Sienkiewicz and Nick Marx demonstrate that in the United States there exists a vast, diverse, and profitable right-wing comedy industry. Its existence has been almost completely overlooked by liberals, who labor under the illusion that comedy is a delivery mechanism exclusively for ideas they support.[19] This is a major conceptual error. Comedy is as neutral as a missile astride the clouds; it can target viewpoints of any political sensibility.

Right-wing comedy comes in many forms and ideological flavors. It could be Greg Gutfeld on Fox fulminating about "woke" colleges. It might be the provocations of Tony Hinchcliffe, the star of the *Kill Tony* podcast who launched a comedic controversy after he referred to Puerto Rico as a "floating island of garbage" during a rally for Donald Trump in 2024.[20]

Moving to the "dank cellar" of what Sienkiewicz and Marx name the "right-wing comedy complex," there's *Murdoch Murdoch*—a web series that espouses a Nazi worldview.[21] The typical episode consists of crude digital cutout animation. Other than the lips of the characters, very little moves. The low-rent aesthetic of the show likely appeals to screenagers unaware (at first) of what they are screening. It also delights those on the Far Right who enjoy *Murdoch Murdoch*'s philosophically tinged anti-Semitic and racist content.[22]

A scene in the episode "Waiting for The Superman" captures the show's brand of humor. A maladroit young male named Skylar attempts, unsuccessfully, to pick up a woman at a Burger King. The woman (a cutout of an Instagram model) ignores the boy's overtures. Her rejection occasions the entrance of one of the heroes of the show, Dr. Murdoch. Adorned in Nazi regalia, SS bolts and all, Dr. Murdoch interjects: "Excuse me, son, I couldn't help but notice you're attempting to lure that vixen over there." Explaining that "today's whore must be dealt with in a different manner," he then whispers instructions into the boy's ear.[23]

The counsel emboldens Skylar, who proceeds to punch the woman in the face. As she sobs on the floor Skylar sneers, "You stupid fucking bitch! You're worthless! That's why your father never loved you!" The cutout image is now of a woman with her nose bloodied and teeth broken. Collecting herself, the victim delivers what must be the punchline: "Listen . . . um, can I give you my number? I know you're kind of an asshole but you're, like, the realest guy I've ever met. That's exactly my type."[24]

Some may label this as not comedy, but misogynistic propaganda. It *is* misogynistic propaganda, yet we cannot disqualify it as comedy simply because it is jarringly offensive. Jarring offensiveness is comedy's stock in trade. Many must find *Murdoch Murdoch* funny, though metrics of the show's popularity are hard to ascertain. As quickly as episodes are posted they are deplatformed because they violate YouTube's "community guidelines." Within hours, they resprout on different accounts like so many mushrooms. It's plausible to estimate that the show's catalog has been viewed millions of times.[25]

Murdoch Murdoch secretes "hate speech" into the body politic. That hate speech—*pace* the counter-speech doctrine—isn't necessarily going to be drowned out by "more speech." In the digital era, incendiary content is the beneficiary of an algorithmic boost. It gets fast-tracked to the screens of those, especially young people, who never would have come across it otherwise. Online, the "good speech" gets overwhelmed by the more viral-friendly "bad speech."

The Consensus is a fundamentally liberal conceit. Fair-minded to a fault, it stands up for the expressive-freedom rights of shows like *Murdoch Murdoch*. The snag is that the fascists who create this content would love nothing more than *to obliterate the liberal order that is presently defending them*. In this regard, The Consensus approximates a suicide pact.

THE DEATH WISH: PORTA DOS FUNDOS

Another reason that The Consensus is coming apart is quite paradoxical. Put bluntly, comedians themselves are part of the problem. They joke so hard, troll so hard, provoke so hard, roast so hard that people—who can access their content with unprecedented ease online—try to censor them.

Take the case of Porta dos Fundos, a Brazilian comedy ensemble with a penchant for blasphemy. Their 18 million subscribers on YouTube clearly enjoy watching the group's short skits in which they singe the country's dominant faith.[26] In their 2013 bit "Oh, meu Deus!," a physician and his assistant make a miraculous discovery while performing a routine gynecological exam. Nestled in the genitals of their patient, they believe, they have glimpsed an image of Jesus Christ. As the woman rests supine in the stirrups, a horde of doctors, nurses, and orderlies come to witness the miracle. Their vaginal vigil stretches through the night as the assorted pilgrims cry, pray, genuflect, and sing while staring at the woman's exposed organs.[27]

Unsurprisingly, in a country where upward of 90 percent of the population are classified as Catholic or Protestant, "Oh, meu Deus!" created an uproar. An even larger ruckus was set off by the group's 2019 Netflix comedy short "A primeira tentação de Cristo" (The First Temptation of Christ), which centered on a gay Jesus and his companion, Orlando.[28]

This heresy prompted one bishop to suggest that Brazilians should cancel their Netflix subscriptions. Marco Feliciano, a Pentecostal pastor and congressman, tweeted, "It's time we took a collective action—churches and all good people—to put an end to this."[29] An extreme far-right group heeded this call and claimed responsibility for a Molotov cocktail attack on Porta dos Fundos's offices on Christmas Eve. A judge soon ordered Netflix to take down the piece, but that was quickly overturned by the Supreme Court, which invoked Brazil's version of The Consensus.[30]

Porta dos Fundos returned fire with a sketch entitled "Jesus hétero." It depicts a young bearded white Jesus who bursts into a church with a firearm concealed under his khaki cargo shorts.[31] The parishioners who were just praying to him a moment prior are stunned by his sudden appearance. They are also stunned by his toxic masculinity.

Jesus comes in hot, placing one of the worshippers in a playful headlock and calling him a "faggot" (*viado*). Frat-boy Jesus then hits on a female worshiper ("I can make a miracle with you. Let's go to my place. You and I"). The Savior's antics are interrupted by the appearance of another Jesus. This Jesus—a Black Jesus—warns that this white Jesus is an impostor, an agent of Satan. As the white Jesus chambers his Glock, the assembled white congregants encourage him to shoot; they're sticking with the Jesus who looks like them.[32]

"Jesus hétero" was released on Christmas Eve 2020, *exactly one year after the Molotov attack of 2019*. Comedians are indomitable. No matter what is thrown at them—including incendiary devices—they will not relent. This is one of the most fascinating patterns I will bring to your attention: the quasi-suicidal refusal of those who make jokes for a living to shut up and back down.

A mini-paradox for those who study comedic controversies is that they are at once funny (because of the jokes—jokes are fun!) and terrifying (because of the consequences of those jokes). Which brings us to the macro-paradox which this book identifies: *Comedy undermines the very Consensus that permits it to thrive.* The Consensus grants humorists broad license to poke, razz, mock, and even humiliate their targets, and comedians gleefully exploit that license. In the process, they so enrage others that they imperil the (beleaguered) Consensus that sustains their comedy.[33]

A SOCIOLOGY OF COMEDY

A comedic controversy begins with a joke. It's an oversimplification to say that the joke's catastrophic aftermath is always a comedian's "fault." The episodes we'll scrutinize have large casts, multiple belligerents, and intricate political antecedents. In addition, these cases are "interactive": the combatants engage and escalate (usually in cyberspace). Instead of focusing on the individual comedian alone, it's better to approach this material sociologically.

The small but growing subfield known as the "sociology of comedy" presently lacks an agreed-upon methodological or theoretical agenda.[34] The few who labor in this area are, apparently, subject to "disparaging sniggers."[35] Years back one wit argued that "among sociologists humor is to be enjoyed only clandestinely, like sex."[36] No one has yet authored the *Prolegomena to the Sociology of Comedy*, and I won't write it here either. Though when that volume is someday published, I hope the ideas in this book will merit inclusion in a footnote or two.

My sociological approach centers on the idea that within comedic controversies *patterned interactions develop between humorists and various audiences.* In most scholarly discussions of comedy, audiences are an afterthought. Instead, researchers concentrate on the comedians—their artistry, their cultural influences, ideological investments, and so forth.

This focus, however, is too narrow for sociologists whose interests extend beyond individuals.[37]

But how does one study an audience? How do we gain insight into people sitting in the dark of a nightclub or staring at their smartphones? The awkward "reaction" shots in filmed comedy specials epitomize this dilemma. The performer on stage "kills" with a banger of a joke. And then—in one of the least visually compelling clichés of the genre—the camera goes "down there": it ventures into the convulsing crowd. We receive a poorly lit, thrawn glimpse of what appears to be a laughing mammal. The mammal, as best we can tell, is happy.

While scholars have displayed ingenuity in trying to learn more about audiences, I am interested in a particular subset: *irate* audiences.[38] Nowadays, these publics can be recognized by the smoldering digital footprint they leave behind. I refer to them as the *actively incensed* or the *coalition of the outraged*.[39]

To understand who they are, let's first identify who they are not. Most people who take umbrage at a joke do so *passively*. They won't really react beyond shaking their heads in disbelief, complaining to a friend, and, most likely, ignoring the offending comedian(s) for the rest of their lives. These passive auditors are of lesser importance to my project.

The coalition of the outraged, by contrast, demonstrates an entirely different response to humorous content that offends them. Its dissatisfaction is made known not through silent withdrawal, but in active, public remonstrance. The responses to Porta dos Fundos—the boycotts, lawsuits, and violence—illustrate this well.

The actively incensed might have preexisted the offensive joke. Think of advocacy groups that monitor anti-Semitism, homophobia, or anti-Asian sentiment. They are sentinels of affront; they scan the horizon for offense, and then some wisecracking comic flashes across their radar. We know the coalition of the outraged by their public attestation of displeasure. Nowadays, the internet is usually where that displeasure is made manifest.

This brings us to the "patterned" part of patterned interactions that develop between humorists and various audiences. Comedic controversies,

I argue, all follow the same general script. The ideal-typical episode starts with a joke that delights some (I'll call them the *coalition of the entertained*) while infuriating the coalition of the outraged.

Crucially, the humorist then recycles the rage of their detractors back into their subsequent comedy. I call this the *meta move* or the *Lenny Bruce Maneuver.* Bruce's tussles with law enforcement over his comedy became part of what he discussed in his subsequent comedy. In fact, he was once arrested after his first set, *only to return a few hours later and make jokes about the experience in his second set!*[40]

Pre-digital Bruce pioneered a phenomenon that is evident in the digital age. A controversy about a comedian's joke thus becomes the basis for their next round of jokes—and more controversy. This results in an acrimonious loop, or what scholars call "a reactionary communication pattern."[41] Comedians who get stuck in this loop, I will contend, are not quite performing comedy anymore. The controversy permeates and alters their art, just as it transforms the behavior of audiences.

The sociology of comedy that follows begins by surveying the somewhat calmer controversies that characterize the United States. Part 1 of this study finds The Consensus to be wobbly in America. Comedians tend to be "canceled" or subjected to an array of what Eve Ng calls "cancel practices."[42] Such was the case with Dave Chappelle (chapter 1), Sarah Silverman (chapter 2), and Kathy Griffin and Shane Gillis (chapter 3). These American comics will help us gain a better sense of the oft-discussed, and problematic, notion of "cancel culture."

In part 2 we move to liberal democracies with their own variants of The Consensus. In India, we'll explore Vir Das's dispute with his government over his allegedly seditious comedy (chapter 4). In Denmark and France we will encounter ghastly violence perpetrated by militant Islamists in response to cartoonists who depicted the Prophet Muhammad (chapter 5). The deliberate attempt of Dieudonné M'Bala M'Bala—an anti-Semitic comic—to undermine The Consensus in France will also be studied (chapter 6). All of these cases invite us to rethink the oft-invoked, and I think oversimplistic, concepts of "punching down" and "punching up."

The conceit that there are comedians who are either stronger or weaker than the people they make jokes about will be critically reexamined.

Part 3 brings us to spaces in which there is no Consensus. In Egypt, the fake news parodist Bassem Youssef made his jokes and was rewarded with exile (chapter 7). In Zimbabwe, brave comedians criticize their government and pay the price, sometimes with physical assaults (chapter 8). We round out our inquiry by looking at North Korea (chapter 9), whose leader, Kim Jong-un, does not abide by any free speech Consensus, be it in his country or any other.

Each chapter probes the volatile and complex triangulation between comedy, the internet, and free speech law. The questions raised do not conduce to easy answers. How has digital technology upended The Consensus? How has social media altered comedy itself? What responsibility does the state have to regulate comedic content and those who threaten it? What is the future of comedic free speech? Perhaps most controversially, I'll ask if comedians may have an obligation to curb their own provocations, to make their jokes more benign in the interests of forestalling chaos.

PART ONE

Comedic Controversies in the United States

ARTISTS GET "CANCELED" BUT THE CONSENSUS HOLDS (FOR THE MOST PART)

ONE

Dave Chappelle

AUDIENCE PARTICIPATION

> [T]hese transgenders . . . these niggahs want me dead. I've gone too far, said too much . . . I'm very worried about it. I'm not even joking. Every time I come out onstage, I be scared. I be looking around the crowd, searching. For knuckles and Adam's apples to see where the threats might be coming from. A niggah came up to me on the street the other day. He said, "Careful, Dave, they after you." I said, "What? One they or many theys?"
>
> DAVE CHAPPELLE
> *The Closer*

WHEN DAVE CHAPPELLE RETIRES, when his body of work is subject to a "retrospective," when his obituary is composed, his running dispute with the LGBTQ community will surely be a key component of his legacy.

Only in recent years has Chappelle come to be known as a homophobic or, in his self-ironizing words, "transphobic comedian."[1] When he started out in the early 1990s, he wasn't recognized as such. Nor was he perceived that way after he walked away from the hugely popular *Chappelle's Show* in 2006 and adopted a less public posture for about a decade.[2] When he made his triumphant return on *Saturday Night Live* in 2016, he still didn't have this reputation, at least not nationally. But soon he began to garner infamy as a comedian who "punched down" on those he derisively labeled "the alphabet people."[3]

The LGBTQ community, for its part, punched back, thus playing the role of what I call "the actively outraged." Although their concerns have been overwhelmingly expressed through peaceful dissent, in one instance a deranged audience member resorted to violence. This occurred during a performance at the Hollywood Bowl in 2022, the perpetrator claiming he was infuriated by Chappelle's anti-LGBTQ jokes.[4] Chappelle recycled the details of the attack into a lengthy bit in a later special, *The Dreamer.* This "meta" reflex, I will show, has now come to characterize much of his comedy, and likely distorts it as well.

The conflict between Chappelle and the LGBTQ community, now about to enter its second decade, has much to teach us about the volatile dynamics of controversial art in the internet age. As I noted in the introduction, comedic controversies are characterized by digitally enhanced "reactionary communication patterns." As the LGBTQ community pushed back more and more on his comedy, Chappelle devoted more and more of his comedy to mocking them.

When all was said and done, the virtuoso stand-up effected what I call a "persona drop." When that occurs, a comedian is not quite performing comedy any more. Their art transforms or mutates into something else, as do the audiences that consume its bitter content.

While Chappelle's comedy changed as a result of his scuffles with the actively outraged, The Consensus held (albeit with some concerning complications) and the comedian was allowed to practice his craft. Alongside Sarah Silverman, Kathy Griffin, and Shane Gillis, three other American comedians covered in this book, Chappelle was subjected to the not necessarily catastrophic consequence of "cancellation." At the conclusion of part 1 I will reflect on what their respective ordeals reveal about the status of comedic free speech in the United States.

THE LOOP: "I CAN'T STOP"

As with many comedians, most of Dave Chappelle's early stand-up (he started performing at fourteen) was never recorded. It is therefore difficult to make accurate, quantifiable statements about how his humor has changed across time. From the available evidence, the best I can conclude is this: throughout his long and storied career, Dave Chappelle always made jokes about sexual minorities. Still, my impression is that the frequency and intensity of this material increased markedly after 2015, as did the frequency and intensity of negative *reactions* to that material. I call this "the loop."

Since 2015, a pattern has emerged that goes like this: Dave Chappelle makes a homophobic or transphobic joke; a group of detractors make clear their displeasure with the joke; Chappelle then "goes meta" by making his detractors' displeasure part of a fresh barrage of homophobic or transphobic jokes. His detractors respond. And on and on it goes.

This loop was first activated after Chappelle emerged from a mild, voluntary public exile around 2015. That year saw the filming of his comeback special, *Deep in the Heart of Texas*. It aired in 2017, and was soon followed by three other Netflix specials featuring Chappelle (*The Age of Spin, Equanimity*, and *The Bird Revelation*).

In all of those performances the comedian spent a good deal of time razzing the LGBTQ community—as in this line, from *The Age of Spin*, about people who transition: "Shit is scary as fuck. If your best friend pitched that to you, you'd be horrified. 'Yo, niggahs, let's go to the hospital and cut our dicks off and make pussies out of them shits.' 'What?! Can't we just get matching jackets or tattoos or something?'"[5]

Fast-forward to 2024—and more of the same:

> To be honest with you, I've been trying to repair my relationship with the transgender community 'cause I don't want them to think that I don't like them. You know how I've been repairing it? I wrote a play. I did. 'Cause I know that gays love plays. It's a very sad play, but it's moving. It's about a Black transgender woman whose pronoun is, sadly, niggah. It's a tear-jerker. At the end of the play she dies of loneliness 'cause white liberals don't know how to speak to her. Sad.[6]

This was not the first time Chappelle displayed an awareness that he was in a "relationship" with LGBTQ people. In the 2019 *Sticks and Stones* he sighed that "the Ts" (his shorthand for transgender people) "hate my fucking guts." Chappelle was weirdly energized by their irritation: "I can't stop telling jokes about these niggahs. I don't want to write these jokes, but I can't stop."[7] Chappelle was describing the "meta" function, a psychological reaction we will encounter frequently in this study. Comedians get so irked by criticisms that they retaliate in their subsequent comedy.

The Closer of 2021 marked a dramatic intensification of the loop. In it, Chappelle spends more than half his seventy-two filmed minutes talking about his dialectical partners. In one segment he recounts a long story about a trans woman, Daphne Dorman, whom he befriended. Dorman defended him on social media against charges of being a transphobe. In return, according to Chappelle, "the trans community dragged that bitch all over Twitter."[8] The abuse, he implies, led Dorman to commit suicide soon thereafter.

Chappelle's account is disputed and seems inaccurate.[9] For our purposes, it's notable that in *The Closer* Chappelle was reflecting on his previous jokes and their emotional fallout. He recounted Dorman's tragedy with the clear intent of demonstrating that he was not a transphobe. But then he went on to make a joke that would certainly strike some as transphobic: "I feel like Daphne lied to me. She always said she identified as a woman. And then one day she goes up to the roof of her building and jumps off and kills herself. Clearly . . . only a man would do some gangster shit like that."[10]

All of this triggered backlash. A few years earlier, in 2016, *The Advocate* was already wondering about Chappelle's "strange resentment of LGBTQ activists." "What is Dave Chappelle's problem with gay people?" asked the *New Republic* in 2017. Commentators suggested that his humor had devastating consequences. "The rhetoric in Chappelle's jokes fortifies the narrative that trans people aren't real and are therefore deceiving cis people," wrote *Buzzfeed*'s Tiq Milan, "and this is almost always the rationale for killing trans people, particularly trans women of color."[11]

The coalition of the outraged wasn't composed only of journalists. Advocacy groups voiced their concerns as well. "Dave Chappelle's brand," read a tweet from GLAAD, "has become synonymous with ridiculing trans people."[12] Private digital citizens also joined the conversation. The following comment on Reddit typifies such reactions: "But he's one note, now. 'Look at me, I'm pressing people's buttons.' Yes you are, Dave, but there's the small matter of it not being funny anymore."[13]

As of today, tearing into the queer community has become Chappelle's shtick, much like the late comedian Jim Gallagher's shtick was smashing melons with a sledgehammer. Chappelle, it seems, cannot stop "beefing" with sexual minorities. Those he mocks, in turn, hurl the rind and pits right back at him. They extend the loop. Then Chappelle extends it more.

BEFORE THE STORM

Chappelle wasn't always enmeshed in comedic controversy. As noted above, it was around 2015 that jokes about sexual minorities became a far more conspicuous component of his performances.

This is not to say that such material was absent in his earlier work. Some scholars detect in Chappelle's more youthful comedy the "performance of a black masculinity that relies upon misogynistic and homophobic rhetoric." Chappelle's thematic interests, as media scholar Novotny Lawrence argues, roughly paralleled those of the hip-hop culture that so deeply influenced him.[14] That is to say, occasionally misogynistic and homophobic material was set within an overarching concern for Black (some might say, Black *male*) suffering.

It's important, then, to understand the comparatively modest presence of homophobic and transphobic humor in Chappelle's earlier work. Most of his material "punched up"—what some define as a process of attacking someone or something more powerful than the person making the joke—at American racism and its attendant absurdities. His breakthrough HBO special *Killin' Them Softly* of 2000 was free of anti-gay material. *For What It's Worth*, from 2004, however, opened by describing San Francisco as "the gayest place on earth." In the same set, Chappelle complained: "Every time white dudes pass out around each other they always do some borderline gay shit."[15]

The rest of the performance, though, had little in the way of homophobic content. When compared with earlier comedians who trafficked boldly in that kind of material (for example, Eddie Murphy, Andrew Dice Clay, Sam Kennison), there was nothing conspicuously homophobic about a Dave Chappelle set.

This brings us to the immensely popular *Chappelle's Show*, which ran from 2003 to 2006. Content analysis of the episodes (at least the ones that are still available for viewing) indicates they are mostly free of material that lampooned sexual minorities, though toward the end of the second season such bits began to creep into the scripted content. There was, for example, a pseudo-*Frontline* exposé about a "Gay America" that featured a gay DMV, gay butchers, gay landscapers, gay KKK, gay boxers, etc. Another episode featured a visual gag about trans prostitutes. Chappelle also starred in a skit featuring a Black president who exclaimed, "That shit is gross!" as he pondered lesbian sex and gay marriage.[16]

Chappelle claims it was around this time that some in the LGBTQ community began to react negatively. In his 2021 special *The Closer* he recalled, "I was doing a nightclub in Oakland sixteen years ago and this is the first time that the trans community ever got mad at me that I knew about."[17] By Chappelle's calculation, that Oakland encounter happened in 2005. There is no record of such an incident in 2005 that I could find, but one did occur in 2010 at Oakland's New Parrish Comedy Club, as related by a spectator who said she argued with Chappelle over anti-queer material and subsequently stormed out.[18]

To complexify matters, let's note that Chappelle's earlier work did not ignore the intersections between racism and homophobia. One of the *Chappelle Show*'s most famous characters demonstrated this awareness. Clayton Bigsby was a blind white supremacist who liberally dropped N-bombs, alongside invectives directed at Jews, Mexicans, Arabs, and homosexuals. Bigsby also happened to be Black.[19] Some scholars argue that with this character Chappelle was "neutralizing" dangerous stereotypes of gay people. That is, by placing homophobic slurs in the mouth of a Klansman (albeit a Black Klansman), Chappelle was, perhaps, recognizing the discrimination the gay community encountered.[20]

How, then, do we properly describe Chappelle's LGBTQ-oriented comedy in the early part of his career, until around 2006? With the aforementioned cautions about his non-recorded materials in mind, I'd argue that although he made derogatory jokes about this community with some regularity, he was better known for engaging with other ideas and themes. Like his hip-hop forebears, Chappelle's slights about women and gay people could be ignored by many because at the time such humor was far less taboo than it is today. Rather, Chappelle was widely admired for the nuance and cleverness of his takes on race and his ability to offer America "a decidedly black sensibility rarely seen in prime-time television comedy."[21]

The general perception was that his politics were fundamentally progressive, his heart was in the right place, and so on. This is no longer the general perception. Why?

"OUTRAGE FUELS VIRALITY"

Dave Chappelle, as we've just seen, was making homophobic jokes in the early aughts. He was just as famous then as he is today. In fact, he was "well on his way to canonization."[22] Chappelle was thriving. In a comedic market far less crowded and atomized than the one we have now, his controversial content triggered no national outcry, no loop.

One explanation is that there is now greater sensitivity to, and less tolerance for, derogatory slurs. Historically marginalized groups are far less hesitant to publicly denounce hateful speech and far better organized to do so.

While all that is true, I would argue that the principal reason for Chappelle's recent notoriety has to do with social media. So let's put aside Chappelle for a moment and ponder the role digital technology plays in comedic controversies.

Homophobic jokes have been a staple of stand-up comedy for decades—and the gay community has made its concerns known for just as long. Take Eddie Murphy. After he lambasted the gay community with slurs and AIDS jokes in his hit special *Delirious* in 1984, a coalition of the outraged emerged and formed a group called "The Eddie Murphy's Disease Foundation," purchasing magazine ads that volunteered to help cure Murphy of his homophobia.[23]

There is, then, nothing new about the actively outraged. What is new is the way the internet radiates and synergizes their discontent. This occurs along three interrelated axes: (1) speed of audience reaction, (2) depth of audience penetration, and (3) increase of audience volatility/engagement. On the speed front, a quip can now move across time and space with unparalleled velocity. "A single tweet with an initial audience of just a few hundred," writes the neuroscientist Molly Crockett, "can quickly reach millions through viral sharing—and outrage fuels virality." The new digital outrage, unlike pre-digital outrage, is not constrained by location or time. It thus bonds together "total strangers living across the globe in different time zones."[24]

The consequences for comedy are major. Once a joke is digitally captured and shared online—a feat unimaginable mere decades back—it can be immediately accessed by anyone in the world with a computer or smartphone.

With the technology in place to rapidly disseminate a joke, the content can almost immediately reach not only the comedian's target audience but *also* those the comedian targeted. This unprecedented capacity has the effect of amassing like-minded individuals who never previously knew one another—and along with it "the potential to amplify moral emotions."[25]

This brings us to the volatility factor. A copious scholarly literature indicates that outrage fuels virality and vice versa. I have yet to see a study of how individual jokes traverse cyberspace (my hunch is that laughing at a group tends to anger and engage people more than simple unhumorous critique does). That said, the influence that offensive or immoral content exerts on listeners has been extensively explored.

This body of work is multifaceted, but for our purposes the key takeaways are as follows. Social media connectivity has a deeply polarizing function. Users may "overperceive moral outrage" when assessing Twitter posts—an error that increases polarization.[26] Those responding to volatile materials—on platforms where reasoned argumentation is rare—may polarize one another. This "creates *reactionary communication patterns*, which amplifies polarization, *creating a vicious cycle* that is hard to break."[27]

We see the pattern at play in Chappelle's *Deep in the Heart of Texas*. During his set he reveals that he had been "attacked online by some gay bloggers and it hurt my feelings." His ensuing comments exemplify a standard Chappelle joke formula which I call "Come Close, Trust me, Take That!" He first tries to lower the temperature by assuring his queer listeners he really likes or respects them. Once in range, he proceeds to insult them anew. The formula is evident as Chappelle insists, "I have no problem with gay people, but I fucking hate bloggers. I'm not saying it because this person was gay, but they was acting like a bitch online." About twenty seconds later Chappelle hits the punchline, which belies his friendly overtures: "I didn't say anything that would allude to gay men not being men. I know you're men. In fact, what could be manlier than fucking another guy in the ass? It's the most gangster shit I've ever heard of in my life."[28]

When comedic bits are blasted into cyberspace they reach various audiences, one of which is bound to be the coalition of the outraged. Their anger and concern exponentially multiply (as might the response from the comedian's defenders). The backlash is likely to land right back in the comedian's social media feed and infiltrate the comedian's psyche. This "reactionary communication pattern" is what I think is transpiring between Chappelle and his detractors, and it is echoed in every case we will encounter in this book.

PERSONA DROP

Social media agitates, accelerates, electrifies, and extends the outrage loops that stretch and circulate between comics and their audiences. All of that crackling negative energy, I argue, *impacts and alters the comedy itself.*

In Chappelle's work this manifests as a "persona drop." That is to say, during his recent performances the comedian sometimes starts talking about himself, *as* himself. He does this as he reflects on his disputes with his LGBTQ critics. He doesn't seem to be "joking." Rather, he's speaking earnestly. He has abandoned his comedic persona.[29]

Persona is an artistic tool, a "self" distinct from an artist's actual self. Part of Dave Chappelle's actual self is being an African American male born in 1973. His childhood was spent between Silver Springs, Maryland, and Yellow Springs, Ohio. He received his high school diploma from the Duke Ellington School of the Arts in Washington, DC. The son of two parents with advanced degrees, he joked he was "the first person in [his] family not to go to college, that had not been a slave."[30]

Part of Dave Chappelle's actual self also consists of what he truly believes about gay people, trans people, ethanol subsidies, what have you. Comedy, however, is not confession. Most comedians are not in the habit of creating art to reveal their innermost, deeply held convictions about social and political issues.

That's where persona comes in. By adopting a persona, comedians are liberated to make observations that they may not necessarily agree with or believe to be true. Persona is a screen, a veil, that grants a comic a moral waiver of sorts. They can utter something truly incendiary and respond (often mostly truthfully) that they were "just kidding."

What is peculiar about stand-up comedy is that the persona is grafted directly onto the artist's actual, corporeal self. The comedian typically uses their real name. They bring their own body to the stage, usually free of masks or makeup that might render them unrecognizable. Using their physical self, mouth, and voice as a platform, they project their persona. Dave Chappelle of flesh and blood adopts a persona on stage. Let's call him "Dave Chappelle" (we use quotes because we must assume he's not identical to the actual Dave Chappelle).

This artist's antagonistic loops with the LGBTQ community, supercharged by internet outrage patterns, have led to persona drops: "Dave Chappelle" recedes into the background, and Dave Chappelle emerges. Since 2017, he's been persona-dropping for large segments of his shows.

"Chappelle" doesn't seem to be "just" joking. In fact, "Chappelle" doesn't appear to be there at all. Rather, Dave Chappelle is now saying something he personally believes to be true. That truth has to do with how sexual minorities are treated compared with racial minorities, particularly Black men.

An example occurs in *Equanimity*, when Chappelle insists he has no issue with transgender people. "My problem," he explains, without any pretense of making a joke, "has always been with the dialogue about transgender people." That dialogue, he maintains, focuses on their feelings. Yet no comparable concern exists in America for the feelings of Black people. Chappelle concludes, "And I cannot shake this awful suspicion that the only reason everybody is talking about transgenders is because white men want to do it."[31]

The reasoning is odd. Surely Chappelle is aware that there are people of color who are gay and trans. But more to our point, the line between joke and personal affirmation has been erased. The real Chappelle is speaking his mind. Dave Chappelle is not a person who dislikes sexual minorities. He only dislikes their position relative to Black people in America.

In *Sticks and Stones*, the same mechanics are evident as Chappelle—not "Chappelle"—points to a double standard. Why was he allowed to say the N-word with impunity on *Chappelle's Show*, but not the F-slur as a derogatory term for gay people? His explanation is less a gag than a statement of what Chappelle views as fact about the entertainment industry: "What I didn't realize at the time . . . is we were breaking an unwritten and unspoken rule of show business. . . . No matter what you do in your artistic expression, you are never, ever, allowed to upset . . . the alphabet people. Those people who took 20 percent of the alphabet for themselves."[32]

Is Chappelle kidding, so to speak? I don't think so. Rather, he has dropped his persona and told us how he truly feels. No longer telling jokes for his entire set, he is toggling between "Chappelle" and Chappelle. And in turn, the controversies that rage around him on social media are reshaping the texture of his art.

STUNTED

Dave Chappelle's ongoing scrimmage with the LGBTQ community has altered both his comedy and his audience. In terms of his comedy, each performance now harks back to the previous performances' controversies. To consume Chappelle's art is to be consumed by the controversies triggered by Chappelle's art![33] When he takes the stage, one now *expects* him to troll his adversaries. In this regard, *The Dreamer* (2024) did not disappoint: "I'm not fucking with those people anymore . . . I ain't saying shit about them. Maybe three or four times tonight, but that's it. Tired of talking about them."[34]

His persona drops have grown more frequent. The shift is changing not only Chappelle, but his friendly audiences as well. Consider Chappelle's 2021 Instagram clip "Stunted" (viewed more than 2 million times). Chappelle—again, as opposed to "Chappelle"—is seated on stage, talking to an adoring crowd. He's imbibing what appears to be an alcoholic beverage, which may account for the lack of coherence that characterizes his forthcoming remarks. He's not really trying to make jokes, which is fortuitous because his audience seems more interested in cheering than laughing.[35]

Their man is railing about the transgender employees of Netflix, the ones who earlier that year protested *The Closer*.[36] But he's not mad at them. This whole controversy is really about "corporate interests." He assures his fans that even though "the media" has framed this as "me versus that community," they should "not blame the LBGTQ community for any of this shit. This has nothing to do with them." In fact, they have been "nothing but loving and supporting."[37]

A few minutes later, and in the spirit of love and support, he offers to meet with the transgender community. One of his conditions is that they "must admit that Hannah Gadsby is not funny."[38] The "Come close, Trust me, Take that!" formula has struck again.

Sipping his drink, the legendary comedian mentions a movie he will soon release, about himself. The film's title (interestingly, given our discussion of persona) is *Dave Chappelle: Live in Real Life*.[39] Getting this project off the ground has been hard, he laments. No movie studio, no festival, "will touch this film." He gives a shout-out to Ted Sarandos, the CEO of Netflix: "He's the only one who didn't cancel me yet." The crowd roars.[40]

He promises to make his film available in ten American cities, so that his fans "can see what they're trying to obstruct you from seeing." Chappelle protests that his voice has been excluded. Suddenly he screams out, "Am I canceled or not?"[41]

His supporters shout back in the negative. Dave exits to raucous cheers. His fans are stoked. His fans are standing up. They are standing *with* Chappelle, in solidarity with Chappelle. They look and sound both happy and angry. But they don't sound like an audience consuming comedy. The gathering has assumed the air of a political rally. Maybe that's because Chappelle has been delivering more applause lines than "Chappelle" has been delivering punchlines.

The audience participates joyously. Are they even aware that in doing so they are protesting another audience, one whose engagement has left its own, quite different mark on Dave Chappelle and his comedy?

TWO

Sarah Silverman

UN-CANCELED, SELF-CANCELED, UN-CANCELABLE

I make rape jokes, but I certainly don't approve of rape.

SARAH SILVERMAN
The Bedwetter: Stories of Courage, Redemption, and Pee

Can stereotypes be mocked by being re-invoked?

HELEN DAVIES AND SARAH ILOTT
"Mocking the Weak?"

LIKE DAVE CHAPPELLE, SARAH SILVERMAN is an accomplished, famous, and highly respected comedian. Like Dave Chappelle too, she has made jokes that gravely offend some who hear them. Unlike Dave Chappelle, she has intensely tangled not with one, but with numerous constituencies. These constituencies are often located on completely different sides of the political spectrum, lending a "bi-partisan" air to her many comedic controversies.

In spite of three decades of altercations, Silverman has managed not only to survive, but to thrive. Through it all she has offered her large fan base many comedic products to consume, ranging from three seasons of TV's *The Sarah Silverman Program* (2007–2010), to her 2010 memoir *The Bedwetter: Stories of Courage, Redemption and Pee* (and the 2022 off-Broadway show based on it), to comedy specials for Netflix and HBO, to her intensely meta TV series *I Love You, America* (2017–2019), to her podcast (launched in 2020), and to assorted gigs guest-hosting late night television shows.

The ideological blast-radius of Silverman's art is wide. This comedian incenses groups as diverse as conservative Christian fundamentalists, gays, feminists, Blacks, Latinos, and Asian Americans, among others. The diversity of her detractors presents us with an opportunity to reflect on the peculiar dynamics of "cancellation." For if "cancel culture" actually exists, how does Silverman continue to flourish? Maybe the phenomenon doesn't really exist. Or maybe it exists and conforms to a logic that has yet to be understood.

Silverman, as we shall see, has *self*-canceled some of her most incendiary content—an act that makes us rethink how "cancel culture" operates. It will also let us continue our reflections on comedic personae, and especially the importance, when necessary, of abandoning a persona and, unlike Chappelle, apologizing sincerely.

THE OUTRAGES TO THE RIGHT

Sarah Silverman often trains her formidable powers of derision on two overlapping groups: Republicans and religious conservatives.[1] Her jokes at their expense are lacerating and, as we shall see, easily reconciled with her personal political convictions.

In her 2007 special *Jesus Is Magic*, Silverman belted out a version of "Amazing Grace."[2] Perhaps "'twas grace that taught" her heart to fear absolutely nothing, for the comedian performed the hymn while positioning microphones near her various orifices. She was undaunted by whatever "dangers, toil, and snares" might prevent an entertainer from rendering a beloved Christian song via her reproductive and excretory organs.

Her ribaldry was also on display in the 2017 special *A Speck of Dust*. There, she performed a bit so egregious it inspires a certain awe. After a flurry of crowd work, she trawled her audience for a male volunteer—"any guys here that believe in God?"—to come to the stage. Once he arrived, she asked him in a tone of earnestness: "So, would you let God come in your mouth?"[3] She followed up by suggesting that if Abraham was willing to sacrifice his firstborn son, Isaac, then surely he would have obliged the Creator's demand for oral pleasure.

In a recent special, *Someone You Love* (2023), she wondered why anti-abortion protesters place gargantuan, anatomically incorrect images of fetuses on their posters. A blastocyst, she notes, is smaller than a pea. "If fetuses were poster-sized," Silverman reasons, "those same people would probably hunt them."[4]

These assaults on the right are not limited to conservative Christianity. One thinks of her 2012 "indecent proposal" to the late billionaire Sheldon Adelson, a major Republican donor. She implored the ultraconservative casino magnate to stop bankrolling the presidential campaign of Mitt Romney. In return, Silverman, an Obama supporter, promised to "scissor you [i.e., Adelson], wearing a bikini bottom, through to fruition."[5]

In the previous presidential election cycle, mindful of a slow, decades-long drift of traditionally Democratic Jewish voters toward the Republican party, Silverman organized "The Great Schlep."[6] This was an endeavor to get liberal Jews to visit their conservative-leaning grandparents in Florida. Once they had made the southward trek to bubbie and zadie's condo in Boca, their task was to convince them to vote blue.

Spewing comic venom upon the right is something that, ideologically speaking, comes naturally to liberal Sarah Silverman. Her act offends conservative Christians—a fact she corroborates in *The Bedwetter* by sharing hate mail received from irate believers.[7] Death threats are not unknown to her. In 2019, on Twitter, she quoted comments made by a Jacksonville pastor: "Have you heard of this comedian, Sarah Silverman? . . . She brags about [killing Jesus]! . . . She is a witch. She is a jezebel . . . I pray that God would give her an untimely death, and it would be evident that it's at the hand of God."[8] In summation, Silverman tweeted: "If I get murdered, start here."[9]

Her anti-Christian and anti-Republican humor, obviously, is not likely to alienate her core audience. Why would liberals, progressives, minorities, LGBTQ folks, religious moderates, and nonbelievers take issue with jokes targeting right-wingers who invalidate their existence? But what distinguishes Silverman is that she doesn't restrict her "kill zone" to those with whom she politically disagrees.

OUTRAGES TO THE LEFT

The critic Paul Lewis has spoken of Silverman's "anti-PC instinct for mocking minority groups."[10] One can glimpse this instinct in her infamous "rape jokes," her asides on the odors of Mexicans, her bit about "Dr. Martin Loser King," her copious references to "dykes" and "faggots"—and we're just getting started.[11]

Silverman has shown no reluctance to comically assail the enemies of her ideological enemies. This means that at times her targets are similar to those of the white Christian conservatives she routinely lambastes. On stage she might even wield the same slurs that they weaponize. This has resulted in fairly substantial and far-reaching comic controversies. The controversies, I will argue, result from the ways in which she uses her persona—ways that confuse some of her audience.

During an appearance on NBC's *Late Night with Conan O'Brien* in July 2001, Silverman expounded on her unique strategy for avoiding jury duty.[12] While munching on grapefruit wedges (provided courtesy of guests Penn and Teller), she sighed that the only fun part of jury duty is "the doody." Getting into her groove, she then pondered various plans for avoiding selection.

A friend had counseled her to write something really inappropriate on her questionnaire for the judge—something like "I hate chinks." Fearful that the court might think she was racist, Silverman eventually settled on the opposite: "I love chinks." "And who doesn't?" she asked with a smile. The audience ate it up.

The president of the Media Action Network for Asian Americans, Guy Aoki, did not eat it up. He demanded an apology from the edgy young comedian the next day.[13] Years later, Silverman related that she was essentially canceled by NBC following the controversy. (The show

Fear Factor didn't cast her. This upset her, even though she never wanted to be on the show in the first place.)[14]

Looking back on the whole episode, Silverman would reflect that "there is nothing more pointless, and nothing less funny, than defending your own material."[15] She learned this lesson on Bill Maher's *Politically Incorrect*, where she, Aoki, and other guests debated the use of slurs in comedy. The segment was tense and unpleasant. It made the white comedians who participated appear thoughtless and entitled, rather than the free speech activists they insisted they were. Maher affirmed his universal right to use the N-word. David Spade remained mostly quiet until he chimed in about his dislike of Black comics making jokes about white people.[16]

In his comments, Aoki drew a connection between racial epithets and the real acts of violence directed against minority communities. Silverman categorically refused to accept that the two might be linked. She ended the debate with an unfortunate joke: "There are only two Asian people I know that I don't like. One is you [Aoki] and the other is my friend Steve who actually went pee-pee in my coke."[17]

A few years later, in 2005, Silverman revisited the controversy: "What kind of world do we live in where a totally cute white girl can't say chink on network television?"[18] Aoki, though, got the last, bittersweet laugh during a completely different comedic controversy. In 2017 he reflected on that encounter with Silverman after a chastened Maher finally apologized for using the N-word.[19]

THE DEMEANING DITZ

Silverman viewed the controversy as a misunderstanding on the part of Aoki and his media watchdog group. What they failed to comprehend, she argued, were the complexities of the technique she uses to perform her art. This technique, she averred, was deployed in the name of anti-racism.

It involves toggling between her *person* and her *persona*, or between Sarah Silverman and "Sarah Silverman." Born in 1970, the Sarah Silverman of flesh and blood grew up in New Hampshire. She is a comedian. She loves dogs, smokes substantial quantities of marijuana, freely discusses her fondness for pornography, breathes air in Los Angeles, and so on.

Silverman's *persona* is a character named "Sarah Silverman" who inhabits Sarah Silverman's body during performances.[20] The views she expresses may or may not be shared by the real person named Sarah Silverman. Person and persona overlap in some Venn Diagram–y sort of space, but they are not identical. Persona requires an understanding from a comedian's audience that the comedian's jokes are, in fact, jokes, and that these jokes are separate from what the comedian may actually believe.

One of Silverman's core personae is what I call "The Demeaning Ditz."[21] This character is a self-absorbed, clueless racist. Beaming a thousand-watt smile as she offends, she is too dumb to understand the inherent stupidity of her words and the anger they foment. Silverman describes her as "a persona at once ignorant and arrogant." Playing this character allowed her "to say what I didn't mean, even preach the opposite of what I believed."[22] All of this is done, of course, with the best of intentions, to highlight problems the real Sarah Silverman sees. The comedian's intent is to expose prejudicial attitudes and behaviors.

This, needless to say, is a morally complicated artistic operation under the best of circumstances. The troubles begin when audiences either cannot, or refuse to, distinguish person from persona, Silverman from "Silverman."

A week after her appearance on *Late Night*, Silverman tried to explain the "I love chinks" punchline to Aoki in an email: "The joke is satirical," she wrote "and the intended point of view is to underline the ignorance people demonstrate when they employ racial epithets."[23] Silverman believes that she was right there with Aoki and other Asian Americans; her intent was to shine a light on irrational hatred. The Demeaning Ditz, then, is a comedic false flag—a tool meant to educate us about racism. Aoki only heard a racial slur.

There are, of course, a few problems with the way she flits between person and persona. For starters, it's confusing. When Silverman mauls targets on the right, person and persona are essentially two perfectly overlapping circles. When she attacks targets on the left (often in the same set), person and persona are pried apart and there is no overlap whatsoever.

One critic referred to Silverman's act as "meta-bigotry," a phrase that nicely captures the complexity of this operation in which a comic self-consciously, winkingly *pretends* to be a mean-spirited, hateful individual.[24] The person is an anti-racist. The persona is a racist. The latter sits atop the former's lap like a hateful ventriloquist dummy. This can induce cognitive whiplash in audiences. It also accounts for an oft-made criticism of Silverman's art: audiences can't tell if "she's exploiting stereotypes or puncturing them."[25] As communications scholar Lacy Lowrey and her colleagues observe, audiences are sometimes unable to identify the manipulation Silverman is performing. When that happens, Silverman inadvertently "risks perpetuating hateful rhetoric."[26]

Let's also recall that some—likely most—audience members might simply not care about the subtle distinction between person and persona. They don't read comedy on a rarefied analytical level. They are not impressed by the craft involved in using screens and masks. They just love to laugh. The slurs, as voiced by The Ditz, give them pleasure. At what point is the comic responsible for the consequences of their audiences' laughter?

Here we encounter a major and underappreciated problem with a racially insensitive persona deployed by an anti-racist artist. It's one thing to use your persona to joke about a minority group in a small comedy club like Yuck Yucks in Fort Wayne, Indiana. It's another thing entirely to make similar jokes in 2001 before a national television audience. And it's exponentially more dangerous to do so today, on a streaming platform in the digital era. Cross-pollinate a racist persona with the immense, unprecedented reach of social media, and complications *will* ensue.

In 2001, and even more so in 2025, an aspersion made in character by a famous comedian about a minority group will be heard by multitudes. Among those multitudes will be submultitudes who harbor irrational hatred toward said minority group. They care less about the joke and its mechanics than about the cruel sentiment it conveys, one that they espouse. These submultitudes, as we are about to see, will likely not know or care that Silverman "preach[es] the opposite of what" she believes.[27]

THE N-WORD AND BLACKFACE

Read charitably, Silverman's Ditz does raise interesting points about culture, politics, and comedy itself. Stimulating thought in her audience is likely what she always aspires to. Her success rate, however, is uneven, and that's because the entire operation she performs is complicated and risky.

Consider the musical number "German Cars," which appeared in the 2005 special *Jesus Is Magic*. The song features Silverman in full 1960s regalia: Pucci dress, white go-go boots, and mod-coiff à la vintage Priscilla Presley. As she walks through a Hollywood studio lot, she strums her guitar, singing about her love for an unknown person ("I love you more than bears love honey, I love you more than Jews love money . . . I love you more than Asians are good at math"). The melody continues with pokes at Blacks, Puerto Ricans, gays (whom she calls "faggots"), and lesbians.[28]

The song then shifts to a completely different problem—an incoherent shift rendered explicable only by footage of the comedian taking a "monster bong hit." Silverman suddenly croons about her unease at Jews driving German cars. She reasons that a Jew driving a Mercedes is like "Patti Hearst siding with her kidnappers" or "South African miners killing diamond-bearing gangster rappers." Maybe, Silverman sings as she wanders across the set, Jews' love of German engineering is "like when Black guys call each other niggers."[29]

At this point the audience (and Silverman) realize she has belted out this racial slur, "hard r" and all, in front of two Black men whom she did not notice standing there. The music stops. The men glare at her in silence, contemplating the insult. Suddenly they start to laugh, leading a relieved Silverman—who a few seconds earlier had looked incredibly uncomfortable and quite dumb—to join in their laughter. They get the joke! The laughter bonds the three of them, as laughter often does.

The laughter bonds the three of them *until* the men suddenly retract their smiles. Now they stare at Silverman with a combination of hurt, anger, and contempt. Silverman tries to recapture the moment and laughs again, but the men will not join her. Left hanging, laughing alone at her own joke that no one finds funny, Silverman turns to the screen, smiles her blinding smile, and ends her song with the outro "CHA-CHA-CHA!"[30]

The scene is offensive, but it does make a point. First, Silverman, who has spent the song (and her career) unloading cruelly on all sorts of identity groups, must reckon with the incontrovertible fact that her jokes are heard by people who have every reason not to appreciate them or to understand why she is making them. Second, Silverman subtly relinquishes interpretive control of the scene; the two offended men force the audience to think not of Sarah Silverman's joke, but of how her joke demeans others. Finally, she concedes that there is no comfortable resolution to the dilemma that her jokes raise. This is evidenced by her self-consciously shallow CHA-CHA-CHA to break the tension created by the silence.[31]

The Ditz persona got Silverman into even greater trouble a few years later. If you wish to watch season 2, episode 3 of *The Sarah Silverman Program*, you're out of luck. That's because it has been scrubbed from the internet. It can no longer be downloaded from the digital archives of *Comedy Central* (where it initially aired in 2007) or on any streaming service or website. All that remains is online snippets of an outrageous skit in which Silverman appears in blackface. The aforementioned submultitudes have taken note: screengrabs of this shocking sketch tend to appear in the social media posts of hard right-wing activists performing "what about" mode (as in, "*My* last tweet was racist? What about the time liberal Sarah Silverman wore blackface?").

It is not clear to me when "Face Wars," as the episode was called, was removed from circulation. The impossibility of screening it, however, helps us to identify a crucial distinction for the study of "cancellation." When contemplating the suppression of art, we must be cognizant of *who* is doing the suppressing. For it appears that executives over at Comedy Central (and maybe even Team Silverman) didn't want this material to circulate and proceeded to make it unavailable. Silverman was coy on the subject, remarking that the episode cannot be seen because of "the Jews."[32]

In this instance, no coalition of the incensed suppressed "Face Wars." The episode was censored not because of an uproar in the African American community and beyond, but because those who created it were concerned about the uproar it *might* create. It was, in other words, an act of *preemptive* self-cancellation, and one likely made with considerations of the artist's commercial longevity in mind.

Artistic censorship, I will argue later, may in some extreme cases be legitimate and necessary. But there is always a downside. The downside here may be the loss of an intriguing set of questions raised by the art itself. In a discussion with podcaster Kevin Hart, Silverman argued the piece was "racist by design."[33] And let there be no doubt, it was extremely racist. Yes, Silverman donned blackface. Yes, she unspooled lines like "I look like the beautiful Queen Latifah." Yes, after being escorted out of an African American church she sighed, "Forsaken by my own people! This is literally my darkest hour."[34]

Everyone remembers the sketch for Silverman's descent into minstrelsy, but that is only half the story. People forget that "Face Wars" also featured a Black actor (Alex Désert) whose storyline paralleled Silverman's. The two characters had made a bet as to who had a more difficult time of it, Blacks or Jews. This meant that Désert was schmaltzed up in "Jewface."[35]

The visual codes surrounding minstrel displays have no exact anti-Semitic parallel. There is no comparable history of gentiles dressing up as Jews in a deliberate effort to mock and humiliate them. That said, the show sure did its level best to innovate in such a space. Silverman describes the episode thus: "I'm in like the most racist blackface and he's wearing paius and a yamacha and a big fake Jewish nose and he's wearing a T-shirt that says 'I Love Money.'"[36]

It's the parallel between the Black and Jewish characters that I find intriguing. Whether the creators of "Face Wars" knew it or not (and I think they knew it), there is a long history of African American and Jewish American conflicts and collaborations. I wonder if the bit was trying to dialogue about this very complicated relationship, one that has resulted in work as serious and varied as Chester Himes's *Lonely Crusade* (1947) and Bernard Malamud's "Angel Levine" (1955).[37] Moreover, the skit is abundantly aware of "Jewish complicity in ... discrimination" against Blacks, as English professor David Gillota points out.[38] The comedy may be offensive, but it's not unthoughtful.

All of this reminds us of a crucial difference between the cancellation of a work of art and the cancellation of an artist. "Face Wars" can no longer be seen. Silverman, though, is thriving. This is what we must try to explain.

APOLOGIES AND PERSONA SHIFTS

Many high-profile male comedians (Dave Chappelle, Chris Rock, Jerry Seinfeld, among others) allege that "cancel culture" is having a detrimental effect on their ability to practice their craft. They complain about prudish audiences, woke closed-mindedness, pearl-clutching, and so forth. Silverman herself has occasionally voiced similar concerns. Reflecting on the left, she once opined: "It's almost like there's a mutated McCarthy era, where any comic better watch anything they say."[39] In a comment to podcaster Bill Simmons she sighed, "I see it on the left, like, this cancel culture that, I call it 'righteousness porn' . . . I see it as a perversion really, you know what I mean . . . it's really, you know, it's um, 'Look how righteous I am.'"[40]

These comics see "cancel culture" as something real and dangerous. Others, however, argue that the concept is either nonexistent or, at best, drastically overhyped. These critics reason that what goes by the name of "wokeness" or "cancellation" is simply audiences doing what audiences have been doing since time immemorial. Namely, shunning artists who offend them.[41]

Wanda Sykes, whose politics are decidedly progressive, made this very claim on Kevin Hart's podcast, when she pushed back at his somewhat leading line of questioning. Sykes asserted, "The idea of cancel culture, it's made up . . . it's always been around, it's always existed. . . . Somebody will say something, or somebody will do something, and then the audience has a right to say whether they like it or not. And that's it."[42]

An adjacent perspective maintains that cancellation's effects are wildly exaggerated. As Osita Nwanevu argued in a 2019 piece "The 'Cancel Culture' Con," the male complainants cited above (among others) continue to perform and post impressive earnings.[43] I'd add that for artists who are *already well established*, the financial effects of being canceled, though tangible, are rarely disastrous. Fame and wealth endow a cultural figure with staying power—a certain resilience and momentum. Leading artists, we might surmise, are "too big to fail." The ordeal of cancellation, however, can make them less big.

A case in point is Louis C. K., who, arguably, was an even bigger comedic star than Silverman. Bigger, that is, until his career imploded in the wake of accusations, which he confirmed, of sexual misconduct. There is no doubt that C. K. was diminished commercially as a result of his #MeToo controversy. Then again, he has made a perfectly fine living and even won critical acclaim in the aftermath of his "cancellation."[44]

In 2022, the controversial artist won a Grammy for his comedy album *Sincerely, Louis C. K.* During his comeback tour the previous year numerous performances were sold out.[45] I'd posit that when an artist is "canceled," they do lose part of their audience. But they will also attract a new public by dint of the attention they received for their transgression.

C. K.'s reputation took a hit. He has clearly suffered some loss of professional stature, platform availability, and income. It is up to others to figure out if those losses were warranted or commensurate with his misdeeds. But the fact remains that he can ply his trade. He remains a profitable artist. So perhaps Silverman, like C. K., has achieved a level of success that assures she will *always* be a viable commercial performer. Unlike C. K., her cancellable offenses have not resulted in a financial loss or a lower profile than she previously had—and now I'll offer an explanation as to why that is.

Some argue that cancellation is real, and others that it is illusory. If it is real, I'd suggest that Silverman's career demonstrates that the condition of cancellation might be reversible or "treatable." An artist can "uncancel" herself. How? By offering an apology. An apology is always good, as is a course correction in the form of a persona reset.

Over the past decade, Silverman has become a contrition machine. In 2021, she expressed remorse for something she'd said fourteen years prior. In 2007 at the MTV Movie Awards, Silverman famously razzed Paris Hilton about her upcoming jail sentence. The prison guards, she suggested, might paint the bars of her cell to look like penises, to make Hilton more comfortable. The audience loved it—especially the punchline: "I just worry she's gonna break her teeth on those things." A notably shaken Hilton was present at the performance.[46]

In 2021 Silverman was repentant: "Here I am, 14 years later, telling you, Paris, that I am really sorry. I was then, and I am much more completely, and with far more understanding, I think, now." She continued: "I can't imagine what you were going through at that time. My understanding of humanity through the lens of my work as a comedian had not yet merged. I'm sorry I hurt you. Comedy, you know, is not evergreen. We can't change the past. What's crucial is that we change with the times."[47]

She has expressed remorse not only toward individuals like Hilton (and Britney Spears), but toward entire classes of people whom she has offended. In 2010 she tweeted a homophobic slur: "I don't mean this in a hateful way but the new bachelorette's a faggot." Eight years later she intoned: "All I can do is learn from it, be changed forever by it, and do what I can to make it right going forward."[48]

A similar overture was made toward rape victims. On her *Jesus Is Magic* special in 2005 she sighed: "I was raped by a doctor. Which is, you know, so bittersweet for a Jewish girl." Looking back on that gag she lamented: "Comedy is not evergreen! There are jokes I made 15 years ago that I would absolutely not make today, because I am less ignorant than I was. I know more now than I did. I change with new information."[49]

The blackface episode discussed above has elicited a slew of apologies. She dredged up the incident in 2017 on her *I Love You, America* TV show, inviting her friend Don Cheadle to explain to her why it was wrong.[50] On her own podcast, as well as those of Kevin Hart and Bill Simmons, she revisited the incident at length.[51] In 2018 she told *GQ*, "I don't stand by the blackface sketch. I'm horrified by it, and I can't erase it. I can only be changed by it and move on. . . . That was such liberal-bubble stuff, where I actually thought it was dealing with racism by using racism. I don't get joy in that anymore. It makes me feel yucky."[52]

One might counter that Silverman's apologies are so frequent as to verge on insincere. Perhaps, but her contrition does seem to correlate with change, even evolution, in her personae. The Demeaning Ditz of yore has been retired, replaced by a much more enlightened, thoughtful "Sarah Silverman." *I Love You, America*, for example, was a series that invested in listening to and building bridges with Red State residents whom Silverman otherwise loved to mock.

Her podcast evinces a similar evolution. The comic spends a significant part of each episode listening to voicemails from her fans. Many of them speak about painful or traumatic experiences in their lives. She listens carefully, expresses empathy, suggests helpful courses of action. Silverman's art has taken a therapeutic turn.

The disappearance of the old anti-PC persona is evidenced in her recent stand-up. My reading of her 2023 Max special *Someone You Love* identified such a shift.[53] Her targets were no longer Asians, Blacks, gays, Mexicans, Puerto Ricans, what have you. Instead she trained her fire on (1) right-wing Christians, (2) those who wish to annihilate Jews, and (3) Jews. While Silverman continued to make fun of her own group, the Ditz and the pain she caused to other minorities seem far behind her. She might be un-canceled, or maybe she's un-cancellable. Whatever the case, Silverman's longevity, despite her provocations, suggests that simplistic notions of cancel culture need to be abandoned.

THREE

Is "Cancellation" Gendered?

KATHY GRIFFIN AND SHANE GILLIS

> Looks like @KathyGriffin, the woman whose fingers got so worn out from trying to satisfy herself that they've fallen off, has me blocked on X so I can't reply to her tweets.
>
> I wonder when the last time Kathy actually felt the touch of a man she wasn't paying for was.
>
> I've never seen such a miserable twat in my life.
>
> JOEY MANNARINO on X (formerly Twitter)

> We recently had this big kerfuffle—this condemnation of Kathy Griffin—for the picture she had of herself holding a head of Trump like a play on Perseus holding the head of Medusa . . . They were selling T-shirts and mugs at the Republican [National] Convention with Trump holding my head. Nobody said a word. Not a word!
>
> HILLARY CLINTON
> *With Her* podcast, 2017

AT FIRST GLANCE, THE COMEDIC controversies of Kathy Griffin and Shane Gillis appear quite similar. Both were embroiled in career-threatening disputes during the first presidency of Donald Trump. Both were immediately deplatformed and excoriated on social media. Both uneasily, and perhaps disingenuously, issued expressions of remorse. Both clawed their way out of the abyss and returned to practice their craft.

The broad contours of their very public trials, undoubtedly, share much in common. Yet the deeper we look, the more evident it becomes that there are substantive differences in their respective ordeals. Some of those differences are of the individual sort. By that, I mean their unique styles as comedians, the content that got them into trouble, and how they charted a path forward while their careers were aflame.

Then there are structural differences, in particular the gender of each artist and the way in which they addressed what I call "the actively outraged." This interaction may explain why Kathy Griffin and Shane Gillis endured strikingly different outcomes after they made jokes that shocked and infuriated their compatriots.

My thesis is that a particular type of sociological explosion is observable when female artists, such as Kathy Griffin, outrage a cultural *majority*. That explosion shakes out differently when a male artist, like Shane Gillis, outrages *minority* groups.

So let's round out our survey of American comedic controversies by comparing two comics who "joked" their way to oblivion and back. One, a middle-aged white woman who "punched up"; the other, a white man half her age who "punched down." From there we will reflect on the state of The Consensus in the United States.

KATHY BEING KATHY? GENRE SPRAWL

On May 30, 2017, comedian Kathy Griffin tweeted a photo of herself holding the bloody, severed head of President Trump by his shock of orange hair. Griffin accompanied the picture with these words: "I caption this 'there was blood coming out of his eyes, blood coming out of his . . . wherever.'"[1] The comment alluded to a tasteless remark that Donald Trump had made about Fox News anchor Megyn Kelly after she moderated a presidential debate in August 2015.[2]

The image is striking for many reasons, not least of which is its inexplicable lack of any comedic signifiers. The fake blood on Trump's face is as striking as the steely blue of Griffin's eyes. The comedian glowers sternly into the camera with post-homicidal smolder. A video made of the shoot itself captures Griffin telling her photographer, Tyler Shields, that they can both expect to go to federal prison.[3]

What, one may ask, is the joke? Here, Griffin careened way outside of her artistic comfort zone—not only in terms of content, but also in terms of form. Her career, after all, was built on a completely different type of humorous sensibility. Griffin is most famous for a reality show called *My Life on the D-List*, which centered on the comedic lengths to which she would go "as she tried to claw her way to A-List stardom."[4]

Every December 31 from 2007 to 2016, Griffin played one of her signature roles—the un-stiff sidekick to CNN's Anderson Cooper. New Year's Eve, the sloppiest evening on network television, synergized with Griffin's uninhibitedly vulgar style. She memorably responded to a heckler in the Times Square crowd, "I don't go to your job and knock the dicks out of your mouth." Another time, she mock-fellated Cooper. Kathy being Kathy.[5]

Prior to the dustup with Trump, Griffin had endured her share of controversy. Her quip about eleven-year-old actress Dakota Fanning going to rehab resulted in her termination as a red-carpet commentator for *E!*[6] Upon receiving an Emmy in 2007, she riffed on celebrities who praise Jesus when they accept awards. As a counterbalance, Griffin exclaimed: "Suck it, Jesus, this award is my God now." The offensive bit was not aired, though word leaked out and Griffin encountered criticism.[7]

Momentarily scandalous as they may have been, these incidents were not political in the strict sense. Griffin was a progressive, an orientation evident in her earlier work with an alternative comedy troupe called UnCabaret. The outfit was mindful of how sexist, racist, and homophobic mainstream comedy could be. She also had a sizable fan base in the LGBTQ community. That said, her body of work showed no record of overtly pursuing an activist agenda.[8]

In terms of form, little in Griffin's background would have predicted that she would offer America a bloody decapitation tableau. She was a celebrity insult comic, not a political satirist. Therein lay her mistake: she reduced Trump to a celebrity, rather than a political figure who inspires almost religious devotion from his followers. For a comedian who made a career out of self-deprecation and off-color jokes about pop culture icons, this venture into agitprop was a radical switch of genre. This was not Kathy being Kathy—at least not as we knew her.

Further, Griffin worked in a verbal medium, and had minimal experience with visual genres. Perhaps if she had more understanding of their unique power to enrage viewers, she would have decided against playing Judith to Trump's Holofernes. The image certainly didn't seem like a gag made by a stand-up. In fact, Griffin's headless Trump composition, in its ferocity and anti-authoritarian intensity, might be more at home in a museum of modern art, or on stage with the Russian performance-art group Pussy Riot, than in a comedian's Twitter feed.[9]

THE INFRASTRUCTURE OF AFFRONT

Whether intentionally or not, the tweet exported Griffin's work to the attention of a brand new audience. A coalition of the outraged formed with preternatural speed and alacrity. This wasn't only because her target was the president of the United States, but because "outrage" is the oxygen, lifeblood, lubricant, umbilical cord, and manna of the MAGA movement. This cohort possesses a truly formidable infrastructure of affront, ready to digitally deploy whenever an insult is tendered (and even when one is not).

The right's response went exactly as one might expect. Donald Trump Jr. wrote, "Disgusting but not surprising. This is the left today. They consider this acceptable. Imagine a conservative did this to Obama as POTUS?"[10] Melania Trump opined, "As a mother, a wife, and a human being, that photo is very disturbing . . . [it] makes you wonder about the mental health of the person who did it."[11] Jenna Ellis, later indicted as a January 6 co-conspirator, seized the opportunity to stampede onto First Amendment moral high ground: "It's crass and ugly and stupid and heartless and disgusting. But it is still free speech."[12] Griffin became a person of interest to the Secret Service and Department of Homeland Security and was investigated for conspiracy to assassinate the president.[13]

Out on Twitter, a maelstrom of rage was evident. One account wrote: "@kathygriffin is the nastiest woman in America! She's the lowest form of life. Scum of the earth! She was birthed in a petri dish!"[14] Actor James Wood pictured Griffin next to an ISIS militant with the caption "Two people with no sense of humor."[15] Another wrote: "Ugly mug of the month right there . . . @KathyGriffin Can't imagine waking up next to THAT skank . . . #KathyISISGriffin #DrainTheSwamp #MAGA."[16]

Hostile words on social media are, potentially, not *just* words; they may create an environment that leads to symbolic and physical violence. Griffin was bullied and doxxed. She received death threats for years afterward. In Auckland, New Zealand, where she was on tour, a Trump supporter hurled a glass bottle at her neck.[17]

The threats against her were quite serious. She learned that the eventual "MAGA bomber" Cesar Sayoc was among the throngs of affronted people tweeting at her. "I think the FBI saved my life," Griffin observed to Jimmy Kimmel. "The FBI did something they call a 'no-knock' to my house, where it's such an imminent threat, they don't even call, they came right over."[18]

The professional impact of the controversy on what some were referring to as "ISIS's favorite comedian" was substantial. She almost immediately lost her gig co-hosting CNN's *New Year's Eve with Anderson Cooper* (who tweeted he was "appalled" by her stunt), and a scheduled tour was canceled, ostensibly because of security concerns.[19]

Griffin was particularly scarred by the critique she received from allies and close friends. "I was vilified by everyone," she fumed. "I was vilified by Chelsea fucking Clinton." (The former first daughter had tweeted, "This is vile and wrong. It is never funny to joke about killing a president.")[20] Griffin continued, "I was vilified by my friend Don Cheadle. I was vilified by people I'd had at my fucking home. Nobody had my back. It happened so fast. I didn't see it coming."[21]

On the same day that she posted the Trump image, May 30, 2017, Griffin tweeted a video of apology:

> Hey everybody, it's me, Kathy Griffin. I sincerely apologize. I'm just now seeing the reaction of these images. I'm a comic, I crossed the line. I move the line then I cross it. I went way too far. The image is too disturbing, I

understand how it offends people. It wasn't funny. I get it. I've made a lot of mistakes in my career, I will continue. I ask for your forgiveness. Taking down the image. I'm going to ask the photographer to take down the image. And I beg for your forgiveness. I went too far. I made a mistake and I was wrong.[22]

We've already encountered apologies in comedic controversies. There was Dave Chappelle's false apology—a prelude to another poke at his critics. There were Sarah Silverman's numerous heartfelt apologies. Griffin offered a new wrinkle on the theme: the heartfelt-but-soon-to-be-retracted apology. Three months later, on August 28, she took it all back: "I am no longer sorry, the whole outrage was B.S." Several weeks later, in an interview with the *Guardian*, she reiterated her retraction. "I totally get it. But in light of everything Trump and the administration have done since, I 100% withdraw my apology."[23]

No contemporary comedic controversy would be complete without meta. In her comeback special *Kathy Griffin: A Hell of a Story*, she relates that Jim Carrey counseled her thus: "Today, you're the most famous comedian in the world . . . you're going to take as long a time as you need to process it and then you're going to put it through your Kathy Griffin comedy prism and you're going to make the story funny and relatable, and you're going to go tell it."[24]

She would spend the next five years of her career doing exactly that. Obsessively, some might say. Just as Dave Chappelle's material morphed after his dustups with the LGBTQ community, Griffin's comedy became increasingly self-absorbed and politically tinged. Like Chappelle, Griffin was drowning in meta, a prisoner of a reactionary communication pattern. Griffin seemed to realize she had wandered off course when she commented, "I just want to get back to making people laugh. More than anything else, that's what has been robbed from me."[25]

Throughout this ordeal, there was a divorce, spells of addiction to pills, a suicide attempt, and eventually a bout with lung cancer.[26] By her own estimation, after the scandal she didn't earn any money for six years and lost a third of her audience. An article about her troubles selling out her shows quotes Griffin pleading, "Buy tickets. . . . Those male promoters are looking to see how I sell and if I sell. . . . When you're a female comedian you'll never sell as well as the boys, no matter what your accomplishments are, blah, blah, blah."[27]

Kathy Griffin, to invoke her own metaphors, went to hell and back. Through determination, talent, and courage, she managed to salvage her career. Today she remains a multimillionaire and has regained some of her previous professional standing. It seems evident, however, that prior to the controversy her comedy was much more dynamic and her professional ceiling much higher.[28]

SHANE GILLIS: PUNCH DOWN PRACTITIONER

"This guy I'm bringing on stage," announced Dave Chappelle, "is so funny he got canceled at the beginning of his career. . . . Please welcome, from *almost Saturday Night Live:* Shane Gillis."[29]

Like Kathy Griffin, Shane Gillis weathered his brush with infamy and reemerged. Unlike Griffin, he reemerged more popular than ever before. In fact, he would rapidly become one of the highest-grossing comedians in the country.[30]

Gillis's woes were caused by a comedic indiscretion from his not-so-distant past. That indiscretion likely would not have been dredged up had he not been selected to join the cast of *Saturday Night Live*. On September 12, 2019, the venerable sketch-comedy program announced its new ensemble members: Chloe Fineman; Bowen Yang, the show's first fully Asian American cast member; and Shane Gillis.[31]

Later that evening, a Twitter account belonging to one Seth Simons linked to a 2018 video of Gillis using anti-Asian slurs.[32] The tweet was soon deleted (the identity of the poster still remains a mystery) but not before news organizations picked up the story.[33] Gillis's pre-*SNL* material provided compelling angles for media consumption. That's because he relentlessly, joyously punched down on minorities—and he did so not from the identity position of a Black man (like Chappelle) or a Jewish woman (like Silverman) but from that of a straight white male.

Among the slew of targets of Gillis and his co-host Matt McCusker on *Matt and Shane's Secret Podcast* were Asian Americans. Commentators were not about to overlook the irony of Bowen Yang's groundbreaking appointment occurring simultaneously with that of a comic who cracked jokes about "chinks" and made fun of Asian American accents. Jeff Yang, a commentator on popular culture, tweeted: "Yeah if you want to know what being a person of color is like, it's literally that for every Bowen Yang–shaped step you take forward, you also take one racist-ass Shane Gillis–shaped step back."[34]

Much of the material regurgitated by the press corps stemmed from a September 2018 episode of Gillis and McCusker's podcast called "Chinatown." During the show, Gillis opined: "Damn Chinatown is fucking nuts," to which McCusker agreed: "It's crazy!" Surfing McCusker's approval, Gillis fared forward: "It's full fucking Chi-na, dude, it's fucking 'Chinee down there." He was not done: "We got in there, we sat down," he exclaimed, "and baby girl [Gillis's alleged girlfriend at the time] was like 'I'm so excited for nooders!' and I was like yo chill chill chill (laughs) . . . yeah and it's full fucking 'Chinee in there."[35]

A few years later, a placid and thoughtful Gillis reflected on his cancellation. "If they were mad about that," he sighed, "there's a lot [more]."[36] There *was* a lot more. In a podcast called *A Fair One*, which Gillis co-hosted with his roommate Tommy Pope, the two comics gave off a distinctly alt-right vibe as they rinsed those who were not white and not male.

In one episode Gillis exclaims, "Get this CNN Jew shit offa here (bursts of laughter). I need some alt-right fuckin' Fox News, dude."[37] Another captured Gillis chanting, "White people! White people! White people! White people . . . white people are the best," while making fun of an "ethnic" bus driver.[38]

The N-word? Sure, Gillis went there. Discussing the prank of ding-dong ditching, Gillis put forth: "Ya nigger knocking?"[39] At other instances, he'd effuse along the lines of "Yo, these guys are so fucking gay!"[40] Factor in copious slights about differently abled people and one understands why his longtime fans on Reddit were concerned that he'd be canceled.[41]

Once the "old" material surfaced, digital retribution ensued. The sociologist Nancy Wang Yuen tweeted, "Woke up thinking about how great we have Bowen Yang on #SNL & pissed that Shane Gillis is triggering my childhood trauma w/ his name-calling & accent mocking. Using centuries old stereotypes is not a 'risk' or 'pushing boundaries.' It's just racist & lazy."[42] *Top Chef* and *Taste the Nation* star Padma Lakshmi remarked, "A great way to not get fired for making lame racist jokes is to not do that."[43] Numerous comedians, among them Asian Americans Jimmy O Yang, W. Kamau Bell, Atsuko Okatsuka, and Sherry Cola, lambasted Gillis's racist language.[44]

Just six hours after being appointed to SNL Gillis was mired in a defensive posture because his past jokes had digital wings. He recounts the odd experience of riding the subway and watching people read about his sensational predicament on their phones. Gillis later related that he was offered an "apology template" by his management team but refused to use it.[45] Instead he posted this rather unconvincing tweet: "I'm happy to apologize to anyone who's actually offended by anything I've said. . . . My intention is never to hurt anyone but I'm trying to be the best comedian I can be and sometimes that requires risks."[46]

SNL issued its own statement: "We were not aware of his prior remarks that have surfaced over the past few days. The language he used is offensive, hurtful and unacceptable."[47] And so it came to pass that on September 16, 2019, four days after news broke of his hiring, Shane Gillis was fired by the most prestigious comedy show in the world.

THE COMEBACK: GOODBYE "STRAIGHT ALEX JONES SHIT"!

And yet five years later, there he was: in February 2024, Gillis *hosted SNL*.[48]

How he rebounded from a professional meltdown that would have finished most artists is a question of interest to our inquiry. In terms of the individual choices Gillis made, a few things stand out. If we are to believe his account of the episode—and he does seem generally credible—he responded with a considerable degree of humility. "I want it to be clear," he explained to Andrew Yang, "I'm not a victim . . . there's a video of me using a slur. There's going to be some backlash."[49] To Joe Rogan he said of his cancellation, "The whole time, I was like, 'I kind of get it.'" Nevertheless, in the aftermath of his very public fall he realized: "I just want to do comedy."[50]

Accepting his fate as a "canceled comedian," Gillis got back to work. Though he did so convinced that his detractors misunderstood him. "It's . . . just not who I am," he observed. "If I was a closeted alt-right dude and they outed me, then it would be hard to fake."[51]

A few months after his cancellation, he received an award for stand-up comedian of the year. Then, together with John McKeever, he released the comedy sketch show *Gilly and Keeves* on YouTube. This project, which has accrued over 100 million views, reestablished Gillis as a marketable entertainer.[52]

The momentum gained from *Gilly and Keeves* cracked open other opportunities, notably a string of appearances on Joe Rogan's massively popular podcast starting in 2021. In that same year, Gillis released a full-length comedy special, *Shane Gillis: Live in Austin*, which has been viewed over 40 million times. In 2023, he released his second comedy special, *Shane Gillis: Beautiful Dogs*, this time on Netflix.[53]

Comedically, *Live in Austin* is likely Gillis's finest hour. Its closest relatives are Dave Chappelle's HBO specials *Killin' Them Softly* of 2000 and the 2004 *For What It's Worth*. All these feature skilled stand-ups making bemused references to odd things about their "own people."

Gillis may have been widely perceived as a racist white guy, but his burns on racist white guys in *Live in Austin* ("all we talk about is eating pussy and fracking") were trenchant. As was his observation about the University of Alabama's 1971 integration of their football team: "A little late for high fives on this one fellas . . . there were literally people on the moon before Alabama had Black guys in their secondary."[54]

And before you knew it, he was hosting *SNL*. His monologue was only mildly meta. "I was fired from this show a while ago . . . don't look that up, please . . . please don't google that . . . I probably shouldn't be up here honestly. I should be home . . . I should be a high school football coach . . . God molded me perfectly to be a high school football coach slash ninth-grade sex education teacher." The remainder of the bit demonstrated the newer, course-corrected Gillis. The humor was mostly self-deprecating, sometimes a tad offensive ("I was gay for my mom . . . [until] the first time I whacked off"),[55] yet it never veered into the alt-right-adjacent swamp of his pre-*SNL* days. Nor did he linger on his cancellation tribulations.

Gillis's thematic shift away from arguably racist material was anticipated in *Gilly and Keeves*, which pointed to a subtle but significant rebrand. Gillis is edgy, but the gratuitous, playground slurs are uttered with a certain air of discretion. The casting aims at racial evenhandedness: Black actors are part of the fun, not the butt of the jokes. Rather, middle-aged white dudes get the brunt of the insults.

One sketch almost reads as a self-parable. Gillis plays the coach of the Chapel Creek Rebels, an all-white football team. At a preseason press conference he boasts that his boys are going to decimate the Black teams they are about to play, football being "a white man's sport."[56] A series of headlines reporting the final scores, however, demonstrates quite the contrary.

At his next press conference the coach reveals that the school board is forcing him to integrate the squad. Game after game, Coach does everything he can to avoid fielding Black athletes. But every time he lets them play, his team wins; when he doesn't, his team gets crushed. After winning the state championship with his Black roster, Coach starts to see the light. He soon informs the "Rebel faithful" that he's been attending a Black church. When we last see him, he is clad in a dashiki and kufi cap. Abandoning the old racist junk is a winning formula for the coach, just as it was for Gillis.

Careerwise, the greatest thing that ever happened to Shane Gillis was cancellation. He went from living in poverty and obscurity to becoming wealthy and famous in the span of a few years. He learned that doing "straight Alex Jones shit" was a commercial dead end.[57] If Kathy Griffin went to hell and back, Gillis seems to have used his time down there to take professional development courses while consuming buffalo wings downed with Pabst Blue Ribbon.

CONCLUSION: EASY TARGETS

At roughly the same moment in American history, two comedians, one male, one female, outraged multitudes, albeit different multitudes. Subsequently, they experienced entirely different professional consequences. Gillis skyrocketed to fame. Griffin is still struggling to regain her footing.

The following equation emerges: a white female comedian who offended, or punched up at, a cultural majority encountered a fate quite different from that of a white male comedian who offended, or punched down at, cultural minorities. These discrepant outcomes raise the possibility that the interpenetrating structural variables mentioned above—that is, gender and the identity of the offended parties—are key operators in comedic controversies.

Put differently, it's extremely hazardous for a woman to stoke the ire of mainstream or majority audiences. Griffin herself has repeatedly raised a variant of this argument (as did Hillary Clinton in this chapter's epigraph), insisting that she was singled out for abuse because she was a fifty-six-year-old female. "I will not be convinced this was not a straight-up case of sexism and ageism," she said bluntly. "I really think Trump went for me because I was an easy target.'"[58]

In terms of female entertainers making controversial, counter-majoritarian political claims and paying a massive toll for doing so, Griffin has some precursors. On a 1992 episode of *SNL*, singer Sinéad O'Connor ripped up a picture of Pope John Paul II on live television. Her protest of the mistreatment of minors in Ireland's Catholic institutions presaged the Church's forthcoming sexual abuse scandal.[59] O'Connor was banned from ever appearing on *SNL* again, and her marketability and visibility as an artist diminished in the ensuing decades.

In 2003, Natalie Maines, lead singer of the female country music group the Dixie Chicks, publicly criticized George W. Bush's imminent invasion of Iraq.[60] "The denunciation of President Bush," wrote musicologists Jada Watson and Lori Burns a few years later, "had a major impact on both the careers and the private lives of the three women in the band. Country music radio refused to play their music, fellow country music artists alienated them . . . the trio continued to be branded as traitors and as unpatriotic."[61]

In each case, a female artist articulated a political position critical of majoritarian sentiments. In each case, they were immediately and massively disparaged, harassed, and deplatformed. O'Connor, who died in 2023, and the Chicks, we should note, were largely spared the social media vitriol—after all, in 2003, never mind 1992, there was no Twitter, no Facebook. Griffin's controversy, in contrast, started with a tweet, and in turn she was digitally savaged.

This gendered online dimension of Griffin's ordeal should not be underestimated. Study after study of "entrenched sexism in media" reveals that women are victimized in cyberspace in distinct and heightened ways.[62] Communications scholar Emma Jane Alice coined the term *e-bile* to describe the misogynistic transmissions she studied. "They target," she writes, "a woman who is, for one reason or another, visible in the public sphere; their authors are anonymous or otherwise difficult to identify; their sexually explicit rhetoric includes homophobic and misogynist epithets; they prescribe coerced sex acts as all-purpose correctives; they pass scathing, appearance-related judgments and they rely on *ad hominem* invective."[63]

Other researchers stress that e-bile is not a function of the victim's fame per se; it is directed, indiscriminately, at *all* publicly visible women online. Griffin, by virtue of her heightened visibility, simply received immensely larger and more lethal doses of such aggression.[64]

A corollary of our women-as-easy-targets hypothesis is that when men mock minority groups they suffer fewer repercussions. In fact, they can do the same to *majority* groups and emerge relatively unscathed. One thinks of Bill Maher, who offended many after 9/11 by implying that the

American military were "cowards," unlike the nineteen suicide-hijackers: "Staying in the airplane when it hits the building, say what you want about it, it's not cowardly."[65] He weathered the storm and went on to a stellar career (see also chapter 2 and Maher's use of the N-word).

My theory about the interplay between gender, offensive content, and majoritarian audiences is just that—a theory. My sample is too small; methodologically, one is never standing on solid ground when n = 1. Further, one could protest that Griffin should not be likened to Gillis. His jokes were, undoubtedly, sophomoric and cruel. Griffin's beheading tweet, however, was abhorrent and demanded a different response.

Griffin was canceled after she veered *way* out of her comedic lane. Gillis was canceled, but for doing what he had done his entire career: making dumb jokes. It was easier for Gillis to recover from his misstep than it was for Griffin. It could also be argued that Gillis was a better comedian, less self-absorbed than Griffin, and so more deserving of a comeback.

Of course, all of this can be true without invalidating the claim that an artist's gender figures prominently in the reception of their art—perhaps even more so when the art is polarizing or controversial. Griffin's plight, as compared with that of Gillis, raises the possibility that social censure has less to do with what is said than with who says it and who responds to its provocation.

With our comedic controversies in hand, let us now return to the question of The Consensus. Our case studies so far suggest that although the free speech guardrails endured a certain degree of "citizen stress," these comics' jokes did not result in investigations, legal penalties, or threats of imprisonment—with the exception of Griffin.

Griffin *was* hounded by the Department of Homeland Security and the Secret Service. She also recounts being detained and questioned upon entering foreign countries to perform, which suggests that Donald Trump's State Department was flagging her to national security agencies across the world.[66] While Griffin's infamous tableau was ill-advised and in bad taste, this type of governmental response seems excessive. It also suggests that The Consensus may soon "go through some things" courtesy of the United States government during Donald J. Trump's second term in office.

The Consensus has, as I just noted, already encountered "citizen stress." Chappelle was assaulted at the Hollywood Bowl. Kathy Griffin was attacked in New Zealand and, like Silverman, subjected to torrents of threats and online vitriol. Silverman, for her part, apologizes to her audience for the metal detectors they must navigate.[67] For now we can conclude that The Consensus mostly defends American comedians from government interference (though this, I repeat, may change). Some American citizens, however, do not abide by The Consensus and its lofty dictates; they don't get the joke, and they make their displeasure known.

Now we turn to three liberal democracies, India, France, and Denmark, where threats to The Consensus come not only from citizens, but also from governments and non-state actors.

PART TWO

Comedic Controversies in Other Liberal Democracies

THE CONSENSUS UNDER SIEGE

FOUR

The Ab/uses of an Audience

VIR DAS

> I come from an India that is going to watch this and say, "This isn't stand-up comedy. Where is the goddamn joke?" And yet I come from an India that will watch this and know there is a gigantic joke, it just isn't funny.
>
> VIR DAS
> "I Come from Two Indias"

"IS IT OK IF I make a small video with you guys before I leave?" comedian Vir Das asked his audience.[1] The crowd at the Kennedy Center on November 12, 2021 roared its consent. Soon thereafter, Das uploaded said small video to YouTube. He surely didn't know that this six-minute post, titled "I Come from Two Indias," would change his life. He probably also didn't foresee that it would trigger a bitter, polarizing national debate in his native India.

Mere hours after "Two Indias" (as it came to be known) surfaced, Das became embroiled in a comedic controversy that raged for months. Alongside calls to ban his performances, some compatriots accused him of sedition—a crime that carries a maximum sentence of imprisonment for life.[2] Some called for the revocation of his citizenship, or even his death.

Others, however, rushed to his defense. These supporters viewed his ordeal as evidence of how India, a constitutionally "secular" nation with its own free speech Consensus, was being theocratized by Hindu religious nationalists.[3]

The entire episode reminds us of what we've encountered in previous chapters. Once again, the internet emerges as an unparalleled accelerant of controversy. We'll also glimpse the swift assembly of a coalition of the outraged. Naturally, a "loop" materialized between Das and his critics whereby the dispute infiltrated his comedy in a meta fashion.[4] And once again a comedian's comportment compels us to ask: is he actually performing *comedy* right now? That's because while performing "Two Indias" Das executed a "persona drop" so intense one could easily forget he was a comedian.

The ructions set off by "Two Indias" present us with some new wrinkles as well. Das experimented with an unusual technique: enlisting his own live audiences in the struggle against his adversaries.[5] His adversaries, for their part, didn't simply express their disapproval of Das's art; they tried to punish him through the country's legal mechanisms. They did the same to other comedians whom we shall meet, such as Kunal Kamra and Munawar Faruqi.

These Indian cases also point to glaring vulnerabilities in free speech protections more generally—vulnerabilities exposed in this event by the actions of Prime Minister Narendra Modi's Bharatiya Janata Party (BJP) and the citizenry that support its *hindutva*, or Hindu nationalist, politics. Now it wasn't only citizens who were challenging The Consensus, but the *state*, whose responsibility, one would imagine, was to defend it as well.

BOLLYWOOD TO BROADBAND AND THE HASMUKH COMPLEX

Vir Das was born in Dehradun, India, in 1979. Almost immediately thereafter, his family "left privilege in New Delhi" and moved to Nigeria, where his father ran a food processing factory.[6] The comedian recollects that their dwelling in Lagos featured "an armed guard with an AK-47 machine gun." "Do you know how many people you would have to murder in India to get that level of security?" asked Das. Then he clarified: "Wait, sorry sorry sorry. I messed up the joke, let me start again: Do you know how senior a politician you would have to be in India?"[7] As we will see, jokes about Indian politicians, especially those affiliated with Modi's BJP, are a staple of Das's comedy.

Due to political upheaval in Nigeria, Das was sent back to boarding school in India when he was eight. During his teen years, he lived with his grandparents in New Delhi.[8] Eventually, Das left to pursue his BA at Knox College in Galesburg, Illinois, where he majored in drama, but he also studied economics to keep his parents off his back. He explored stand-up comedy in his senior year, writing and performing a show called "Brown Men Can't Hump."[9]

From there Das returned to India, where he would soon make a name for himself in Bollywood. Of the many movies he acted in between 2007 and 2017, one, *Delhi Belly*, had an audience of 500 million people. Conversely, another film he starred in, *Maastizaade*, which Das describes as "a horribly regressive, sex comedy script," was a major flop.[10]

The ups and downs in motion pictures drove him back to the United States, where he began to focus more on comedic genres, including stand-up. In a 2023 discussion with Marc Maron, Das refers to clips he started posting on the internet after his Bollywood stint and before his infamous Kennedy Center set: "I had done ten YouTube videos," he told Maron, "just kind of like pieces, spoken word pieces, etc . . . [poems] about class differences, about privilege."[11]

To better contextualize these pieces we might mention that earlier in India, Das co-created and starred in a Netflix series called *Hasmukh*. It's the story of a small-market comedian (played by Das) turned serial killer. Hasmukh can only overcome his stage fright and "slay" on stage by murdering a villainish person before each performance. The premise, as I see it, points to the belief of some comedians that they speak, or joke, truth to power, vanquish bad people, and make the world a better place through their art—let's call that the "Hasmukh Complex."[12] I sometimes wonder if numerous humorists, ranging from Lenny Bruce to the Zimbabwean performers we'll meet in chapter 8, suffer from this noble affliction.

In any case, Das's platform shift from Bollywood to broadband platforms like Netflix and YouTube aligns with changes in the entertainment landscape of contemporary India. Sociologist Kavyta Kay points to the phenomenon of "media disruption" whereby "the Indian screen is undergoing a transformation through the emergence of a new wave of online channels since 2008." This "decentering" of Bollywood has had massive implications for how comedy is created and consumed in India.[13] While Bollywood remains a central cultural reference point, the advent of streaming has led to more content creators and generated new audiences. This shift changed the form and content of Indian comedy.

Das's YouTube clips that he called #TenOnTen (2021) were usually stand-up sets filmed in a club or in front of people watching on Zoom. Posted at the height of the COVID era, these bits explore a variety of issues. For our purposes two interrelated themes of interest emerge across this body of work. The first is trenchant criticism of India's Hindu nationalist government. This theme sometimes merged with the second one, about how Modi's BJP had fostered a culture hostile to free speech and comedy.

In one episode titled "Who Has Freedom of Speech?" Das deftly mimicked Modi's unique drawl and speech cadences. Elsewhere, he tarred the prime minister as a "Gujarati uncle," a reference to the state Modi once governed—and, importantly, the scene of a massacre of Muslims that took place on Modi's watch.[14]

These jests were often fused with complaints about the state of freedom of expression in India. Referring to a Hindu mob that had ransacked a club and roughed up a comedian (see below), Das exclaimed: "If your faith is so rattled by a joke, is it really that strong? You believe in your God. You worship your God. Leave my jokes alone . . . You think your God doesn't have a sense of humor . . . He made *you!*"[15] In another segment about jailed comedians he fumed, "You tell us an Indian comic got slapped, we don't ask by who but by what: sedition."[16]

In Das's view, a comedian has a responsibility to make people laugh and a corresponding obligation to say what the powerful don't want to hear.[17] Thus in a video titled "Jokes for the Dead" he exclaimed, "My job as a comedian is to talk about the elephant in the room. And I am not going to not do my job because the elephant is a dead one."[18] Das was alluding to the death toll from COVID—a shockingly high number, which Modi's critics accused him of increasing through negligence.[19]

These YouTube materials came before Das's Kennedy Center performance. Perhaps by the time he took the stage in Washington, DC, his Hasmukh Complex had already placed the comedian on his adversaries' radar and they were ready to pounce. It's certainly plausible. But as we shall see, Das's earlier work, controversial as it might have been, does not fully explain why "Two Indias" ignited the outrage it did.

"MAKE SOME NOISE"

"Two Indias," the "small video" made at the Kennedy Center in 2021, was a spontaneous bonus track, not part of the "Manic Man" world tour proper.[20] Das decided to tape the segment after the show, with his audience present, and post it to the internet as a one-off.

Das hired a wedding photographer off of Craig's List to film the piece. The cinematographer revels in wide-angle shots of the audience.[21] Das, as we will see, makes his audience part of his comedy and politics. Those in the packed theater are all standing. All are masked in accordance with pandemic-era guidelines. They seem to be intensely focused. They are also perhaps a bit confused as to what precisely Das is doing. And let there be no doubt: what Das is doing *is* confusing—at least for a stand-up comic.

"Two Indias" has two main targets, one approached with affection and one with vitriol. As for the former, Das chides his compatriots sweetly. "I come from an India," he sighs, "that is Hindu, and Muslim, and Christian, and Sikh, and Parsi, and Jew, and when we all look up at the sky, we only see one thing together . . . the price of petrol." He also chides Indians' complacency: "I come from an India that will not shut up and yet I come from an India that will not speak up."[22]

Yet aside from measured pokes at his compatriots, the segment is shot through with sharp rebukes of the powers that be. Das's reflections on his second target, the current government, are occasionally droll. One can plausibly muster a chuckle when he asides, "I come from an India that has the largest working population under thirty on the planet but still listens to seventy-five-year-old leaders with 150-year-old ideas."[23] During other parts of the bit, however, it doesn't seem that the artist is at all interested in garnering laughs.

What was the audience to make, for example, of this observation, one minute into the piece: "I come from an India where we worship women during the day and gang rape them at night"?[24] The comedian was scratching at national wounds. An epidemic of violence against women and sexual assault has been widely chronicled in the Indian press. In 2019 alone, 32,000 rapes were reported. Two months prior to Das's performance yet another horrific rape and murder of a woman had seized headlines across the nation, a case notable both for its brutality and because the victim was a member of a lower caste.[25]

Das received his biggest applause of the night when he observed, "I come from an India where we take pride in being vegetarians and yet run over the farmers who grow our vegetables."[26] Here, he was giving voice to widespread discontent over recent government policies that essentially privatized the once heavily—and many would say successfully—regulated agricultural industry.[27] The immediate pain was experienced by farmers in Punjab, who took to the streets to demonstrate their displeasure. According to Punjabi farm leaders, the stress and circumstances caused by the new laws led directly to the deaths of more than seven hundred farmers. Specifically, Das noted an alleged incident in which protesting farmers were run over by a politician's SUV and killed.[28]

While the Kennedy Center audience reacted positively, it is important to recall there was no discernible punchline here. Das delivered the remark in a tone of unrelieved moral seriousness. It wasn't a joke. All of which harmonizes with the fact that "Two Indias" radiates a sense of dread; it insinuates that India is losing its way.

Das, however, has not lost hope. In a deft act of demagoguery he closes his set by enlisting his live audience to send a message to those he has just criticized. "I represent a great people," he exclaims:

> Great people who built a great thing that is turning into a memory. And I know that you believe in that India like I believe in that India. Because

> I see it in your eyes and you are in this room tonight. So before I leave your country I will leave this stage and I will put this camera on you and you. Make some noise for the India you want to live in, because I promise you that this is the Kennedy Center, but tonight it is our fucking house. So make some noise for India.[29]

They did indeed make noise. Their noise would radiate across the globe via the internet. Soon, there would be much more noise.

GHAR KI BAAT, GHAR MEIN RAHE

Das posted "Two Indias" to YouTube and went to sleep. He woke up to a media frenzy. Within just three days the video was viewed more than 2.5 million times.[30] The comedian would report that he and his family had received nearly 50,000 death threats.[31] Then again, the incident rocketed his popularity. He later claimed that because of the hullabaloo he gained 1.8 million new followers between the ages of eighteen and twenty-five.[32]

A coalition of the outraged almost immediately assembled itself. It was not, his detractors insisted, *what* Das said that angered them, but *where* he said it. His critics locked in on one particular trespass. A well-known Hindi aphorism goes, "Ghar ki baat, ghar mein rahe": matters of the house should remain in the house. Das, many charged, had violated the rule by lampooning India on foreign soil. How ironic, given that in "Two Indias" Das pointedly observes: "I come from an India which will accuse me of airing our dirty laundry." [33]

According to Indian law, citizens can inform the police of crimes that come within their cognizance in a First Information Report (FIR). In Mumbai, a lawyer for the ruling party filed an FIR, and then took to Twitter: "I don't mind if he makes mockery of Indian politicians but he made a mockery of India, which is my country, my pride. He hurt the sentiments of India." The complainant continued: "If an Indian goes outside the country, I want him to show the positive side . . . He must apologize to India."[34]

In Delhi, a citizen tweeted: "@thevirdas has made a desperate attempt to tarnish India's image internationally. For this, I have lodged an FIR against Vir Das with the DCP [New Dehli police]. We have to respond to this well-planned and organized conspiracy [to defame the nation]. #ArrestVirDas."[35]

In the opinion of Ashoke Pandit, a Kashmiri filmmaker, Das imperiled national security interests with his monologue: "I see a terrorist in this man called #VirDas. He is one of those members of a sleeper cell who has waged a war against our country on a foreign land. Should be immediately arrested under #UAPA [Unlawful Activities Prevention Act] and tried under terror laws."[36]

That Das's performance amounted to a grave offense was a complaint made by a Bollywood actress, Kangana Ranaut, on Instagram: "When you generalize all Indian men as gang-rapists[,] it gives rise and encouragement to racism and bullying against Indians all over the world ... such creative work targeting an entire race is soft terrorism ... strict actions must be taken against such criminals."[37]

Das's critics wanted him tried on the charge of sedition. His accusers claimed he had violated section 124A of the Indian constitution.[38] A legacy of British colonialism, the law was updated in 2018 to define sedition as "an act that brings or attempts to bring into hatred or contempt, or excites or attempts to excite disaffection towards, the Government established by law in India by words, either spoken or written."[39]

Leaving aside whether this is a just law, we should note that Das does seem to have contravened 124A. It wouldn't take a legal genius to argue that after criticizing the government *and then asking his audience* to "make some noise for the India you want to live in," the comedian was "exciting disaffection" toward the government. Fortuitously, attempts to try Das on sedition did not come to pass.

Notable is Das's technique of conscripting his audience into his controversies. We saw him urge his crowd to "make some noise" at the Kennedy Center. In his #TenOnTen segment "Who Has Freedom of Speech?" he empowered his audience again: "The scariest sound that this establishment can hear is not the wording of my jokes, it's the energy in your laughs. It's not the statement I make, it's the agreement in your lungs. The target isn't my microphone, it's your throat. It is. And if you consider what laughter is, which is just the involuntary exhalation and inhalation of air, you think you don't have freedom of speech? Bitch, you don't have freedom to breathe."[40]

As with Dave Chappelle, Das's meta move involves identifying his adversaries as well as his supporters—who happen to be in the theater with him. This "us versus them" vibe certainly endows a comedic controversy with drama. But in an India whose Consensus is crumbling, it presents some obvious dangers. In general, as I shall argue in my conclusion, it's a practice that comes with considerable risks.

"COME AND DARE TO BATTLE ME, OR ELSE . . ."

Das had supporters. They usually emerged from politically predictable quarters, especially the Congress Party, rival of the BJP. A controversial Congress Party leader, Shashi Tharoor, tweeted that Das was "a stand up who knows the real meaning of 'stand up' is not physical but moral."[41] Another Congress stalwart, Abhishek Singhvi, expressed reservations about "Two Indias" on nationalist grounds, but defended the comedian nonetheless. "Vilifying the nation as a whole in front of the world is just not done!" but, he continued, "my agreeing or [not] with Vir Das['s] words . . . is irrelevant. What is condemnable, despicable & unpardonable is his being subjected to complaints. He has violated no law & [should not be] harassed."[42]

Das's most ardent defender was Das himself. As we saw in earlier chapters, comedians commonly use their own art to address controversies created *by* their art. In an interview about his Netflix special *Landing*, Das made this very point, arguing that artists who create controversies get stuck "in a feedback loop." He then clarified that he would not succumb to such a fate: "I set a rule when I was doing the special, which is your content may have become controversy, but controversy will never become your content."[43]

Two things must immediately be said. First, *Landing* is very good. Second, self-awareness is not Vir Das's strong suit. *Landing* is, in fact, in near-constant dialogue with Das's controversy. As a work of art, it lives and breathes within the fore and aft of the feedback loop. Das even brought dirt from India and sprinkled it on the stage. Why? So that he no longer could be accused of defaming the nation abroad: he was literally standing on Indian soil!

Throughout *Landing* Das mentions the feelings of despair he felt over the "Two Indias" ordeal. He thought his career was over, and even experienced suicidal thoughts.[44] The comic sighs: "The headlines had, 'Vir Das is a terrorist.' And I just remember thinking, 'This is so insulting to actual terrorists.' Can you imagine how terrorists feel? They're like, 'Bro, this guy? We choreograph acts of violence ten years in advance, but now we have to do spoken word performance, apparently.'"[45]

Yet Das's most provocative punch to his many detractors—and evidence that, *contra* Das, his content *was* his controversy and vice versa—is subtle. In another bit, Das chides Indians in the diaspora for being critical of Indians in India. He urges them to "come home and witness modern India in all of our chaos but our infinitely larger beauty. Come home!" Das rails against being lectured "from abroad about what it means to be Indian." Then he issues this taunt to these outsiders, with his middle finger raised: "In the words of every Mumbaikar I know, 'Come and dare to battle me, or else fuck off.'"[46]

At this point in *Landing*, something strange happens as the camera radically switches its orientation. Now, it is behind Das, middle finger still aloft, affording us a view of his audience (and evoking the crowd shots we saw in "Two Indias"). We see what Das sees. To wit, a huge, smiling, enthusiastic crowd, strangely visible because the house lights have been turned up. We are looking at them as they are looking at Das. Suddenly Das, whose back was in our frame, turns around to face the camera, the delirious audience in the background. He breaks the fourth wall with an exaggeratedly demented smirk, as if saying to his many critics: "Come and dare to battle me—and my followers—or else fuck off."[47]

And yes, he flipped off his critics while standing on Indian soil.

Vir Das was frequently threatened with, but never tried on, charges of sedition.[48] In the years since "Two Indias" dropped on YouTube Das has become internationally famous. Aside from *Landing*, he launched his "Mind Fool" tour and has ambitious projects in the works.[49] As of 2025, Vir Das is doing just fine.

Freedom of speech in India, by contrast, is doing less fine.[50] The historian Tripurdaman Singh has argued that the Indian constitution, unlike its American counterpart, "enables and underpins a vast armory of coercive laws . . . dedicated to promoting executive power."[51] Singh contends that free speech liberties in India, far from being constitutionally entrenched, are subservient to whoever controls the executive branch (a state of affairs that finds some parallels with Donald J. Trump's attacks on universities, law firms, and even comedians in 2025). Since 2014, the executive branch has been in the hands of the BJP. Under Modi's leadership, there has been a stark crackdown on journalism, scholarship, and art that is critical of his government.

The ruling party has devoted considerable judicial ingenuity in deploying existing laws to punish those who express opposing ideas. Sedition charges against the internationally known writer Arundhati Roy are just the tip of the iceberg. Watchdog groups in India have chronicled a sharp rise in such prosecutions under the Modi government.[52]

The government is not only interpreting existing laws in aggressive ways that chill free speech, but drafting new ones as well. In one sense, this is not unexpected. The advent of the internet has necessitated a rethinking of free speech laws across the globe as nations wrestle with the radical possibilities of cyber-speech.[53] The new legislation proposed by Modi's government does this and more, geared as it seems to be to reduce free speech, especially speech critical of India's majoritarian religion and the ruling party.

In April 2023 the Indian Ministry of Electronics and Information Technology proposed a new regulation that would force media platforms to remove content about the "business of the Central Government" that is "fake, false, or misleading."[54] Menacingly, the new rule established a government-run Fact Checking Unit (FCU) to assess whether any violations of the act occur. In other words, the *government* would be the arbiter of whether statements about the government are true or not. Once the FCU rendered that decision, it could order "false" information scrubbed from digital platforms.

Such legislation, needless to say, undermines every aspect of The Consensus.

Kunal Kamra, a stand-up comedian with a large following in India, challenged the directive.[55] He argued that the proposed regulation violated a 2000 law which granted social media platforms safe harbor from liability claims for user-generated content. Kamra also maintained that the "business of the Central Government" provision would infringe on free speech and the right of political satirists such as himself to make a living.[56]

Kamra, like Das, inserted the controversy swirling around him into his own act. In his *Be Like* series on YouTube he describes how the Supreme Court slapped a contempt violation on him over a tweet critical of the court. His lawyer advised him to apologize. Kamra told his delighted audience that he issued the following "apology" (via WhatsApp): "Dear Supreme Court. Forget yesterday's talk. You can swing on my cock."[57]

Kamra went on to write an affidavit to the Supreme Court in which he unspooled a virtual manifesto about the functions of comedy. Going full Hasmukh, Kamra championed "comedy's tenet of comforting the afflicted, and afflicting the comfortable." He continued: "Constitutional offices—including judicial offices—know no protection from jokes. I do not believe that any high authority, including judges, would find themselves unable to discharge their duties only on account of being the subject of satire or comedy."[58] Reflecting on the free speech atmosphere in India, Kamra subsequently observed: "If you want a career in the arts in India . . . you should hide your opinions. Or befriend many, many lawyers."[59]

In March 2025 Kamra created another national controversy after remarking that a leading politician from Maharashtra state was a "traitor." A video featuring the comment went viral. Soon the club in which it was filmed was attacked and destroyed by a pro-BJP mob. Explicitly threatened, Kamra went into hiding as comedians bemoaned the collapse of India's free speech Consensus.[60]

Kamra has a large national following. Like Das, he is a Hindu in a majoritarian Hindu country presently ruled by a Hindu nationalist party. When the comedian in question is not well known or is a member of a minority, controversy may have more serious outcomes. Take the case of Munawar Faruqi, a once-obscure Indian stand-up who is a Muslim. In January 2021, Faruqi was performing in Madhya Pradesh when he was interrupted by an individual who accused him of having made disrespectful jokes about a Hindu deity (Faruqi had taken down the 2020 YouTube video in question before that performance). The accuser happened to be the son of a mayor affiliated with the BJP.[61]

Faruqi and the heckler went back and forth, with Faruqi protesting that he had made more Muslim jokes than Hindu ones and that he regretted the original YouTube gag. The heckler seemed satisfied and exited the club. A woman called out to the comedian, "Sir, listen to me, Hindus and Muslims are brothers." The crowd applauded. Someone shouted, "Munawar, we are with you!"[62] The comedian raised his arm in a gesture of appreciation.

But not everyone was with Munawar on that particular evening. Within a few minutes police entered the club and arrested Faruqi. Videos show him and his colleagues being beaten by a mob. Accused of making "indecent" remarks about Hindu deities, Faruqi was said to be in violation of the Indian Penal Code, including Statute 295A, which concerned "deliberate and malicious acts, intended to outrage religious feelings of any class by insulting its religion or religious beliefs."[63] The penalty carried a four-year prison term.

As *Time* magazine put it, Faruqi was "arrested for a joke he didn't tell."[64] His case bounced around the lower courts (where he received little in the way of sympathy). Finally the Indian Supreme Court intervened and pronounced the charges against him "vague." In all, he spent thirty-seven days in prison before being granted bail.[65] Aside from showing us that the BJP does not refrain from attacking artists, the episode demonstrates the ways in which identity intersects with free speech. In comedic controversies, some identities (think of Kathy Griffin) render performers more exposed to legal persecution. As Kamra said in support of Faruqi, "It is not what Munawar said, it is who he is."[66]

"A GIGANTIC JOKE"

In the United States, comedic controversies mostly play out in "civil society." Social media posts, op-eds, press releases, boycotts, are the ways in which the coalition of the outraged expresses itself.

In present-day India those things happen as well. What's different is that actors may also appeal to the state when experiencing comedically induced outrage. What's also different is that the Indian government, far from merely playing a mediating role in comedic disputes between citizens, *becomes part of the fray*. Jokes are literally being policed.[67]

Are Indian comedians entering their Lenny Bruce era? I refer, of course, to the legendary, transgressive American comedian, who was so hounded by law enforcement that he committed suicide in 1966. Within a few years, American free speech laws were radically liberalized. The question for India is whether censorship is "just a phase," or the beginning of an era which Das might call "a gigantic joke" that isn't funny.[68]

FIVE

Charlie Hebdo

THE TERRORIST'S VETO

> [T]he simplicity of punching up or down posits a Manichean moral perspective where one party is evil, the other good—when in reality all relationships are based in a very complicated web of power structures with its own unique set of ethical challenges. In most conflicts, rarely is a singular oppressor outed as a Machiavellian Goliath universally recognizable to all.
>
> GRANT JULIN
> "What's the Punch Line? Punching Up and Down in the Comic Thunderdome"

THE COMEDIC CONTROVERSY SURROUNDING the French satirical magazine *Charlie Hebdo* (*Charlie* for short) differs from the ones we've discussed so far in a few significant dimensions. First, scale: "*L'affaire Charlie Hebdo*" quickly went global, inflaming passions worldwide. Geopolitically speaking, the episode was consequential in a way that Dave Chappelle's "alphabet people" bit, for example, was not.

Second, the magazine's caricatures of the Prophet Muhammad resulted, both directly and indirectly, in mass casualties. An attack at the Paris headquarters of *Charlie* on January 7, 2015, resulted in twelve dead, including one of the magazine's editors, satirical caricaturist Stéphane Charbonnier. Within forty-eight hours, another gunman murdered a police officer and four shoppers at a Jewish supermarket in the same city. The carnage didn't stop there. Subsequent massacres in France triggered a redoubling of French military engagement in Iraq and Syria, which resulted in the deaths of hundreds, if not thousands, more.

This would not be the first time Muslim extremists waged violence in reaction to art they considered blasphemous. The fatwa issued by the Iranian cleric Ayatollah Ruhollah Khomeini against Salman Rushdie in 1989 for his novel *The Satanic Verses* furnishes one example.[1] Another is the international mayhem triggered by images of the Prophet Muhammad published in the Danish newspaper *Jyllands-Posten* in September 2005. We will take a look at that case because it is inextricably bound to what transpired in France a decade later. And what transpired a decade later, I will argue, demands that we think more critically about terms like "punching up" and "punching down."

Finally, the *Charlie* episode resurrected a question that liberal democracies thought they had entombed in the Sepulcher of Forgotten Civic Debates. Namely, should certain forms of artistic expression be preemptively censored to preserve public safety? Are governments morally obligated to decree, "*You can't make this joke. It's too dangerous. We just can't laugh at that!*"?

JYLLANDS-POSTEN: AN EXPERIMENT GONE WRONG

To understand the *Charlie Hebdo* tragedy of 2015, let us first explore the ructions sparked by a conservative Danish newspaper, *Morgenavisen Jyllands-Posten*, in 2005–2006. "It is hard not to marvel," writes political scientist Jytte Klausen, "at how 12 little cartoons could cause so much trouble."[2] Klausen produced a definitive account of that trouble in her 2009 study *The Cartoons That Shook the World*. Ironically, her publisher, Yale University Press, refused to print those twelve little Danish cartoons—which is troubling because Klausen's scholarly monograph was *about* those twelve little cartoons. This indicates (1) just how incendiary said content was and (2) how risk-averse American cultural institutions are compared to their European counterparts.[3]

The *Jyllands-Posten* affair began in 2005 when a rumor circulated in Danish journalistic circles that a children's book author could not find anyone to illustrate images of the Prophet Muhammad.[4] Some Danes believed this difficulty exemplified a free-speech dilemma; namely, self-imposed censorship stemming from fear of Muslim fundamentalist reprisal. The concern was not unfounded. In some forms of Islam, though not all, iconographic representations of the Prophet are prohibited.[5] As the Rushdie case fifteen years earlier indicated, the publication of content considered blasphemous by some could lead to substantial security complications.[6]

The rumors of self-censorship came to the attention of the editors of *Jyllands-Posten*, a newspaper known to be conservative and with a somewhat anti-immigrant editorial policy. According to Klausen, however, the tone of the journal had recently done a "flip into a libertarian view."[7]

The newspaper decided to conduct an experiment of sorts.[8] In order to ascertain whether a climate of self-imposed repression existed in Denmark, it solicited images of the Prophet from Denmark's union of newspaper illustrators. Their response to the invitation (or lack thereof) would be the measuring stick by which to gauge self-silencing. The editor entrusted with the task, Flemming Rose, later claimed: "I commissioned the cartoons in response to several incidents of self-censorship in Europe caused by widening fears and feelings of intimidation in dealing with issues related to Islam."[9]

Rose invited forty-two members of a national association of illustrators "to draw Muhammad as you see him."[10] All who submitted to *Jyllands-Posten* would have their content published and be paid a small fee. The initial invitation, I should note, included no explicit instruction to satirize or ridicule Muhammad. This affair, then, is not a comedic controversy per se. *Jyllands-Posten*'s motivations may have been provocative, but there was no explicit remit to provoke through humor.

Of the forty-two invitees, twelve submitted.[11] Not all interpreted their charge in the same way. Some seized the opportunity to criticize *Jyllands-Posten* itself. Others proffered art that was cryptic and difficult to interpret. A few of the images, however, struck some as Islamophobic, such as one showing the Prophet atop a cloud yelling, "Stop! Stop! We have run out of virgins!" to a group of suicide bombers.[12]

But it was cartoonist Kurt Westergaard's submission that was destined to convulse the world. Here, a bearded individual (perhaps I am the first commentator to note that the caricature looks like a self-portrait?) stares inscrutably to his right. He wears a turban that morphs visually into a lit bomb. Printed on the explosive device are the Arabic words of the *shahada*, or Muslim profession of faith. It was this image that "seared its way into the public consciousness and came to represent them all."[13]

THE APOLOGY. THE UNREST

Over the days and months following the September 30, 2005, publication of the twelve cartoons, there would be diplomatic strife, boycotts, threats, mass protests, and death.

Prior to rehearsing these grim highlights, we should recall Klausen's more nuanced narrative. She points out that neither "the Danes" who supported the publication's cartoons nor "the Muslims" who opposed them were of one mind as to what should be done. Gradations of opinion were evident in all camps. There were Danish and non-Danish Muslims who were not offended by or even particularly interested in the controversy. There were non-Muslim Danes who wished the cartoons had never seen the light of day. Within Denmark, anyhow, there was robust civil debate and a general absence of violence against minorities.[14]

The cartoons, however, spread rapidly beyond Denmark's borders, through two conduits. The first was social media—whose capacity to transmit and amplify incendiary content we have already seen.[15] The second was a group of four Danish imams who personally transported a dossier of cartoons, including inflammatory images *that were never published in Jyllands-Posten*, to various Muslim-majority nations.[16]

The exposure resulted in a cascade of protests and disturbances. The newspaper, its staff, and the cartoonists were subjected to numerous death threats. Muslim advocacy groups such as the Organization of Islamic Cooperation and the Arab League, along with Muslim-majority countries the world over, protested the images. The prime minister of Denmark, Anders Fogh Rasmussen, repeatedly rebuffed demands that he apologize.[17] By January 2006 a boycott of Danish goods had taken root in Saudi Arabia, before spreading across the Middle East. These economic sanctions created considerable stress for export-dependent Denmark.[18]

An apology, as we have seen, is a standard feature of controversies such as this. With the crisis gone global, *Jyllands-Posten* editor-in-chief Carsten Juste tried to make amends. In an early February statement titled "Honourable Fellow Citizens of the Muslim World," he wrote:

> In our opinion, the 12 drawings were sober. They were not intended to be offensive, nor were they at variance with Danish law, but they have indisputably offended many Muslims for which we apologize.... Maybe because of culturally based misunderstandings, the initiative to publish the 12 drawings has been interpreted as a campaign against Muslims in Denmark and the rest of the world. I must categorically dismiss such an interpretation. Because of the very fact that we are strong proponents of the freedom of religion and because we respect the right of any human being to practise his or her religion, offending anybody on the grounds of their religious beliefs is unthinkable to us. That this happened was, consequently, unintentional.[19]

The apology did not achieve its intended effect. By late February, Danish (and some Norwegian) consulates and embassies in Beirut, Jakarta, Teheran, and Damascus were ransacked and burned. Violent demonstrations led to deaths in Indonesia, Afghanistan, Somalia, Kashmir, and Nigeria. The violence spread to dozens of countries, resulting by Klausen's count in at least 248 dead and 800 injured.[20]

All sorts of other actors joined the fray.[21] In April, Osama Bin Laden chimed in with a lyrical threat: "If there is no check on the freedom of your words, then let your hearts be open to the freedom of our actions."[22] In some sectors of the Islamic world the cartoons were framed as a "Zionist-crusader war on Islam."[23] Pope Benedict, for his part, inflamed and medievalized the situation when he quoted a remark made by fourteenth-century Byzantine emperor Manuel II Paleologus, who charged that Mohammed "spread by the sword the faith he preached."[24]

The materials, of course, had their defenders as well. Newspapers across Europe republished the images in solidarity with *Jyllands-Posten* and in support of free speech (though few in the United States followed suit). One of these was a small French satirical magazine of the left, known as *Charlie Hebdo*.[25]

SOMETHING IS SACRED

Charlie Hebdo dive-bombed into the *Jyllands-Posten* affair like a comic book superhero—or archvillain, depending on one's point of view. Its plunge was not a crass attempt to "cash in" or exploit a controversy for publicity. The intervention made perfect sense given the magazine's history and mission. As editor Stéphane Charbonnier (or Charb) argued in an essay written shortly before his murder, *Charlie* had been mischievously publishing caricatures of Muhammad since well before the unrest in Denmark.[26]

Founded in 1951 as *Hara Kiri*, the satirical journal took its present name in 1970.[27] Throughout its run (1970–1982, 1992–present), *Charlie Hebdo* has abided by the conviction that everything can—indeed, *must*—be ridiculed. In the words of Cavanna, one of its stable of illustrators, "Nothing is sacred. Principle Number 1. Not even your own mother, not the Jewish martyrs, not those dying of famine . . . [L]augh at everything, everything, ferociously, bitterly, to exorcize the old demons."[28]

As the historian Jane Weston has noted, for *Charlie* "any subject, however taboo or sensitive," is considered fair game. It prides itself on its own rudeness, irreverence, nastiness, and idiocy, and as a result has garnered a well-deserved reputation for "provocative excesses." One of its self-descriptions, naturally, is "bête et méchant" (stupid and mean).[29]

It is, however, inaccurate to claim, as did some critics, that *Charlie* disproportionately aimed at Muslim targets. Content analysis conducted by sociologists Céline Goffette and Jean-François Mignot concluded that the magazine was "not obsessed by Islam."[30] Although there have been shifts, especially under different editors, *Charlie*'s ideological stances have been generally clear and consistent: anti-government, anti–

powers that be, anti–right wing, anti-racist, anti-capitalist, and most importantly for us, anti–traditionalist religion.[31]

In terms of what it was *for, Charlie* defended free speech, viewing it as a core component of republican French identity. Despite being a frequent critic of the state, especially its ruling political class, *Charlie* was adamant that unimpeded artistic and intellectual expression was a sacred national virtue—one the staff and contributors were self-deputized to defend.[32] In so doing, they were valorizing France's classical republican values. *Contra* Cavanna, whom we quoted above, the state's commitment to free speech *is* sacred.

Unsurprisingly, *Charlie*'s scatological brand of humor did not translate to mass appeal. Prior to 2005, the magazine was decidedly "niche." It was little known outside of France and circles of cartoon aficionados, and perennially hovered on the verge of bankruptcy.[33] None of that, of course, prevented it from savaging its enemies. Since its reemergence in 1992, it had been sued some 48 times.[34] The complainants included representatives of the Far Right, various Catholic and Muslim associations, and other aggrieved individuals.[35]

Charlie was in the business of being outrageous. It didn't stumble into the Muhammad cartoons affair like *Jyllands-Posten*, but giddily sprinted onto the battlefield. All of which is to say, it is perfectly understandable that a magazine devoted to criticizing religion, not to mention upholding the Gallic ideal of near-total expressive liberty, would opine, loudly, on a controversy that was roiling the entire world.[36]

RACIST? ANTI-ISLAM? ANTI-ISLAMIST?

In early 2006, in an act of solidarity, French newspapers like *France Soir* and *Libération* republished the Danish cartoons.[37] *Le Monde,* for its part, published its own original, rather meta image of the Prophet composed of the words "I must not draw Muhammad."[38]

Charlie republished the *Jyllands-Posten* cartoons in its February 8, 2006, issue (number 712).[39] Not to be outdone by the stodgy *Le Monde,* the journal went the extra mile with a cover that featured the Prophet, exasperated and sighing, "It's hard being loved by assholes."[40] Jonathan Ervine, a professor of French studies, has noted a tendency of analysts to focus solely on *Charlie*'s (incendiary) cover art. But issue 712, like many others, contained much more in the way of content. This included thoughtful essays about free speech, reflections on Islamic theories of iconography, and so forth. Too, there was an image by the illustrator Georges Wolinski of the smiling Prophet exclaiming, "It's actually the first time that the Danes have made me laugh!"[41]

None of that prevented some in the French Muslim community from taking offense. In July 2006 the Grand Mosque of Paris and the Union of Islamic Organizations of France (UOIF) sued *Charlie* and its then-editor, Phillipe Val, for "publicly abusing a group of people because of their religion."[42]

Different countries have different free speech regulations. Blasphemy laws exist in Denmark, but they lie in a "dormant" state.[43] In France, blasphemy is not a punishable offense; one can criticize religion as one sees fit. So *Charlie*'s representation of the Prophet Muhammad ran afoul of no French restrictions.

It *is* illegal in France, however, to incite hatred against a group because of their race or religion, per article 33 of France's 1881 penal code. These laws, which have been amended throughout French history, currently forbid any insult (*injure*) "towards a person or groups of persons on the basis of their origins or their belonging or their non-belonging to an ethnic group, nation, race, or religion."[44]

The plaintiffs in the 2006 case tried to frame *Charlie*'s Muhammad cartoons as attacking all members of a group along racial and religious lines. "In France," argued Francis Szpiner, representing the Grand Mosque, "racism is not an opinion, it is a crime. . . . The issue is not the principle of caricaturising the Prophet, but a racist aggression against French Muslims, telling them they are terrorists."[45]

Val countered that this wasn't an attack on all Muslims as a group; rather, the cartoons' target was radical, militant Islamists specifically.[46] The magazine also pushed back on the equation between racism and

Islamophobia. Given that *Charlie* had long aligned itself with anti-racist causes, the cartoonists bristled at this link. Charb, for one, attacked the logic thus: "The strategy used by minority group activists masquerading as anti-racists is to pass off blasphemy as Islamophobia and Islamophobia as racism."[47]

Indeed, if anyone was racist, the magazine's editors argued, it was those who were castigating *Charlie*. "It is racist to imagine," Val alleged, "that they [Muslims] can't understand a joke."[48] Charb made a similar point: "Asserting that Islam is not compatible with humor is as absurd as claiming that Islam is not compatible with democracy or secular governance."[49]

The trial, which occurred in February 2007, garnered immense national and international attention.[50] The judges ultimately ruled in favor of *Charlie Hebdo*, conceding that although the cartoons were offensive, the magazine's satirical history suggested no "deliberate intention of directly and gratuitously offending the Muslim community."[51] Judge Jean-Claude Magendie made another Consensus-friendly point: no one was forced to purchase the magazine or to look at the images. The courtroom burst into applause at the ruling.[52]

Victorious and vindicated, *Charlie* proceeded apace with its takedowns of religious fundamentalists. The journal hit its stride with a November 2011 issue claiming to be guest edited by the Prophet Muhammad himself, who exclaimed in a cover illustration: "100 lashes if you don't die of laughter!"[53] Not only that, but the title of the magazine was changed for the edition from *Charlie Hebdo* to *Charia Hebdo*, a play on "Sharia law," the religious customs, laws, and guidelines outlined in the Quran.

One day after that issue's release, *Charlie*'s offices were firebombed and completely destroyed.[54] There were no injuries, but Hebdo's higher-ranking editors, including Charb, were subsequently placed under police protection. The assailants were never found.[55]

Undaunted, the magazine continued doing what it had always done. One cover featured two men (one a Muslim) smooching, with a caption that read, "Love is stronger than hate." Another pictured a member of

ISIS preparing to behead the Prophet Muhammad. Then there was one of Osama Bin Laden decked out in an Elvis Presley get-up insisting he was still alive (though by that time Bin Laden had been dead for months).[56]

And then came the terror which seems increasingly commonplace when art enrages fundamentalists. On January 7, 2015, two brothers, Cherif and Said Kouachi, accessed the journal's office and killed twelve people—eight *Charlie* journalists, two police officers, a caretaker, and a visitor.[57] According to reports, the gunmen "listed off the names of their [journalist] targets before shooting them execution-style."[58] The next day, an acquaintance of the brothers, Amedy Coulibaly—they had met in prison—murdered a police officer and four people at a Jewish supermarket in Paris.[59] The attackers claimed to be affiliated with Al-Qaeda Yemen and ISIS, respectively.

All of this occurred within the context of an ongoing "violent relationship" between France and various Islamic terrorist outfits, including French operations against the Islamic State in Iraq in 2014.[60] In response to the *Charlie* assault, France then increased its overseas engagement with militant Islamists, launching airstrikes in Syria in September 2015.[61]

Two months later, on November 13, 2015, Islamist terrorists raided Paris's Bataclan Concert Hall, leading to the "deadliest peacetime [attack] in French history," with 130 dead and nearly 400 injured.[62] The following year, on Bastille Day, a truck rammed into a crowd in Nice, killing eighty-four.[63] The justification for both acts, according to the perpetrators, was French intervention in Syria and against the Islamic State (of Iraq and Levant). All of which underscores that the attack on the cartoonists was not an isolated event, but part of a series of escalating antagonisms between France and militant Islamists.

"LIBERAL FASCISM" AND "MORAL INJURY"

We have now familiarized ourselves with the basics of what must be the most tragic comedic controversy in history. Of interest to us are the

TABLE 1 Anti-*Charlie Hebdo* activists

Types of Response	Examples of State Actors	Examples of Nonstate Actors
Violent Reaction	Iran Mauritania Pakistan	Al-Qaeda Boko Haram ISIS/ISIL Islamic Jihad
Peaceful Protest	Egypt Jordan Türkiye	The Catholic League #JeNeSuisPasCharlie Pope Francis Post-Colonial Professoriate

audiences that were enraged by *Charlie's* art. The caricatures invoked a coalition of the outraged that was larger and more geographically far-flung than anything seen before. This coalition was also wildly diverse.

To understand its diversity, we should think of the anti-*Charlie* activists along two axes: (1) state actors versus non-state actors, be they terrorist organizations or groups within civil society, and (2) those who peacefully objected to the cartoons versus those who resorted to violence (see table 1).

Let's work our way through the quadrants. Various countries, among them Egypt, Türkiye, and Jordan, issued statements condemning the cartoons, though they did not condone, endorse, or engage in violence.[64] In contrast, several nation-states, including Pakistan, Iran, and Mauritania, did justify or engage in violent reprisal.[65]

Non-state actors that rushed to militantly defend the Prophet's honor included, aside from Al-Qaeda, ISIS/ISIL, Boko Haram, and Islamic Jihad.[66] There were also "lone-wolf" assailants who acted as individuals, though they may have been radicalized by these other groups.

This brings us to our final and most interesting quadrant: non-state actors that expressed their displeasure with the cartoons in an entirely peaceful manner. In France, these included Muslim civic associations, conservative Catholic groups, and anti-racist organizations.[67] After the massacre, a response to the #JeSuisCharlie coalition emerged called

#JeNeSuisPasCharlie (there was also a group called #JeSuisAhmed, honoring the Muslim police officer slain by the terrorists).[68] While appalled by the violence, the #JeNeSuisPasCharlie movement was acutely aware of surging anti-Muslim sentiment.

In this quadrant, the most salient figures, however, were intellectuals across the globe. An astonishingly high percentage of academicians who wrote about the *Charlie Hebdo* affair were deeply critical of the caricatures. These scholars were almost always on the far left end of the political spectrum. The irony, of course, is that *Charlie* was widely perceived—and perceived itself—as situated on the Far Left. Ever since its *Hara Kiri* days it had acquired a well-earned reputation as a bastion of anti-racist, anti-capitalist, and anti-authoritarian agitation.

The Left, however, had been mutating and fracturing for decades. In the Academy, especially among the elite faculties, a "postcolonial" Left had achieved a substantial presence. Its fissures with an older Left, and liberals in particular, became manifestly evident during this controversy.[69] This cohort of academics and intellectuals is deeply critical of The Consensus.

Postcolonial thinkers reserve their most trenchant critique not for conservatism or the Far Right, but for liberalism (what some call "liberal fascism").[70] These scholars affirmed that the cartoons were Islamophobic. Insofar as most French Muslims are of African origin, the Islamophobia accusation meshed with charges of racism.[71] But their critique went further.

Numerous postcolonialists interpreted the episode as a displaced clash between a former colonizer and its former subjects. The cartoons, in their opinion, mocked people whom France had once brutally colonized and subsequently uprooted, impoverished, and sequestered in its suburban ghettos.[72] Images like *Charlie*'s caricatures, in the words of one scholar, were "belittling . . . the faith of those who already felt deeply vulnerable within French society."[73] Put another way, the cartoons were doing the cultural dirty work of punching down on powerless immigrant communities tethered to France by a history of imperial domination.[74]

A somewhat adjacent critique was leveled by the sociologist Emmanuel Todd, who described those who demonstrated in favor of the cartoons (the #JeSuisCharlie movement) as "Zombie Catholics." These xenophobic, white, middle- and upper-class French citizens, most of whom were lapsed Catholics, Todd alleged, "pour scorn on the religion of the weak."[75]

This brings us to free speech, an issue that exemplifies the massive rupture that has developed between the postcolonial Left and traditional liberals.[76] The former maintain that because free speech laws—part of what we have identified as The Consensus—were born of majoritarian white, Western Christian societies, they favor such citizens to the disadvantage all others.

Many of these scholars thus cast doubt on the very concept of free speech, viewing The Consensus as simply another instrument of occidental oppression. For them, free speech is an "imaginary" (a common postcolonial term for something the West believes is real), powered by "first world privilege and Eurocentric sentiments."[77] This Enlightenment value of expressive liberty for all is, in truth, a "mere mask . . . for racism and imperialism."[78] The Consensus, then, is upheld only by the powerful whom it alone serves.

It follows from this that the free speech playing field is not even. The anthropologist Saba Mahmood speaks of a double standard by which hateful content directed toward Muslims but not others is excused (an idea pursued in the next chapter). In Mahmood's estimation, French free speech law permits forms of expression that disregard the feelings of entire categories of citizens (particularly Muslim citizens).

These citizens, according to Mahmood, experience intense psychic pain when the figure of Muhammad is disparaged or even iconically represented.[79] She refers to this as "moral injury," and suggests that no system of (Western) law can balm the wound it creates. "The notion of moral injury I am describing," Mahmood writes, "no doubt entails a sense of violation, but this violation emanates not from the judgment that the law has been transgressed but that one's being, grounded as it is in a relationship of dependency with the Prophet, has been shaken." The nature of the trespass is intense, so much so that its "wound requires moral action."[80]

It is not clear what type of "moral action" Mahmood had in mind. Yet her larger point is that these cartoons, sanctified by systems of law and a free speech Consensus forged in a Christian society, are uniquely and existentially unsettling to French Muslim citizens.[81]

PUNCHING DOWN?

Another intriguing dimension of this controversy concerns the notion of "punching down." Usually punching down is construed as a comedic attack on an individual or group with less social power than the humorist(s) can claim.[82] The *Charlie* affair exposes the limitations of this conceptualization.

For purposes of argument, let's posit that the magazine was, in fact, punching down on French Muslims. Let's also assume that by caricaturing the Prophet, *Charlie* inflicted "moral injury" on them. Even so, we must still recognize that a few French Muslims with ties to militant non-state actors resorted to extreme violence to avenge the slight. Gunning down was their answer to punching down, inflicting fatal injury their answer to moral injury.[83]

This suggests that "punching down" requires some qualifiers. The ability to issue a comedic punch may be a function of power, but power is not a zero-sum game. It would be ludicrous to claim that the terrorists who murdered seventeen people in January 2015 were truly powerless.

When we look at these events from the cartoonists' perspective, we see more reasons to tread cautiously. As far as *Charlie*'s illustrators were concerned, they were actually punching *up*. They had gleaned from the Salman Rushdie and *Jyllands-Posten* affairs that they were vulnerable to militant state and non-state actors equipped with arsenals of deadly weapons. A credible threat of violent reprisal existed every time they drew their caricatures.[84]

The cartoonists refused to relent. Instead they punched up at militant Islamists, armed and dangerous people with a considerable degree of raw power. It might also be said that they simultaneously punched *down* on French Muslims with no connection to, or sympathy for, militant Islamists.

Thus we see that any analysis of punching down must factor in a spatial dimension—one that has been widened by the advent of the internet. In Denmark, *Jyllands-Posten* was conceivably punching down when it commissioned provocative cartoons that were sure to offend members of the nation's tiny Muslim community.[85] But then the images migrated to the Middle East and beyond. Suddenly this asymmetrical relation of power was reversed. Now Denmark's economy and its embassy personnel were the endangered minority, not to mention the cartoonists themselves.

Jyllands-Posten's editor Flemming Rose observed that "power is not static."[86] The insight is worth considering. Jokes, barbs, and slights are no longer isolated to one cultural or national space. Social media has shattered existing comedo-spatial norms, by radiating content quickly across the globe. This, too, upends the dynamics of punching up and punching down. The point is that in comedy it is not always easy to assess who is the perpetrator and who is the victim, who has the power and who does not.

THE "ASSASSIN'S VETO"

A few days after the January 7 attack, a surviving *Charlie* cartoonist drew a caricature in a state of anguish. Luz's image featured a weeping Prophet Muhammad holding up a "Je suis Charlie" sign.[87] A caption above the distraught figure read, "Tout est pardonné": All is forgiven.[88] The frame is striking, haunting and cryptic. It is also very *Charlie;* a close glance reveals what appears to be male genitalia in the shape of the turban on the Prophet's head.

This was obviously not an apology. Luz—who mentioned to an interviewer that he believed his Muhammad caricature spoke to him, saying:

"We'll get out of this mess because you're still here to draw me"—was not backing down.[89] "We have the right," Luz thundered, "to do anything and to do anything we want again, and to use our characters as we see fit."[90] Later he announced he was done drawing the Prophet Muhammad, though the magazine continues to publish incendiary images to this day.[91]

Such dogged refusal to issue even a cynical, strategic apology underscores these artists' ferocious commitment to their principles (compare it to the pseudo-apologies and "apology templates" we saw in earlier chapters). They truly believed in free speech, truly abhorred fundamentalist religion, and were willing to suffer the consequences of their convictions. They were defiant toward those who threatened them. "What I'm about to say," declared Charb, "is maybe a little pompous, but I'd rather die standing up than live on my knees."[92] Another editor wrote, "If we say to religions 'You're untouchable,' then we're screwed."[93]

"L'affaire Charlie Hebdo" pitted absolute believers in French conceptions of expressive liberty against absolute believers in a fundamentalist iteration of the Islamic faith. The antagonists were like two immovable granite blocks, albeit somehow cartoonishly accelerating toward each other at high speed. Neither would blink or back down.

The resultant collision raises a dilemma for democracies: Should artistic expression be limited when public order is endangered?[94] If certain comedians were hellbent on making jokes that would spawn violence, would the authorities be justified in preemptively making the gags illegal and silencing the comics?

Jurists refer to this as the "heckler's veto," a term that has now evolved into the "assassin's" or "terrorist's veto."[95] It comes into play when those who don't like a certain type of speech threaten a "disruption of public order."[96] If the government capitulates and shuts down protected expression in the name of safety, then a bad actor will have exploited "an extraconstitutional method to curb speech."[97]

In the twentieth century, The Consensus prevailed; liberal democracies consistently, courageously overrode such vetoes. France, as we saw, has been stalwart in not succumbing to such threats. In the United

States, the same has been generally true. "The First Amendment in modern times," observes a scholar of American law, "generally stands against acceding to the power of heckling counter-protesters to shut down messages with which they disagree. . . . Modern First Amendment doctrine places the burden on the listeners to avert their eyes, close their ears, or simply walk away."[98]

In light of the *Charlie Hebdo* affair, however, I predict an erosion in the willingness of liberal democracies to override the veto. The Consensus is wobbly. Bans on certain types of incendiary jokes may be in our future, because the collective will required to combat such censorship is not as robust as some might imagine. And this is not merely because people, understandably, fear violence. It is also because sizable numbers of law-abiding citizens do not necessarily support the robust free speech protections that prevailed in the twentieth century.[99]

Religious conservatives of all stripes fall into this category. We should recall that in France many traditionalist Catholics, like their Islamist counterparts, have complained bitterly about *Charlie*'s cartoons.[100] The late Charb observed with dismay that these two groups, who otherwise despised one another, were allied in their abhorrence of blasphemous speech. "Catholic fundamentalists," he exclaimed, "await every triumph by Muslim fundamentalists in their fight against Islamophobia with both voracity and jealousy."[101]

It would be a mistake, however, to assume that support for barring controversial comedy will come uniquely from the Right. Research has demonstrated that younger populations, including those leaning left, differ markedly from their predecessor generations on the issue of free speech. Survey after survey indicates that Millennials and members of Gen Z are far more willing to suppress types of expression they consider hateful, be it against religious minorities, sexual minorities, or other groups.[102]

Restrictions on free speech might also find a receptive audience in the business sector, where commitment to expressive freedom has always been uneven at best. We learned from the Danish example that an economic boycott was devastating to the nation's economic well-being. It seems plausible that corporations across the globe might decide that the bottom line trumps the unfettered right of an oddball cartoonist to draw testicles on some revered figure's head.

Finally, we should never overestimate the commitment of politicians to the defense of The Consensus. When *Charlie* published the Danish cartoons in 2006, French president Jacques Chirac made it abundantly clear that he did not appreciate their work, calling it "overt provocation."[103] One can easily picture conservative governments and courts finding ways to restrict controversial comedy in the name of safety.

In fact, such restrictions are explicitly mentioned in the foundational legal documents of many countries. In France, article 10 of the Declaration of the Rights of Man announces, "No one shall be disquieted on account of his opinions, including his religious views, provided their manifestation does not disturb the public order established by law."[104] In the hands of more conservative governments, such public order provisions could quickly be used to suppress potentially dangerous jokes.

Shortly after the *Charlie Hebdo* massacre, a variety of news outlets debated republishing Luz's "All is forgiven."[105] *Jyllands-Posten*, for one, declined to participate.[106] When asked why, Flemming Rose observed that "we [*Jyllands-Posten*] caved in."[107] He went on: "Violence works. . . . Sometimes the sword is mightier than the pen."[108]

SIX

Dieudonné M'bala M'bala

POSTCOLONIAL PROVOCATEUR, CONSENSUS DESTROYER

> Liberté-égalité-fraternité turlututu, chapeau pointu et mon cul sur la commode!
>
> DIEUDONNÉ M'BALA M'BALA

IMMEDIATELY AFTER THE *CHARLIE HEBDO* terrorist attacks, the hashtag #JeSuisCharlie went viral. It quickly became a digital totem representing multitudes of people traumatized by the massacres in Paris. Amid this moment of intense collective grief, France's most controversial comedian took to Facebook and posted a most unusual message: "*Je me sens Charlie Coulibaly*" (I feel like Charlie Coulibaly).[1]

The cryptic phrase alluded to at least three things. It was partly a reference to the magazine *Charlie Hebdo* and its slain cartoonists. It was partly a reference to the growing #JeSuisCharlie movement.[2] It was also conspicuously—and shockingly—a reference to Amedy Coulibaly, the militant who had just murdered a policewoman and four Jewish shoppers in Paris.[3]

As we shall see, the remark may be a touch more subtle than it initially seems. Still, such subtleties were not widely recognized. And understandably so. Many were unwilling to give the comedian the benefit of the doubt, including the French authorities who promptly arrested him for "condoning terrorism."[4] Perhaps that was because the individual who wrote "*Je me sens Charlie Coulibaly*" is the world's most notorious anti-Semitic insult comic.

Dieudonné M'bala M'bala is a fascinating and beguiling artist.[5] His diverse and international "coalition of the entertained" numbers in the millions. Dieudo, as he is sometimes called, is a masterful performer and a spellbinding orator. When listening to him speak—and he seems to be *always* speaking, either as a comic, an interviewee, a defendant, or a candidate for elected office—it's difficult not to be impressed by the preternatural lucidity of his oratory.

Yet those rare talents have been pressed into the service of an irrational obsession: for two decades running, this "shock-comic" has advanced an unrelenting critique of Jews, Judaism, and Israel.[6] This critique is enmeshed within a broader assault on secularism, individualism, liberal democracy, rights-based discourse, France, Western Civilization, the Enlightenment, and so on. If academic postcolonial studies had an official comedian, it would surely be Dieudonné M'bala M'bala.

Dieudonné's complaints, like those of *Charlie Hebdo* before him, are somewhat hypocritical. Like the cartoonists we discussed in the previous chapter, he benefits from France's free speech Consensus while excoriating all of the democratic ideas and institutions that make it possible. Then again, every national free speech Consensus is riddled with double standards, and France is no exception. Dieudonné relentlessly seeks those contradictions out. He then skillfully uses comedy and digital media to identify those discrepancies and publicize his concerns. Along the way he has become a multinational free speech martyr and "a lucrative commodity."[7]

What results is a complex comedic controversy that has lasted for a quarter century. Yes, his anti-Semitic jokes are reprehensible. Yes, they potentially pose risks to public safety. But yes, it is also true that the comedian is railing against free speech norms that seem unfair and double-standardish.

What also results is a warning of sorts. While pressing his case, Dieudonné has forged unusual political alliances between the Far Left and Far Right. This new coalition poses unique threats to the increasingly vulnerable Pre-Digital Liberal Free Speech Consensus.

"MY VOICE AT THE DISPOSAL OF CERTAIN CITIZENS"

Dieudonné M'Bala M'Bala was born in France in 1966 to a Cameroonian father and a French mother from Brittany. After his parents divorced, he was raised by his mother, Josiane Grué, a professor of sociology.[8]

Dieudonné describes his childhood in the Paris suburbs as uneventful. When an interviewer asked about his experience with racism, he said: "I never really suffered from it. I'm perfectly integrated."[9] Then again, his identity as a "métis" or mixed-race person placed him in the "non-white" category of France's rigid system of racial assignment. His mother claimed this sensitized him to forms of discrimination both major and minor that obtain in the Fifth Republic.[10]

His first run of commercial success occurred from 1991 to 1997. During this period he worked with his childhood friend, a Jewish comedian named Élie Semoun. Their collaboration featured everything from forgettable skits about gay butchers to some true gems lampooning French provincials (one bit about a town obsessed with an odd shoe-throwing sport is especially memorable).[11] Dieudonné flashes considerable actorly skills, especially the ability to play the calm, dry, straight man to Semoun's uber-animated characters. (To those raised on American comedy, the French counterpart can seem awfully theatrical and, well, ear-splitting. Indeed, those like Dieudo who stage one-man shows often appear to be competing for the title Loudest Man in Gaul.)

The duo's most substantial humor probed French multiculturalism, with a focus on those living in *les banlieues* and *les cités*—the socioeconomically disadvantaged suburbs and the affiliated housing projects where many Muslim, Black, and Arab citizens of France reside.[12] One of their most famous sketches was "Cohen and Bokassa."[13] With its obvious symbolic referents, the bit is widely described as an effort to counter France's debilitating stereotypes of Jews and Blacks. Semoun, playing Cohen the Jew, razzes Bokassa with taunts about bodily odors, welfare checks, and chimpanzees. Dieudonné, playing Bokassa the African, exclaims that the Germans should have finished the job, mocks Cohen's circumcision, and so on.

To a contemporary American viewer, this skit is cringe-inducing. The 1990s French audience, however, ate it up. It was a different era, no doubt. Though clearly, in this majoritarian white, Catholic country there existed a public eager to witness two minorities blasting each other with crude stereotypes.

By 1997 the comedians drifted apart.[14] Dieudonné's commitment to anti-racism now came to the fore, as did his penchant for seeking elected office. His first run was for a legislative position in the village of Dreux, about fifty miles west of Paris. The comedian articulated no particular policy platform; the objective of his candidacy was simply to counter the dominance of the town's far-right candidate, Marie-France Stirbois.[15] She represented La Front Nationale (FN), the party of Jean-Marie Le Pen, well known for its xenophobic, anti-immigrant, and anti-Semitic positions.

"Dreux is the town of the fascist revival," the comedian charged in media appearances.[16] When interviewed about his candidacy, Dieudonné showed himself to be a thoughtful artist, cognizant of systemic racism and intent on effecting change. His thoughts were clear—so clear. In measured tones, he equated his comedy to "placing [his] voice at the disposal of certain citizens."[17]

The cameras followed him to "les quartiers difficiles," the immigrant neighborhoods that no politician visited and the state had forsaken. He chatted amiably with the locals. In the end, his campaign, which lacked any formal planks or infrastructure, garnered roughly 8 percent of the vote.[18]

In the late 1990s, Dieudonné was a rising star. His outsize talent had earned him the respect of his peers in comedy and theater. His art was not particularly scandalous. His political focus was anti-racism, in which he joined a plethora of liberal groups in French civil society. Naturally, these included Jewish groups.

"ISRA-HEIL!"?

At the turn of the millennium, a new theme became evident in Dieudonné's work: Jews.[19] Prior to outlining his rationale for the shift,

I'll mention that it can usefully be situated within the context of major international events. Relevant here are the Second Intifada in Israel and Palestine, the 9/11 attacks, and America's ensuing "War on Terror," all of which shook up, altered, and polarized the political convictions of many citizens the world over.

These seismic geopolitical events also spawned a wealth of conspiracy theories involving Jews. Scholars speak of "the new anti-Semitism" (or *la nouvelle judéophobie*).[20] One feature of this attitude (leaving aside how "new" it is) is extreme anti-Zionism, which views all Jews as agents of Israel and its diabolical partner, the United States.[21] Demographically, the new anti-Semitism presents another twist: whereas the redoubt of older anti-Semitism was among white Europeans of the Far Right, this newer version gained a stronghold among Islamists, immigrant communities, and the radical Left.[22]

Dieudonné, for his part, traces his newfound interest in Jews to a professional setback. In his telling, he wished to make a film about French complicity in the slave trade called "Code Noir."[23] The studios balked. This led him to draw a comparison that had recently gained currency among African Americans in the United States: Jewish suffering was respectfully commemorated while Black suffering was ignored.[24]

This allegation is fundamentally true. However, Dieudonné then synergized the claim with others of more dubious validity. "Code Noir," he alleged, was scotched *by the Jews*, who exploited the memory of the Holocaust to erase the suffering of Blacks.[25] In a now-infamous 2002 interview he alleged:

> The descendants of the Jews continue to be given a free pass because of what happened during the Shoah. We, the Blacks, never got anything because certain Jews refuse to let our suffering be placed on the same level as theirs! I won't allow myself to rank victimization, because I believe that human suffering is the same in all tragedies, and that's the human condition. But I believe that the Jewish Lobby hates Blacks, really![26]

In 2003, Dieudonné performed a routine on a popular comedy show, *On ne peut pas plaire à tout le monde* (You Can't Please Everyone).[27] He took the stage adorned in a black ski mask, military fatigues, and some facsimile of the type of hat worn by an Orthodox Jew, with plastic sidecurls or *payot* spilling out on either side of his head. Playing the role of an Israeli settler, Dieudo urged the youth of *les banlieues* to convert to Judaism and "join the American-Zionist axis of good."[28]

The so-called *colon-facho* (fascist settler) bit was uneven, and the comedian himself later called it "relatively mediocre."[29] At its conclusion, he raised his arm in a gesture of physical comedy so poorly executed that many failed to even notice it. Upon review, he appeared to be making a Nazi salute and perhaps saying, "Isra-heil!"

Initially, the show's host and other guests dapped him up, congratulated him, and lauded his immense talent. As controversy spread in subsequent days, however, that praise got walked back. Dieudonné was soon accused of public defamation of a racist nature.[30] After years of winding its way through the French judicial system, the case was finally dismissed in 2007. The judge could not discern if Dieudo had actually said "Isra-heil!"[31]

Nevertheless, his transformation from the anti-racist days of the 1990s was now complete. In the words of one commentator, he had "drifted into pathological antisemitism and conspiracy theory."[32]

"THE AIDS OF JUDAISM"

Dieudonné M'Bala M'Bala has lampooned all sorts of folks: politicians of all stripes, pygmies, white people, Catholics, Muslim extremists, African political leaders, the LGBTQ community, Asians (Chinese people in particular), French speakers of African and Arab descent, entertainment figures, and on and on. That said, for two decades he has fixated predominantly, consistently, and often viciously on Jews. The Jewish community took note, leading to battles with the comedian that would periodically convulse France.

Dieudonné strenuously denies that he has anything against Jews. He is, he insists, "neither a Nazi, nor an anti-Semite."[33] No, he's not assailing the entire community—only the Jewish lobby, or "mafia," that controls

France.[34] He's not making fun of the Holocaust; he's simply pointing to the "instrumentalization" of Holocaust suffering by "Zionist" groups.[35]

It is difficult to take Dieudo's disavowals seriously. The newspaper *Le Monde* put it best: Dieudo is a "master of ellipses," skilled at claiming something he says does not mean what people believe it means.[36] It would take a separate book to chronicle all of his slights. What follows is something of a compilation of his greatest anti-Semitic hits, divided into four types of targets. (As with most anthologies, it is incomplete.)

High-profile Jewish individuals: Dieudonné often targets prominent French Jews. He had a field day with the travails of economist and politician Dominique Strauss-Kahn, who was accused (charges were later dismissed) of sexual assault in a New York hotel.[37] Riffing on reports that police found Strauss-Kahn's semen on his victim's dress, Dieudonné added that it had also been found on the carpet, the ceiling, in the parking lot, and so forth.[38]

Grimly, he made jokes about Ilan Halimi, the young Jewish phone salesman who was kidnapped in 2006 by an anti-Semitic gang called "the Barbarians."[39] The hostage takers tortured and mutilated Halimi for weeks before leaving him to die in the street.[40] During a 2014 show Dieudonné was recorded as saying, "[if they] exhume Ilan Halimi they're going to find my DNA in his asshole."[41] He was later fined for posting a video in which he called for the release of Halimi's murderer, Youssouf Fofana.[42]

The Jewish people: Another thematic slight centers around observations about the Jewish people as a collective entity, such as when he remarked that Jews "founded their empires and fortunes on the trade in Blacks and slavery."[43] In 2002 he observed, "For me, Jews are a cult, a swindle."[44]

The Holocaust: The Shoah, or the attempted extermination of the Jews between 1939 and 1945, is a staple of this humorist's anti-Semitic material. He adheres to a "zero-sum" conception of memorialization: when Jews commemorate the Shoah (something he calls "memorial pornography"), it somehow diminishes our ability to recognize the suffering of other peoples, notably Africans.[45]

Holocaust denial, or what the French call "négationnisme," is illegal in France.[46] Dieudonné, however, has surrounded himself with an entourage of highly controversial negationists[47]—though he denies that he himself is a negationist. In a manner reminiscent of right-wing American figures such as Tucker Carlson, he claims he's simply "asking questions."[48] Maybe, he suggests, the number of murdered Jews wasn't *precisely* six million. Maybe there were fewer gas chambers than alleged. Who knows?[49] Dieudonné's musings helped make fringe conspiracy theories go mainstream—or as one scholar phrased it, he was creating "negationism for the masses."[50]

Then there were what can only be called Holocaust-themed stunts, like his creation of "La Quenelle," an inverted Nazi salute. The gesture took on its own digital life, becoming a form of derision that multiplied exponentially. His fans, including many celebrities, posted selfies of themselves "sliding a quenelle" (*glisser la quenelle*) in front of synagogues, Auschwitz, and other Jewish-related sites.[51]

In the same vein, he performed a sketch called "Shoananas" (combining *Shoah* with the French word for pineapple). As a catchy children's tune plays in the background, his sidekick (Jacky Sigaux), dressed in concentration camp fatigues and bearing a huge yellow star, comes out shaking maracas. The two men dance exuberantly.[52]

The state of Israel and Zionism: In Dieudonné's telling, the problem is not Judaism per se. The real problem is a small elite of Jewish Zionists who completely control French society. Zionism, which he called "the AIDS of Judaism," is the connective tissue that brings together the comedian's various anti-Jewish planks.[53] Prominent Jews and their lobby, he contends, exploit the memory of the Holocaust to advance their nefarious interests in France and, by extension, Israel. In this way of thinking, Holocaust commemoration is a strategic act meant to indemnify Israel from critique. "The Zionists," he declares, "have claimed a monopoly on suffering."[54]

Dieudonné maintains that a comedian's job is to expose human folly, and in his view there is no human folly greater than Zionism.[55] His anti-Zionism, though, was not confined to his art and interviews. In 2004, 2009, and 2012, he ran as a candidate for anti-Zionist parties in the EU and the French parliament (he also made a run for the presidency of France in 2002).[56] In 2009, on a "resistance weekend," he visited Iran and met then-President Mahmoud Ahmadinejad.[57]

Perhaps his most outrageous anti-Zionist art, however, was the song "Palestine." The routine, far less well known than his other provocations, appeared in his show *J'ai fait l'con* (I'm being a jerk).[58] Dieudo plays Hamid, a twenty-two-year-old Palestinian suicide bomber. To the accompaniment of guitar, Hamid sings of his displacement at the hands of Israelis:

I was born here	Je suis né ici
On this slice of the Mediterranean	Sur ce bord de Méditerranée
In this paradise, suffused by the sun	Dans ce paradis ensoleillé
Palestine, Palestine	Palestine, Palestine

Hamid recounts what has led him to perform the murderous act he is about to commit:

They killed my father	Ils ont tué mon père
And then my uncle	Et puis mon oncle
And my brother	Et puis mon frère
They burned the house	Ont fait brûler la maison
Destroyed the gardens and orchards	Détruit jardins et plantations
To set up their settlers	Pour y installer leurs colons

Art plays a conspicuous role in this bit. Hamid's soliloquy invokes songs, melodies, and instruments:

Melody of people on the journey	Mélodie des gens du voyage
Music of the uprooted	Musique des déracinés
It helped me forget the pain	Elle m'a fait oublier le mal

In fact, Hamid's coming act of terror *is* a work of art. He fancies himself a musician, an orchestra conductor staging a performance whose final bars will be percussive and explosive:

And here I am now	Et me voilà maintenant
A bomb taped to my stomach . . .	Une bombe scotchée sur le bidon . . .

I am going to make you dance	Je vais vous faire danser
Happy settler	Joyeux colon
To the sound of my cannon	Sur le son de mon canon
Today I am the conductor	Aujourd'hui je suis chef d'orchestre
Tuning my note to the sound of time	Réglant ma note sur celle des temps

The guitar accelerates to a fevered cadence as the macabre tune comes to its climax. Hamid descends from the bus, focuses on his prey, and concludes his song with a bang:

I smile to a kid	Je souris à l'enfant
And at the end of street	Et puis au milieu de la rue
I see you, beautiful stranger	Je te vois, belle inconnue
It's you	C'est toi
I chose you	Je t'ai choisi
Shall I grab you by the waist	Vais-je tu prendre par la taille
And make our innards dance?	Et faire danser nos entrailles?
Your eyes locked on me	Ton regard que me fixe
You understand	Tu comprends
Your pocketbook falls to ground	Ton sac qui tombe
An apple rolls out	La pomme qui roule
Move back?	Reculez?
It's too late, sweetie	Il est trop tard, petite
My finger tenses up	Y'a mon doigt qui se crispe
Since the two of us can't live with one another	Puisqu'on ne peut vivre tous les deux
Let's die together	Crevons ensemble

WHEN THE STATE IS PROFANED

Not surprisingly, the Jewish community constituted a major part of Dieudonné's coalition of the outraged. On a few occasions, Jewish protesters interrupted his performances.[59] During a trip to Martinique in

2005 the comedian was assaulted by four Israeli nationals who were subsequently arrested.[60] In his show *1905* he claimed he was attacked by Jewish militants in Paris.[61]

These physical altercations, however, are far less frequent than his countless legal and media scuffles with Jewish groups that he sees as part of the mafia.[62] These include the CRIF (Conseil Représentatif des Institutions Juives de France), LICRA (Ligue Internationale Contre le Racisme et l'Antisémitisme), and the UEJF (Union des Etudiants Juifs de France).

Dieudonné has been challenged by local and national authorities as well. He is no longer permitted to enter the United Kingdom.[63] Morocco would not let him perform there in 2015.[64] A year later, he was sternly warned not to ply his wares in Montreal.[65] After performances in Switzerland and Belgium, he was found guilty of inciting racial hatred.[66]

Which brings us to his native France, where the coalition of the outraged includes his own government. French prosecutors have pursued Dieudonné for two decades. Authorities have fined him, banned his shows, arrested him; they have tried to have him imprisoned, but to no avail. So much for the omnipotence of the Jews and their mafia!

To American observers, this governmental reaction to mere speech acts, especially *comedic* speech acts, may seem odd. In the United States, what is commonly called "hate speech" is granted a wide berth; denigrating a given religious, racial, or ethnic group is generally legal, as long as there is no imminent threat of violence and individual members of the group are not singled out.[67] In France, by contrast, the "legal system can readily accommodate a very illiberal view of freedom of speech."[68]

It would require a separate chapter to chronicle all of the charges leveled at Dieudonné by the state, not to mention the media spectacles they engender. Just a few examples will be offered here.

Let's start with the "public order" provisions built into France's foundational documents (see chapter 5). These imply that (unspecified) security considerations may trump expressive liberties. In 2013, Dieudonné's show *Le Mur* was banned in cities across France by Interior Minister Manuel Valls after a hidden camera in his theater revealed him wishing that a Jewish journalist had lived in the era of gas chambers.[69] The shows in which the Quenelle was slid were similarly deemed a threat to public safety and banned.[70]

Then there is the 1972 Loi Pleven, which "provides protection against acts of racial discrimination, as well as three categories of racist speech (incitement, libel, and *injure* or abuse)."[71] In 2005, Dieudonné made the aforementioned "memorial pornography" remark.[72] For this he was tried, convicted, and eventually fined 7,000 euros.[73] In 2006, he was assessed a 5,000 euro fine for "inciting racial hatred with comments comparing Jews to slave traders."[74]

Most saliently, there is the ever-controversial Loi Gayssot of 1990,[75] a "memory law" that effectively makes Holocaust denial punishable by fine or imprisonment.[76] In 2014, Dieudonné was ordered to remove a video about the Quenelle from YouTube, risking a fine of 500 euros for each day he did not. Undeterred, he let the clip remain, in which he claimed to "know nothing about the gas chambers." Judge Marc Bailly "ruled that one of the passages" from the video "breached French law on Holocaust denial and another one amounted to incitement to racial hatred."[77]

As noted above, Dieudonné's "Je me sens Charlie Coulibaly" post led to his arrest for supporting terrorism. He defended himself by saying that he deplored "without restraint and without any ambiguity" the events of January 7.[78] His invocation of Coulibaly, he alleged, had to do with his sense of being treated like a "terrorist" in his own country.[79] Having drawn our attention to this subtlety, one still wonders why he felt kinship with a man who had just murdered Jews and a police officer.

"THE LIE OF DEMOCRACY"

Dieudonné has targets other than the Jews. As one journalist put it, he has declared "war on France."[80] He mocks not only the government, but the nation's lofty values of free speech, equality, *laïcité* (what we would call “secularism”), and human rights.[81] Not restricting himself to the Hexagon, he then broadens his critique to all liberal democracies, the Enlightenment, and Western civilization itself.

Here the comedian links up with the postcolonial theorists discussed in the previous chapter. These researchers evince “a profound distrust or complete rejection of core principles of universalism, secularism, liberalism . . . as irredeemably false universals that mask racist, imperialist assumptions and reinforce existing power dynamics.”[82] Postcolonialists are fond of “mapping,” “interrogating,” and “problematizing” the West’s triumphant narratives about its political and cultural legacies. Dieudo does that too, though his medium is comedic quips, barbs, and asides rather than rarefied academic discourse.

The Enlightenment, as he jokes in the epigraph, is overrated. Elsewhere Dieudo points out that its leading lights in France—Montesquieu, Diderot, Rousseau, Voltaire—were all racists.[83] The comedian spends a good deal of time on the conception of “rights,” one of the delicate flowers of Enlightenment thought. For Dieudonné, as for his academic postcolonial counterparts, the West is less interested in granting and protecting rights than in weaponizing a *discourse* of “rights.”

This discourse assisted Europeans in plundering, brutalizing, and dominating all others. In one of his shows he reframed the Declaration of the Rights of Man of 1789 as really being about “the rights of white men.”[84] More darkly, Dieudonné recently mused: “This civilization is built on a lie . . . the lie of democracy, the lie of human rights . . . This system is an enormous lie.”[85]

France prides itself on a form of secularism called *laïcité* that aspires to treat all citizens equally while minimizing the role of religion in public life.[86] In his show *1905*, however, Dieudonné pretended to spit in the face of *laïcité* after delivering this monologue:

> *Laïcité. Laïcité.* What are you talking about? So according to you we’d all be able to leave the cozy nest of our religions, our communities, our ethnicities to find ourselves all united in some sort of universal citizenship? My fucking ass. How stupid do you think we are?[87]

Here again he overlaps with postcolonial theorists who have criticized secularism (in far more sober language) for decades.[88] Later he exclaimed, "I don't believe in *laïcité*, I don't believe in equality, I don't believe in all that."[89]

If he doesn't believe in "all that," he certainly doesn't believe that secular France, or any Western country, defends the free speech rights of religious citizens equally. An example comes to mind. When *Charlie Hebdo* trampled on Muslim sensitivities, it was glorified for defending the values of Republican France, yet when Dieudonné tackles the Holocaust, specific laws subject him to criminal prosecution.

This is likely why he seeks to provoke courtroom showdowns about the Gayssot law, which criminalizes Holocaust denialism. He could ask, reasonably, why no Muslim version of this edict exists prohibiting denigration of the Prophet and thus protecting the sensitivities of another French minority group. One could respond, just as reasonably, that France does not recognize blasphemy as a crime; penalizing false historical claims is different from penalizing what is heterodox to some Muslims.[90]

Yet Dieudo's repeated charge of a double standard is not to be taken lightly. Why do the nation's laws always seem to align against the interests of Black and Arab citizens of France? Why, he asks, is the Holocaust the paradigmatic case of "crimes against humanity," but never the African slave trade?[91]

Dieudonné is a postcolonial provocateur in two senses. First, he renders into the key of comedy (and anti-Semitism) the melodies of postcolonial theory. The ensuing libretto is so relentlessly critical of his country's self-perception and its version of The Consensus that it's no wonder he has become "the black militant artist the French secular republic loves to hate."[92]

Second, he has garnered an immense postcolonial fan base, composed mostly of a Brown, Black, and Arab France that has long complained of being treated like second-class citizens. One observer likens him to "a Robin Hood of freedom of expression with people in the *banlieues*."[93] That postcolonial fanbase, as we shall now see, is dangerously conjoined with another.

It's 2024 and Dieudonné M'Bala M'Bala is under house arrest for a 2019 conviction. He's confined to his home, but not on account of violating any speech laws. This time, he's been penalized for tax fraud and money laundering.[94]

The authorities have placed a bracelet on his ankle. He proudly displays this piece of carceral hardware to the assorted podcasters, YouTube hosts, and influencers who interview him. The contraption, he claims, perfectly embodies the plight of the Black artist in French society.[95] He considers it a medal of honor that links him with "the voice and energy of his 'ancestors,'" individuals such as Nelson Mandela and Muammar Qaddafi.[96] The electronic manacle reminds him: "I am a slave, I am a Black man who is considered an animal."[97]

His incarceration has not stopped him from speaking—speaking a great deal, in fact. One of the themes of this book is that "cancellation" in liberal democracies does not effectively prevent comedians from communicating with their audiences. Canceled artists can always express themselves (and sell their art) on their own websites. Too, there exist alternative media outlets eager to platform controversial voices. Even while under house arrest, even while canceled, and even while being a pariah, or what the French call "*infréquentable*," Dieudonné can radiate his views far and wide.

And what views they are! He believes all persons of African descent in France and the diaspora should return to their ancestral homelands.[98] Everyone should just dwell among their own people forevermore (he himself intends to retire from comedy soon and move to Cameroon).

He's in with anti-vaxxers.[99] He speaks reverently of Russia. Vladmir Putin, he says, is a patient man, but his patience is wearing thin.[100] World War III, Dieudo believes, is imminent. There won't, he sighs, be a World War IV.[101]

Then there's the LGBTQ community. In a bit from his show *Gilets Jaunes*, one of his characters wonders why these people can't do whatever it is they do in private? In Africa, after all, these things—these *queer* things—are done behind closed doors, away from the public eye, unlike in Strasbourg, where man-on-man sex takes place in the street.[102]

In a podcast he points out that homosexuality is forbidden in Cameroon's public spaces.[103] It's not clear if he means that simply being gay is forbidden in public, but that would seem to suit him just fine. He believes the salience of LGBTQ propaganda signals a "moral collapse," as well as the end of Western supremacy with its unrestrained individualism.[104] The gays, he says, are aggressively forcing their values on his children and all French children. Dieudo is very worried about the children.

He was once speaking to somebody who told him that some scientist claimed that the earth has recently rotated slightly off its axis.[105] Maybe, he sighs, this accounts for the proliferation of all this LGBTQ stuff, which he views as unnatural. He stresses, of course, that he has nothing against those people.[106] But some (not all, of course) in the LGBTQ community are part of the mafia that runs France.[107] They are becoming his new Jews.

As for the Jews, he's very disappointed in them. He issued an apology to the Jewish community in 2023,[108] writing: "I also want to ask forgiveness from all those I may have hurt, shocked, harmed through some of my acts of artistic expression. I am thinking in particular of my compatriots in the Jewish community, to whom I humbly admit I went too far. It's true, I sometimes went too far and acted outrageously, indulging in inappropriate provocations."[109]

A few Jews forgave, but most could not put aside decades of vicious insults. Most Jews remember his 2004 *Mes excuses* (My Apologies) where Dieudo went meta: far from apologizing, he took accusations about his anti-Semitism and recycled them right back into the show, mocking Jews generally.[110] The Jews are wary of Dieudo's contrition.

No matter. He reasons that he performed his duty as a Christian. Christianity is a religion of forgiveness.[111] Dieudo followed Christ's example. He couldn't do more than that.[112] Now he thinks the Jews should ask *him* for forgiveness.[113] He wonders aloud if the best thing for the Jews wouldn't just be to convert to Christianity.[114]

The reader may notice that ankle-bracelet Dieudonné sounds awfully conservative. In fact, this turn to the right had been years in the making. It started in 2007 when he shocked his followers by reconciling with, and befriending, Jean-Marie Le Pen. Yes, *that* Jean-Marie Le Pen: the leader of France's nationalist Right—pro-colonialist, an unrepentant xenophobe and avowed foe of the country's immigrant communities.[115] The fiery politician was a scion of a long line of snarling Gallic nativists who exclaimed, "*La France aux français*" (France for the French).[116] The "*français*" in question being white Catholics. French people of Maghrebian, Sahelian, and Caribbean extraction—or Jewish people—are decidedly not part of that France.

Dieudonné, as we saw above, ran, and railed, against a Front Nationale candidate in 1997. Yet there he was a decade later singing the praises of the FN's leader. In 2007, Dieudo even let it be known that Le Pen—who himself had been convicted of Holocaust denial—was his son's godfather.[117] It seems they found common ground in their hatred of the status quo—a status quo that both allege is controlled by the "Jewish mafia."

We've already pondered the fact that a comedian has "constituencies." But Dieudo is unusual in that his constituencies occupy opposite sides of the political spectrum.[118] He has an organic "postcolonial" fan base, but ever since his alliance with Le Pen he has had a following on the Far Right as well. His "incredibly heterogeneous audience" includes French citizens with African and Middle Eastern roots who excoriate France as a white, racist monoculture *and* whites who wish France would become that monoculture again.[119]

This is the most unusual coalition of the entertained we've yet to encounter. Though maybe it won't stay unusual for long. In liberal democracies today, the Far Left and the Far Right share an adversary around whom they form a pincer, one we might refer to by various, overlapping terms such as "the Center," "the mainstream," "the status quo," "*la classe politique et médiatique*," "the elites"—or liberal democracy itself.

Perhaps Dieudo's diverse, populist coalition represents a new development. Within liberal democracies, the center and its free speech

Consensus are under siege from the flanks and the fringes. In France, the Far Right and the Far Left can laugh together at Jewish jokes. Their common cause raises the possibility that in another country they might unite over barbs aimed more broadly—at immigrants, Muslims, gays, and other minorities. It also raises the possibility that The Consensus, fighting on two fronts, is in great trouble.

PART THREE

No Consensus

JOKES IN NON-DEMOCRATIC SPACES

SEVEN

"I'm Just a Satirist"

POLITAINMENT AND BASSEM YOUSSEF

All I did was make jokes.

BASSEM YOUSSEF
Revolution for Dummies: Laughing through the Arab Spring (2017)

ONE DAY IN THE FUTURE, people might view satirical news programs like *The Daily Show* with the same puzzlement we experience when we watch footage of mid-century comedic duos. Google acts from the 1940s, like Abbott and Costello, and give their bits a watch on YouTube. You'll likely have many questions. Questions like: Is this supposed to be funny? Why are the comics screaming? What are they even saying? Why is the audience laughing so hard? And why is everyone wearing fedoras?

Comedy, more than any other art form, bears the linguistic markings and cultural quiddities of the era in which it is performed. Maybe that's why old routines seem so much more "archival" to contemporary observers than old tunes or canvases. Music and paintings from the Abbott and Costello era, like Thelonious Monk's "I Mean You" or Piet Mondrian's *Victory Boogie Woogie*, usually don't leave people today scratching their heads. A relic like Abbott and Costello's "Two Tens for a Five," by contrast, seems encased in the amber of its day.[1] I'm not sure why. But it does raise the possibility that the comedy we adore today might flummox our grandchildren tomorrow.

In this vein, I wonder what people in the year 2075 might make of *The Daily Show* and the countless domestic and international spinoffs of the franchise it spawned. What, our grandchildren may ask, prompted so many comedians in the early twenty-first century to dress as newscasters and get all shined up?[2] Aren't comedians lounge-around-in-stained-sweats sorts of folk? Yet back in grandpa's day they appeared in suits, properly knotted ties, and tailleurs, their hair neatly combed.

A related set of questions for posterity concerns why these shows "plagiariz[ed] the aesthetics of the media."[3] What impelled these artists to perform on soundstages that looked exactly like newsrooms? Why did they go so far as to adopt the camera angles and entire visual vocabulary of cable and network news? Why did they work so hard to mimic the flashy chyrons and eye-popping graphics seen on CNN and Fox News? Why bother with all those fake correspondents and fake guests?

There is, of course, a difference between real news and the fake news these comedians are performing—including the live, loud studio audience.[4] Though even those tittering spectators don't undermine the "newsiness" of these productions. Which is another thing that might bewilder those of the future: people actually got their news from these clever clown shows.

A final query that our descendants might pose about satiric news shows of the early 2000s concerns whether they had any socially redeeming value *beyond* entertainment. Is this comedic genre a boon to liberal democracy? Is it needed in nondemocratic societies? Does it demonstrate comedy's capacity to effectuate positive change, right wrongs, build a better future? Such claims, to the best of my knowledge, were never made about Abbott and Costello—though they are often made about parodic news.

In this chapter, I hope to offer some appropriately nuanced responses to these questions. To do that, I use the example of Bassem Youssef, an Egyptian news parodist whose jokes got him into a world of trouble. Youssef's saga kicks off part 3 of this study, where we survey comedy in nondemocratic spaces—spaces where there is no Pre-Digital Liberal Free Speech Consensus and where Western-style free speech laws are not observed.

The comedic genre that we examine here goes by a variety of names: political TV satire, televised political satire, satire TV, satire news, news parody, parodic news, and on and on.[5] Elsewhere it might be referred to as "fake news"—which I prefer in part because of all the sinister multivalence it evokes in the wake of Donald J. Trump's appropriation of the term.[6] All of these designations are part of a broader cultural phenomenon that scholars label "politainment" or "politicotainment," which we shall encounter momentarily.[7]

Researchers trace the origins of fake news to British programs of the early 1960s like *That Was the Week That Was*. The concept quickly migrated to Canada (*This Hour Has Seven Days*) and Germany (*Notizen aus der Provinz*, or Notes from the Periphery).[8] A pivotal moment in the genre's evolution was the "Weekend Update" segment of America's *Saturday Night Live*. From the mid-1970s to the 1990s, cast members such as Chevy Chase, Jane Curtin, and Dennis Miller, among others, normalized and popularized the gimmick of comedians delivering the news while masquerading as journalists.[9]

The north star, gateway, and watershed for this genre, however, is *The Daily Show*, a franchise that came into its own when Jon Stewart took over the "anchor's desk" from Craig Kilborn in 1999.[10] Throughout the close and contested American elections of the new millennium, *The Daily Show* achieved huge popularity, and Stewart himself became an iconic figure both in the United States and abroad.[11] After a sixteen-year stint, he stepped down in 2015, but returned to part-time hosting in 2024.

In the United States, *The Daily Show* generated spin-offs such as *Last Week Tonight with John Oliver, The Colbert Report, The Nightly Show with Larry Wilmore, Full Frontal with Samantha Bee*, and *The Opposition with Jordan Klepper.*[12] All these shows were ostentatiously liberal in their perspective. Eventually, conservative broadcasters recognized the power of this medium. The Fox News channel began to produce its own imitations. As Matt Sienkiewicz and Nick Marx point out in their study of right-wing comedy, Fox productions like *Watters' World* and *Gutfeld!* embody "the same aesthetic strategy" as their liberal precursors.[13]

For our purposes, the key fact is that the genre of fake news is popular across the world. This comedic technology was adopted globally and then customized locally (or "glocalized").[14] The list of nations with facsimiles of *The Daily Show* is long. It includes those where there is a Consensus (e.g., Germany, the UK, Italy, India) and those where there is no Consensus (e.g., Egypt, Iran, Iraq, Nigeria, Zimbabwe). In some cases, the international versions replicate the look and structure of *The Daily Show*. In some cases the hosts themselves mimic Stewart's mannerisms or physically resemble him. And in some cases, as we are about to see, all of these things happen at once.

THE OMNI-BLUR OF POLITAINMENT

A substantial body of academic analysis has focused on news parody. In terms of our interest in comedic controversies, a few core ideas are relevant. The first is that while these news parodies ostensibly critique politics, *they may be just as critical of the broadcast media*.

As media analysts Geoffrey Baym and Jeffrey Jones note, televised political satire is geared to "expose the artifice of news."[15] Journalism itself in these shows is depicted not as objective and independent, but as "subservient to societal structures of power and authority."[16] News parody's ultimate impact, then, may be to undermine popular faith in the media.[17]

By taking on two theoretically distinct targets—political figures and the media—fake news becomes uniquely subversive in authoritarian states where the media is tightly controlled by, if not an outright mouthpiece of, the government. Naturally, being like liberal, sassy Jon Stewart in an illiberal, unsassy environment can be hazardous to the career and safety of purveyors of news parody. Put differently: where The Consensus does not exist, news parody is dangerous.

And confusing. This leads us to a second dimension of the genre, something I refer to as "omni-blur": the fact that these parodies relentlessly mix together things that are assumed to be distinct from one another. As I mentioned above, fake news is a subgenre of politainment. One standard definition of this term is "the blending of politics and entertainment" whereby the "entertainment industry exploits political topics in various entertainment formats."[18]

That's just the beginning of the blur, however. Fake news also gleefully jumbles what is real and what is not. The "anchor," after all, is often "reporting" a true news story, only to comically reframe it seconds later. In a 2024 episode of *The Daily Show*, for example, Stewart shared real footage of President Joe Biden slowly old-man-shuffling out of a press conference. He then rolled the video again, posing it as the intro sequence to a seventies-style sitcom, replete with a theme song and bubbly Carter-era graphics, introducing old man Biden as a character named "Colonel Butters."[19]

Omni-blur extends to the performers who deliver the news as well. As media scholar Amber Day observes, "Their work functions as political speech in itself, affecting the direction of public discourse while elevating the parodist to the level of legitimate political expert."[20] To Day's point, fake news always raises a question for me: could it be that this comic, whose core competency is (let's say) making jokes about genitals, is "sincerely" trying to advance a substantive, well thought out point about a complex political issue?

Fake newscasters are often likened to "court jester" types.[21] As Stewart once enthused, "We have no power."[22] Perhaps. But that assertion is belied by findings that stunned political and media elites in the early 2000s. Namely, a significant portion of Americans—some 12 percent—were getting their news from *The Daily Show*.[23] People really like their fake news, confusing and blurry though it may be. Their support endows the fake newscaster with a certain power and cultural leverage.

Another confusion synthesized by this art form concerns the actual political commitments of those who create the parody. Jon Stewart describes himself as neither liberal nor conservative "but passionately opposed to bullshit."[24] Elsewhere, he has self-identified as a representative of "the distracted center."[25] This seems a bit off. Stewart's body of serious work suggests that he is a liberal. But that is beside the point. What matters is that fake news abounds in irony, feints, and misdirection, which may extend to the political positions of the hosts.

All of this blurring creates delight for some audiences. For some, it is confusing. And for others, it inspires punitive rage.

"JON STEWART ON THE NILE"

Bassem Youssef is an Egyptian fake newsman who inspired punitive rage not only among his enemies, but also among *the enemies of his enemies.* Naturally, Youssef had legions of fans: his short-lived (2011–2014) television show *Al-Bernamig* ("The Program" in Arabic) was among the most watched in the history of Egypt and even the Middle East.[26] At its height, some 30–40 million viewers screened its weekly episodes.[27]

Of all the global Jon Stewarts that starred in far-flung facsimiles of *The Daily Show*, Bassem Youssef is the Jon Stewartiest of them all, his "closest clone."[28] "Youssef," write scholars Joel Gordon and Heba Arafa, "mimics Stewart's body language, facial expressions, and comic timing to a disarming degree."[29] The news parody programs that Youssef created and hosted, first *B+* (2011) and then *Al-Bernamig*, were directly modeled on *The Daily Show*. Youssef refers to Stewart as his "biggest inspiration."[30]

Stewart, for his part, greatly admires the man who has been variously dubbed "the Jon Stewart of Egypt," "the Jon Stewart on the Nile," and the "the Jon Stewart of the Middle East."[31] He interviewed Youssef on *The Daily Show*, blurbed Youssef's book *Revolution for Dummies*, and appeared as a guest on *Al-Bernamig*. Of his Egyptian counterpart the American comedian said: "He hosts his program in a country where freedom of expression is not settled law. He helps carve out space through his show to help that country understand the importance of dissent and satire's role."[32]

Leaving the similarities and mutual admiration of the two comics aside, the fates of their comedic projects were quite different. *The Daily Show with John Stewart* was broadcast for a decade and a half on Comedy Central. The media and entertainment conglomerate Viacom was its steady and profitable corporate overlord for almost all that time (though now the show is owned by Paramount Global, whose cancellation of "The Late Show with Stephen Colbert" in July 2025 prompted charges of political meddling).[33] Youssef's *Al-Bernamig* ran for just three seasons, bouncing from channel to channel until no Egyptian network would carry it.[34]

As with Stewart, Youssef's fake news made him internationally famous and earned him many awards and accolades. But unlike Stewart, his satire led to all sorts of personal and professional travails—legal challenges, arrest warrants, interrogations, and attempts to jam and censor his programs. There were physical threats to him, his colleagues, and his family. All of this punitive rage led in 2014 to his exile from his native Egypt.

Youssef's fake news journey began during the Arab Spring of 2011. At the time, he was contemplating coming to the United States to practice as a cardiac surgeon in Cleveland (wherein lies another difference between Stewart and Youssef). But even before the massive demonstrations against Egyptian president Hosni Mubarak were picking up steam in January 2011, Youssef was experimenting with digital content creation.[35]

On February 11, 2011, Mubarak stepped down. One month later, Youssef launched the pilot episode of *B+*, which he posted on YouTube. Filmed from Youssef's laundry room, the show's segments were unusually direct by Egyptian standards.

Youssef has commented that while there is a rich tradition of political satire in Egypt, it tends to avoid saying the obvious.[36] His show did not avoid the obvious, no matter how critical of the powerful the obvious might have been. If, moreover, politainment is characterized by a critique of the media, *B+* delivered that by the metric ton. Its host skewered the way the pro-democracy protests were being reported by Egypt's notoriously unobjective and state-aligned news agencies. The segments, usually just a few minutes in length, accrued millions of views.[37]

Suddenly famous in what was widely (and wrongly) assumed to be a new era of democratization, the rising star was approached by numerous media outlets. Cleveland and medicine could wait; the affable physician was positioned to actualize his dream of bringing *The Daily Show* to Egyptian audiences. He sought a real professional staff, a real network to platform him, and a real fake news studio. By August 2011, *Al-Bernamig* had launched.[38]

FAKE NEWS IN AN AUTHORITARIAN STATE

"When someone is in authority," Youssef once remarked in a very Consensus-like way, "you make fun of them."[39] Throughout the Arab Spring the comedian stayed true to his creed. In accordance with the mandates of fake news, he placed Egyptian journalists in his sights, mocking the media's inaccurate and condescending coverage of the protests that roiled the region.[40]

News parody's other target, political actors, were duly razzed as well. In early 2011 he focused on the burgeoning Islamist coalition in Egypt, whose superior organization and infrastructure made it a frontrunner in any post-Mubarak reconstruction.[41] Surveying its membership, he exclaimed: "Salafists! Now it's complete! No wait! There's still one element missing. No one has mentioned them yet." Youssef then cued the Hezbollah anthem to play in the background as he roll-called the new coalition: "That's more like it! Now the conspiracy is complete. Salafists, Muslim Brotherhood, Mossad, Hezbollah. This is a real revolution!"[42]

In June 2012, the Islamist Muhammad Morsi attained the presidency in a democratic election. Even with a new authority figure in place, Youssef did not relent. Political Islamists are not generally known for appreciating a good roast—at least not when they are the ones getting cooked, sliced, and garnished. Predictably, they were not well disposed to Youssef's jibes. And no, they were not about to overlook the fact that

Al-Bernamig was carried on a relatively new and independent station (ONTV) owned by a Coptic Christian millionaire.[43] This meant that Youssef, a moderate Muslim, was making fun of fundamentalist Muslims on a Christian-owned platform.

That November, Youssef switched to a new carrier, CBC.[44] As this was happening, protests reignited in opposition to the heavy-handed fundamentalist policies of the Morsi government. Once again, *Al-Bernamig* covered these events with gusto. The host noted how the same media tropes heard during the Mubarak days about the anti-government demonstrators were now being mouthed by the ruling Muslim brotherhood. Clip after clip of Islamists claiming that they had infiltrated the protests and found drugs, alcohol, vaginal disinfectant, sex paraphernalia, and, oddly, cheese triangles were mocked by Youssef.[45]

President Morsi and his Islamist policies provided much material, with Youssef's gags sometimes drifting out of comedy into social commentary.[46] In one episode, Youssef thundered: "Just like you don't consider us Muslims, we don't consider you sheikhs or scholars."[47] Nor was any punchline intended in his aside that "Islam is bigger and more welcoming and better than how you represent it."[48] A guest on the show, the comedian Ali Kandil, trod similar ground as he poked fun at the Muslim call to prayer.[49]

Tensions came to a head in what would become one of *Al-Bernamig*'s most famous visual gags. Here, Youssef ridiculed a rather large hat that Morsi had worn to a ceremony in Pakistan. The image of the host walking to the anchor's desk balancing a cap almost as large as himself went viral. Soon thereafter, Youssef was arrested and charged with "insulting the president and Islam."[50] Naturally, he attended his hearing adorned in the comic headgear amid throngs of onlookers and selfie-seekers. He was fined and released on bail.

By early 2013, Morsi stirred panic that he would theocratize Egypt's government. In March, the Tamarod movement formed in opposition to the administration.[51] A few months later, Egypt's "first experiment in democracy" ended in a military action as Morsi was overthrown by Field Commander Abdel Fattah al-Sisi.[52]

Was it a coup or a revolution? Youssef favored the former assessment. With a new authority figure to ridicule, the comedian got to work on the interim government of Adly Mansour, widely assumed to be a placeholder until an election that would "democratically" bring al-Sisi to power.

In October 2013, *Al-Bernamig* aired a controversial sketch featuring a male actor dressed as a woman. Her name was Gamaheer, or "The People."[53] Crammed with sexual double entendres, the skit managed to mock everyone from Gamaheer's former lovers (the Islamists), to the next man up (the incoming regime of al-Sisi), not to mention the fickle Egyptian electorate.[54]

Al-Bernamig's constant critique of the interim government earned its host visits from state intelligence services. His corporate broadcaster grew nervous, likely facing threats as well. Youssef claims that many of the so-called liberals who supported him when he mocked the Islamists abandoned him when he trained his invective on the army and the al-Sisi regime. He abruptly canceled the show. "The Program doesn't have a space," Youssef explained. "It's not allowed."[55] As scholar Tarek Masoud notes, the show, "which had been so effective in subverting the Morsi Presidency, could not survive a month in the post-coup political environment."[56]

Youssef was visiting Dubai in 2014 when he learned that his producer's father had been arrested. At roughly the same time, a judge levied a massive fine against the increasingly isolated host of *Al-Bernamig* (Youssef believes the unusually harsh judgment in this arbitration case was manipulated by the government). He returned to Egypt, packed his bags, and fled the country before he could be placed on a no-fly list. He has never returned.[57]

AL-BERNAMIG'S AUTOPSY

In just three years, Bassem Youssef became the most famous and most polarizing comedian in the history of the Middle East. In the long run, his project, his *intervention*, will likely impact the free speech culture of the region for decades. *Al-Bernamig* will provide a heroic benchmark of what political satire can sound like in a country where many are fearful of its insolent, contrarian cadences.

In the short run, though, Youssef's endeavor to bring American-style parodic news to Egypt was unsuccessful. For the most part, it failed for the same reason that the Arab Spring quickly devolved into the Arab Winter: the lack of a political, legal, and economic infrastructure within Egypt that could support widespread citizen demands for rapid democratization.[58] That in itself was a result of Egypt's history of colonialism, a tragedy that hellspawned decades of authoritarian governments. Politainment will always struggle to breathe outside of a liberal democracy.

News parody, by design, functions as an act of *mass* communication (unlike stand-up comedy, which usually takes place in a club seating a few dozen people). Its remit is not only to emulate the news but to reach the same vast audiences that consume the news. To achieve this end it requires large technical teams, huge financial investments, corporate sponsorship, network support, broadcasting licenses, and so forth.

Fake news is thus difficult to produce and easy to deplatform. A controversial news parodist can be shut down by the network or nervous advertisers.[59] In a country with a shaky democratic footing such as Egypt, the government can deploy its vast powers, directly or indirectly, to unplug the program. One way to explain Youssef's failure absolves him of blame: within a political economy like that of contemporary Egypt, any sort of subversive mass communication—or what scholars call "culture jamming"—is destined not to last for long.[60] It's impressive that *Al-Bernamig* lasted as long as it did.

Yet Youssef can perhaps be blamed for not "reading the room." He was beholden to an understanding of comedy's function that could only fail in the political space he was occupying. He acted (courageously) *as if* there was a free speech Consensus in Egypt. In so doing, he antagonized powerful people and groups. He trained his talents of derision on Islamists, anti-Islamists, the old guard media—Youssef targeted them all! He once quipped that if Copts ran Egypt, he'd make fun of them too.[61] In terms of ethical comedic practice, this is commendable. Yet admirable as this punching up may have been, it was ultimately suicidal.

There is a twist in all this that lends a nuance to our understanding of "punching up," of meting out comedic justice on behalf of the majority, or even the masses. The punch-up artist mocks the tyrant, the oligarch, the arms dealer, the sexist CEO. In theory, one punches up for the greater good and for the good of a large section of the populace.

In retrospect, Youssef's punching up had a paradoxical effect. When he was enfilading the media, Mubarak, and the Muslim Brotherhood, his fan base of liberal, secular Egyptians championed him. At that moment, his devotees were committed to the robust free speech protections that Youssef himself endorsed. They continued to support him throughout the tumultuous twelve months of Islamist rule. Then came Field Commander al-Sisi and the military who imprisoned Muhammad Morsi.

The violent transition of power had an unexpected impact on public opinion. Youssef recounts with considerable bitterness that many in the liberal secular camp seemed at peace with al-Sisi's regime and its authoritarian tendencies (even his own parents tended to side with the new anti-Islamist and anti-democratic replacement).[62] This may be because Egyptians were so traumatized by the looming specter of Islamist rule and by the rise of terrorist death cults such as ISIS across the region.[63] Youssef, for his part, criticized everyone. He remained true to his democratic principles.

But perhaps he was simply naive about what was possible in the moment. Or maybe he had less to fear? Let it be noted that Youssef possessed the requisite social and economic capital to flee the country, something that most of his fellow citizens could never dream of. Should the al-Sisi regime collapse, it was *they*, after all, who would suffer the terrors of homicidal death cults. Youssef, for his part, would soon be in Los Angeles pursuing a career in stand-up.

An autopsy of *Al-Bernamig* reveals many causes of death, one being that various Egyptians in power never wanted it to exist in the first place.

Another is that Youssef's lacerating satire may, in the end, have lacked crucial support from the disempowered as well. This reminds us that one can punch up and infuriate not just a powerful minority, but *a majority*—those who supported the al-Sisi coup—as well. Nor should we underestimate Egypt's lack of a free speech Consensus as a factor explaining Al-Bernamig's demise. Youssef wasn't of his moment, like Abbott and Costello, but well ahead of his time.

THE MIX, THE BLUR

Back before he was tearing into President al-Sisi, Bassem Youssef tore into President Morsi with this screed: "Gas and alcohol don't mix. Like English and Arabic don't mix. Like religion and politics don't mix . . . The drunk doesn't do the driving."[64] Let's run with that mixed metaphor for a moment, because it has implications for fake news parody.

Politainment, I have argued, is a genre that does a lot of mixing. Parodists blur the distinction between news and entertainment, fact and fiction, real and fake, serious and funny. This mixing creates hilarity, yes; but it also creates unintentional confusions and consequences. I say "unintentional" because I'm not sure the parodists always mean for these confusions or consequences to occur. Nor do they seem aware that they might be hazardous to the democratic project that they claim to defend.

Fake newscasters scumble the line between comedy and journalism. Two scholars have made the astute observation that politainment shows are actually "rival news organizations" to their mainstream counterparts, providing their viewership with actual newsworthy information.[65] To quote Amber Day, they "incorporate the real into the satiric."[66] Watching back episodes of *Al-Bernamig*, it becomes clear that Youssef wasn't only parodying the headlines; he was "doing" journalism.

His team performed investigations. They took deep dives into the activities of the nation's leaders. In the process, they often unearthed previously unknown footage of said leaders making hair-raisingly incendiary comments. Some episodes covered parliamentary proceedings.

"We were like the Egyptian version of C-SPAN," exclaimed Youssef. He even embedded himself in the protests in Tahrir Square, a cameraman in tow, and shared the footage with his viewers.[67]

At other points, the show demonstrated that meta quality that often characterizes contemporary comedy. Throughout this book we've seen comedians cycle the very controversies they created back into their art. *Al-Bernamig* displayed this tendency as well. During Morsi's Islamist regime, Youssef regaled his audience with tales of lawsuits that had been slapped on him. He went on to show clip after clip of Islamists insulting him.[68]

Fake newsmen are eager to point out that they are not newsmen at all. They are comedians. Full stop. In his memoir, Youssef sighs: "I am no political analyst, no global thinker, and no credible source of information."[69] As the chapter epigraph indicates, Youssef contends he is just making jokes. Nothing more.

Al-Bernamig, however, wasn't just satire. Youssef was plugging a hole, rectifying a failure of Egyptian media, government, and civil society. His show thus performed an important and responsible journalistic function. Yet as healthy as this comedy–public service hybrid might be, it also has drawbacks. Comedians, unlike journalists, are not held to standards of objectivity; they are not accountable to anyone else for errors in their reportage. Nor should they be. They're comedians, not journalists. Or are they?

In *Revolution for Dummies*, Youssef recounts an anecdote that might have led him to interrogate his insistence that he was "just" a satirist. In the aftermath of a gruesome mass casualty event in Port Said he was approached (in Cairo) by a mourner who implored him, "We need you to avenge us . . . you are the only one that speaks in our voice."[70]

A question that Youssef might have probed is: How did it come to pass that these people believed that a mere satirist was their surrogate, their retribution?[71] Were the mourners confused about Youssef's role? And if so, why? Some scholars assert that audiences implicitly understand the artifice, or "mimesis," of fake news.[72] I'm not sure about this; all that blurring *must* have an impact on the audience.

If audiences are confused, maybe the entertainers are too? One of the confusions that fake news foments, as I noted above, concerns the actual role of the parodist. My concern with the genre is that its practitioners seem not to fully grasp what *they* are actually doing. Yes, the "host" is satirizing. But the host is *also* reporting news, unearthing news, and creating news. All of that journalism is shot through with the host's obvious political commitments. This tends to confuse audiences and, apparently, the parodists themselves.

EIGHT

Premeditated Provocation and Zimbabwe's Pseudo-Consensus

[W]e know that political comedy is a taboo in Zimbabwe, hence artists are aware of the risks involved.

CARL JOSHUA NCUBE
In Kennedy Nyavaya, "Carl Joshua Ncube Receives Death Threats" (2016)

Politics as well, you, you can joke about politics. [W]hen you're not on stage you . . . start talking in hushed tones, . . . you're worried about who's listening. But onstage you're shouting it out . . . so yeah, that's what happens. It's different, stage and off-stage. You get this bravado from nowhere, once you're off it's gone.

SHARON CHIDEU
Interview with Amanda Källstig, "Humouring the State? Zimbabwean Stand-up Comedians as Political Actors" (2021)

IN AUGUST OF 2019, MEDIA reports circulated globally about a harrowing attack on a popular Zimbabwean comedian.[1] According to news accounts, Samantha Kureya, whose stage name is Gonyeti, was kidnapped from her home in Harare by masked gunmen. She was then stripped, beaten, and forced to ingest raw sewage. After the perpetrators fled, a traumatized Kureya somehow found her way to safety.[2]

The identity of her assailants has never been conclusively determined. It is widely suspected, however, that those responsible for the violence were aligned with the Zimbabwean government.[3] This supposition, as we shall see, is based on the fact that these authorities have an extensive track record of not taking kindly to criticism—like the type of criticism

Gonyeti and her comedy troupe BUSTOP TV were known to mete out with aplomb.[4]

In this chapter we will use Gonyeti's ordeal to explore how some comedians operate in less-than-ideal free speech environments. In these places there is no functional Consensus like the ones we observe in liberal democracies. Though as we shall see, the authorities themselves often claim otherwise, insisting that they ardently support expressive liberties.

Social scientists refer to Zimbabwe's government as a "hybrid regime."[5] A hybrid regime "mix[es] democratic and autocratic features," often toggling back and forth between those poles across time.[6] Such governments "fulfill the democratic requirement of minimally free and fair elections."[7] Too, they usually possess the external trappings of a democracy, like a constitution, a judicial system, and legislative bodies.

At the same time, hybrid regimes such as the one in Zimbabwe "violate democratic principles in many other spheres of government—some of them drastically so," and tend to display "systematic deficiencies" when it comes to civil rights.[8] Freedom of speech, as one might imagine, has a rough go of it in any system with autocratic components. Under such circumstances, where autocracy and democracy are melded, any expression of dissent is a perilous act. It goes without saying that cracking jokes and viralizing them on the internet invites aforesaid peril.[9]

Zimbabwe's status as a hybrid regime will help us consider a comedic paradox. In this young nation, it has always been hazardous for citizens to speak unkindly of the president and his ruling party. Dissenters have been subject to surveillance, censorship, arrest, imprisonment, and extralegal state violence.

And yet, even though there is considerable political repression in Zimbabwe, there are also comedians, like Gonyeti and her colleagues, who will lampoon that repression, regardless of the consequences. Political comedians making jokes about their rulers and rulers who wish to silence political comedians—the two exist in a sort of bewildering embrace. Or maybe it's a chokehold. But however we characterize that relationship, we can only be stunned at the strange, courageous, quasi-suicidal defiance of some comedians.

There are good reasons to suspect that individuals affiliated with the Zimbabwean government were involved in the abduction of Samantha Kureya. But since transparency and accountability are not typically part of a hybrid regime's skill set, the evidence remains circumstantial.

A few data points, however, suggest the complicity of the state's security apparatus in the attack. The political scientist Amanda Källstig, who studies the Zimbabwean stand-up scene, learned from her sources that Kureya's captors "ordered [her] to perform military exercises." This type of punishment is characteristic of the nation's armed forces.[10] Elsewhere it was reported that Kureya's abductors allegedly screamed, "You are too young to mock the government . . . You are being paid to mock the government."[11] Such behaviors track with the ruling regime's long history of menacing its detractors. (The attack itself took place during a period when opposition figures nationwide were being harassed and persecuted.)[12]

If her assailants were in fact linked to the authorities—an allegation that those authorities vehemently deny—then what provoked them?[13] The answer: political comedy and social critique.

Gonyeti is a star of the BUSTOP TV troupe, which describes itself as "a youth-run Zimbabwean media house." "We are widely known," their mission statement announces, "for our satirical skits that go viral as they comment on economy, political and social issues that affect society."[14] From their inception in 2014 to the present, the group has created over a hundred filmed sketches. Aside from satirical content, the company also produces serious pieces about social issues and occasionally crafts multi-episode soap operas.

The ensemble's aesthetic is low-tech and unpretentious. A typical episode lasts a few minutes and transpires in just one space, like a bedroom, porch, kitchen, backyard, public street, or field.[15] It usually features two or three cast members speaking to one another while standing still or sitting. The dialogue-driven skits appear to be a mix of improvised banter and scripted content. There is very little in the way of flashy camera work or special effects.

BUSTOP TV's sketches are mostly performed in the Shona language, though the actors sometimes lapse into English. Of the dozens of videos I reviewed, fewer than 10 percent were captioned or translated. One controversial piece—plausibly the piece that drew the authorities' ire (see below)—was performed mostly in English.

BUSTOP TV's videos are usually posted to its Facebook page and YouTube channel—which brings us to social media, always an accelerant of conflict in today's comedic controversies.[16] For artists in Zimbabwe and across the continent, these platforms have increasingly provided a broadcast space outside of state-run and -supervised media.[17] And that's a potentially dangerous space! Especially in hybrid regimes, where the government tends to crack down on voices of opposition and critique. By taking political comedy to the internet, BUSTOP TV joins Africa's swelling ranks of "social media dissidents."[18]

Not all of BUSTOP TV's satire, however, is directed at the government. My viewing of their posted material suggests that they are equally focused on domestic life and its trials. A number of videos feature couples locked in bitter arguments.[19] Their disputes sometimes take a dark turn when a male character physically assaults his female partner (though in a few instances the opposite occurs).[20] Often these episodes end with a final screen imploring viewers to prevent violence against women.[21]

Elsewhere, the group's targets include corrupt members of civil society. One sketch, "Bogus Lawyer," follows a woman from a small town seeking to speak to a prosecutor about her physically abusive husband. She is intercepted by the bogus lawyer. After sizing the yokel up, the attorney tells her that he knows the prosecutor; if she wants to meet him, she'll have to pay him—the bogus lawyer—which she does.[22] Other skits cover the dangers of misinformation, or how to obtain a passport.[23]

These sketches, as with a good deal of BUSTOP TV's catalog, have the feel of a public service announcement. In fact, since 2019 (the year Kureya was attacked) more and more of their episodes have been sponsored by organizations whose activism aligns with the message of the video. We'll return to that. First, let's discuss the episode that probably got Gonyeti and her colleagues into trouble.

It is difficult to pinpoint what about Samantha's Kureya's work with BUSSTOP TV might have triggered a gang, likely associated with the government, to kidnap her. But if there is one episode in particular that might have sent them over the edge, it would be her 2016 sketch "Order and Law: Special Women Unit."[24]

The skit is framed as an interview made by a skeptical journalist questioning a public official in English. In it, we see the "REC" symbol on the screen, reminding us that we are watching something recorded—ostensibly by the offscreen journalist whom we faintly hear but never see. Gonyeti's fellow cast member Magi (Sharon Chideu, whom we met in the second epigraph above) is dressed in a police uniform. Apparently a spokesperson for the force, she is vehemently denying the reporter's insinuation that recent videos of cops brutalizing citizens have anything to do with the Zimbabwean law enforcement that she represents.

"Those videos that have been circulating on the social media," she protests, "they're not ours." Refusing to accept blame, she continues: "They have been doctored by our detractors in the West just to tarnish our name." The skeptical journalist asks the spokesperson why the filmed police officers were speaking Shona, a language almost exclusive to Zimbabwe. The outraged official responds, "Shona is an international language!"[25] She thus implies that non-Zimbabwean Shona speakers may have been responsible for those (doctored!) videos of the police assaulting civilians.

The spokesperson then attempts to soothe us viewers by saying, "We are very peaceful. We do not promote violence . . . I would like to assure the nation," she declaims in a confident tone, "that we do not promote violence all." We'd likely be more willing to trust her if it weren't for the fact that throughout this entire recording another uniformed police officer (played by Gonyeti) has been manhandling two teenagers with a nightstick.[26]

Gonyeti does so with a maniacal glee that might have made Moe of *The Three Stooges* envious. I should also mention that Gonyeti's stage name roughly translates as "large truck used for hauling."[27] In "Order and Law," she uses her heft and physicality deftly.

During Magi's full-throated denial of police misconduct, Gonyeti chops, kicks, and smacks the supine boys. She cracks one in the head with her baton. She crushes another's testicles with her foot. "She only applies minimum force," exclaims Magi as she proudly surveys the beatdown.[28]

The sketch clearly intends to problematize police brutality and the government's penchant for disinformation. I also wonder if "Order and Law" doesn't have a more subtle subtheme. Namely, the passivity of the Zimbabwean public in the face of corrupt, abusive, and violent public officials.[29]

At one point during the beatdown, Magi exclaims: "It's a normal day . . . People are enjoying. The kids are playing . . . this is because of us."[30] The camera quickly pans to a crowd nearby, which, unbeknownst to us (the viewers), has been observing the whole interview and assault. Is BUSTOP TV implying that the Zimbabwean public, in its unwillingness to intervene, is complicit in its own misery?[31]

I also wonder if the high proportion of children in the crowd doesn't allude to the future of Zimbabwe. Then again, I am not sure it the crowd was placed there on purpose. It is impossible to tell if the gathering of onlookers is affiliated with the BUSTOP TV ensemble or whether they are just passersby observing the filming.

It gets even more meta. This 2016 "Order and Law" sketch is about police who taunt and brutalize citizens yet deny any involvement, insisting that the whole thing is fake. In 2019, Gonyeti herself was likely subjected to just such police brutality. Yet the authorities denied any involvement in the affair. For good measure, they insulted her, as when a reporter for one of the state-run newspapers, the *Herald*, opined: "There is strong suspicion that the alleged abduction [of Gonyeti] on the night of August 22 was stage-managed for political expediency or to raise the stock of the controversial drama queen."[32]

Throughout this book, we have seen comedians "go meta." What's weird about this case is that the *government* got meta with BUSTOP's jokes. Individuals affiliated with the Zimbabwean government may have reprocessed their own outrage at the *fictional* violence depicted in this comedic skit by inflicting *non-fictional* violence upon Gonyeti.

"THE CHAUVINISTIC COLOSSUS"

At this point in our inquiry I need to articulate a strongly held opinion: BUSTOP TV's subversive comedy was virtually guaranteed to infuriate Zimbabwe's leaders. I don't see how these talented, brave artists failed to recognize that. It strains credulity that they didn't know what they were up against. And what they were up against was "an authoritarian, repressive, and violent state . . . intolerant of any dissent."[33]

BUSTOP TV came into being in 2014, toward the end of the seemingly interminable reign of President Robert Mugabe. This "chauvinistic colossus" ruled Zimbabwe for "an uninterrupted period of thirty-seven years and seven months."[34] One scholar refers to him as "the person who liberated and destroyed Zimbabwe altogether."[35]

When Mugabe came to power in 1980, he was widely hailed throughout Africa as a freedom fighter. He and his Zimbabwe African National Union–Patriotic Front (ZANU-PF) party began as a liberation movement intent on ridding the country of British colonialism. Their signal achievement was rendering the racist state of Rhodesia defunct, thereby gaining true independence for what would become Zimbabwe.

Mugabe and ZANU-PF's abiding ideological assumption, according to historian Sabelo J. Ndlovu-Gatsheni, was that "Zimbabwe needed to be destroyed to be rebuilt."[36] The project of "Mugabeism," Ndlovu-Gatsheni argues, was "anti-colonial," but it was not "decolonial." As a governing ethos, therefore, it continued to embrace violence, racism, tribalism, sexism, and patriarchy, or the full arsenal of repressive colonial technologies.[37]

Many of these qualities were on gruesome display during the state-driven "Gukurahundi" massacre of the Ndebele people in the early 1980s. Gukurahundi (which means "the rain that washes away the chaff") was the name of the North Korean–trained Fifth Brigade deployed by Mugabe.[38] The carnage they inflicted in Matabeleland is estimated to have cost twenty thousand lives.

That and countless other human rights abuses drew Mugabe to global attention. Although initially he was on "cozy" terms with Western leaders, his reputation slowly changed.[39] Mugabe, once the freedom fighter, soon led Zimbabwe in a starkly anti-democratic direction. His country thus joined the wave of backsliding governments throughout the continent that civil society organizations monitored, criticized, and sanctioned. Mugabe and his ruling party became pariahs, at least in the opinion of liberal democracies.

The longstanding criticism he received from the West, as well as his experiences with colonial oppression, had a strong influence on Mugabe's foreign and domestic policy. Internationally, he eventually embraced relations with China as part of his "Look East" approach.[40] Internally, Mugabe's fury at his detractors in former metropoles helped to shape, and ultimately deform, the free speech landscape of Zimbabwe. It is to this point that we now turn.

"OUR DETRACTORS IN THE WEST"

In the "Order and Law" video, as we have seen, the police spokesperson made reference to "our detractors in the West." The quip poked at a common talking point in Mugabe's lexicon. For a Zimbabwean citizen to criticize the regime was to be an "unpatriotic sell-out," an agent of foreign, pro-colonial interests.[41] Thus ZANU-PF tarred opposition parties, like the Movement for Democratic Change (which had a habit of winning elections), as being in cahoots with imperialists.[42]

"Order and Law" was calling attention to how Zimbabwe's rulers justified their disregard of legitimate dissent. To wit, any criticism was simply nonsense cooked up by seditious citizens who were agents, either witting or unwitting, of Western hegemony. Mugabe and his party believed that "political dissent and divergence were . . . not only unpatriotic, but an attempt to defy the natural order of Zimbabwean politics."[43]

As a result, ZANU-PF (which is still in power today) has a decades-long track record of using legal and extralegal means to "muzzle dissenting voices and create a civil society that aligned itself with" the ruling party.[44] Criticism of Zimbabwe's leaders, as one might imagine, was completely off limits.[45] Scholars liken the country to a surveillance state.[46] To this end, it was outfitted with a formidable apparatus of coercive violence to maintain "internal security."[47] This was used to punish and imprison opposition parties, elected officials, judges, journalists, and citizen activists.

It was into this "laughscape" that BUSTOP TV plied their wares. Gonyeti and her ensemble were incredibly courageous to practice political comedy in this environment. For her efforts, she was subjected to extralegal punishment by armed groups likely associated with the government.

It is crucial to recognize, however, that a hybrid regime uses "legal" mechanisms to stifle dissent. In Zimbabwe, censorship has been accomplished, in part, through what are known as "insult laws." Insult laws, alongside hate speech laws, are a genre of legislation usually inherited from a nation's former colonizers. Created to inoculate those in power from criticism, they tend to thrive in hybrid regimes.

Such rules, in the words of law professor Badala Tachilisa Balule, ensure "the protection of the honor and dignity of holders of specific government offices, institutions, [and] national symbols."[48] Insult laws, Balule further notes, take no heed of the truthfulness of a claim. In other words, it doesn't matter if a critique of the government is factually accurate; the perpetrators will run afoul of a law like the Public Order and Security Act (POSA) anyhow. The government can punish any statement, factually true or not.[49] The impact of these laws on free speech in a given country can be immense, adversely impacting everyone from politicians to journalists to artists to political satirists.

POSA was Zimbabwe's insult law. Operative between 2002 and 2019, this regulation reworked an older Rhodesian stipulation against criticizing the president. POSA, according to Jamal Jafari, "prohibits making any false statements prejudicial to the government, or . . . undermin[ing] public confidence in defense and law enforcement agencies." Naturally, Jafari continues, the government determines what may be a "false statement."[50] It was in this suffocating environment that BUSTOP TV began its work in 2014.

In 2017, Mugabe was deposed by his former vice-president Emmerson Mnangagwa. Some refer to that transfer of power as "the coup d'état that was but was not."[51] When he assumed leadership, some Zimbabwean artists and intellectuals imagined that the censorship and repression of the Mugabe days would be relaxed. Gonyeti herself told the BBC in 2018, "I just hope in Zimbabwe we have the freedom to talk about the president without being in trouble, the freedom to talk about anyone without the police coming after you . . . I just hope that it will change."[52]

Unfortunately, that change has not come to pass. The ZANU-PF party is still in power, and the so-called "New Dispensation" of Mnangagwa's presidency has in many ways replicated the flaws of his predecessor.[53] Gonyeti's abduction, it should be recalled, occurred in 2019, two years into the new regime.

THE PARADOX OF PREMEDITATED PROVOCATION

Zimbabwean comedians are fond of saying that in their country there is "freedom of speech, but no freedom *after* the speech."[54] It's a great aphorism, but as with many great aphorisms, it can use some fine-tuning.

To begin with, Zimbabwean comics seem weirdly undaunted by obvious risks, such as what might transpire "after" the speech. One humorist, Tonderai Zinyanga, boasted to a news agency about his various political provocations: "By imitating late President Mugabe," he explained, "I wanted to draw people's attention to his brutality." But Zinyanga didn't stop with Zimbabwe's first autocratic leader: "I still do the same about current President Emmerson Mnangagwa under whom tyranny has continued."[55] Zinyanga is no outlier. As Amanda Källstig observes, "Zimbabwean stand-up comedy has not only survived a repressive regime, but flourished in it."[56]

In Zimbabwe, it is dangerous to poke fun at the government, yet some comedians know this, suffer from it, *and proceed to do it anyway.* These artists do it within Zimbabwe's borders, which is substantively different from ridiculing the powers that be from abroad (as expat Zimbabweans are known to do).[57] For want of a better word, there's something oddly "premeditated" about their provocation. Comedian Carl Joshua Ncube, who himself has received death threats, observes that artists in Zimbabwe "are aware of the risks involved."[58]

Call it "the paradox of premeditated provocation." Gonyeti has lived (and nearly died) in this paradox. And she is not alone. Magamba TV is an ensemble that offers up politainment (see chapter 7).[59] Their work often lampoons the stiff, stodgy, "propaganda-centered news" of the state-run Zimbabwe Broadcast Corporation.[60] Magamba's experiences "after the speech" have been unpleasant—its offices raided, its computers confiscated, its staff hounded by state security agents.[61] Yet still they continue to roast their powerful targets.

These examples of comedians exercising freedom of speech, despite being aware of the repercussions, raise a question: Why does the government permit *any* of it? Why is there a "before" in which critics crack jokes at the government's expense? Why don't the powers that be deploy their massive arsenals of coercion and burn all comedy clubs to the ground? Why don't they criminalize laughter? Why don't they preemptively sterilize every class clown, every stand-up comedian? Why is "before" even possible in a hybrid regime?

One major reason is capacity. It would take a gargantuan investment of the state's operating budget to comprehensively monitor citizen speech, whether digital or nondigital.[62] Even more resources would be needed to arrest rulebreakers and then try them in court (or systematically brutalize them via paramilitary groups). Hybrid regimes, no doubt, would very much like to eliminate comedy that is critical of them. Their dilemma is that even with their "extensive censorship infrastructure," they usually don't possess the means or institutions to do so comprehensively.[63]

In light of these structural limitations, we might speculate that the authorities in Zimbabwe have opted for a more cost-effective strategy of selective crackdowns. Thus Gonyeti was attacked in order to "send a message." By making an example of a high-profile target, they may have hoped to chill other critical voices, causing satirists to think twice before being so brave in the "before."[64]

And then there are optics. Hybrid regimes often insist that they are champions of free speech, that they abide by a principled Consensus. Zimbabwe is no exception: in its official communications, the nation is pro-democracy and pro-comedy too! Nick Mangwana, permanent secretary of the Ministry of Information, has averred that the government "supports freedom of expression as it is enshrined in our constitution; artistic expression, satire or even dark comedy, is part of that freedom."[65]

Pressed by journalists about political satire in Zimbabwe, Mangwana uttered all the requisite affirmations and even championed what I would call a Pseudo-Consensus: "You cannot make a comedy without poking fun at someone, even if it is the president; that's the work of comedy, it has to be fun . . . It only cannot be fun if it then starts to, for instance, mock someone who is disabled."[66]

"Fun," according to Zimbabwe's permanent secretary of the Ministry of Information, is what this is all about! The current president, incidentally, is known for having a little fun on the job as well. In his speechcraft, Emmerson Mnangagwa often makes jokes about politically sensitive issues (such as the Gukurahundi massacre).[67] Perhaps this public commitment to free speech, comedy, and fun restrains the authorities to a certain degree. Might this pro–civil liberties posture limit their ability to censor all opponents?

This brings us back to the comedians who persist in spite of obvious dangers. Our question remains: Why are they undeterred by the whole grim "after" part of the Zimbabwean free speech experience? One possibility is that these artists *actually believe in those democratic ideals which their hybrid regime espouses*. When humorists in Zimbabwe are asked about their work, they sound like patriots who want to contribute to civic improvement. One comic, Victor Mpofu, known as Doctor Vickela, says, "It is my duty to heal our community, and to challenge those in power."[68] Carl Joshua Ncube, whom we met above, opines that Zimbabwean comics "represent an idea, an idea of freedom; freedom of speech."[69]

In Zimbabwe, satirists poke and aggravate the beast that is their government. They perform this heroism because they believe it is the right thing to do. They are brave. They are defiant. And to a certain degree they are, yes, foolish.

Maybe that foolishness is powered by dynamics that are unique to comedy as an art form. In the second epigraph above, Sharon Chideu (who played the police spokesperson in "Order and Law") speaks of the "bravado from nowhere" the rush of invincibility she feels when taking the stage.[70] It's as if the wall of laughter emanating from her appreciative audience will protect her from the tumultuous "after." Perhaps some comedians wildly overestimate the security benefits provided by their coalition of the entertained. Maybe the ability to induce warm, appreciative, collective laughter leads them to believe they are somehow immune from cold, brutal, coercive power.

This feeling of laugh-induced invincibility may explain why Gonyeti will not relent. Right after her attack, she got back in the saddle. In a 2020 video called "Tsamba Yekuendesa Kumba," she and Magi play two vendors who are trying to get permits from a government bureaucrat to operate their stalls. During their back-and-forth, they complain that they were recently beaten by the police. This sends the bureaucrat into a rage: "You got beat up," he shouts, "for not following COVID-19 regulations!"[71]

In the same year, Gonyeti and her crew thought it might be a swell idea to make a video alluding to a graft controversy that had engulfed President Mnangagwa and his son, "a COVID-19 equipment tender corruption scandal," as scholars Trust Matsilele and Wishes Mututwa put it.[72] Elsewhere the ensemble made a video featuring an abusive—and perhaps insane—police officer threatening Magi and Gonyeti with a saw.[73]

Gonyeti had freedom of speech and freedom after speech. Now she may have a little *more* freedom after speech. Looking at the closing credits of BUSTOP TV episodes following the attack on Gonyeti, I noticed something new. From 2019 onward, the ensemble's work has been sponsored in a manner that rarely occurred prior. Sometimes local or regional advocacy groups partner with BUSTOP TV.[74] Elsewhere, European and international NGOs are backing their productions.[75] In a few instances transnational development organizations and non-governmental organizations—the International Republican Institute (IRI), the European Union (EU),

Oxfam, UKAID, USAID, and the UN Development Programme (UNDP)—have funded BUSTOP TV's content.[76]

The link with international organizations is certain to irk the ZANU-PF and the Mnangagwa government, who routinely accuse their domestic opponents of being in cahoots with "imperialists." The "Order and Law" video mocked that accusation. And now those "detractors from the West" are providing material aid for BUSTOP TV's grand experiment in free speech!

It's already ironic that the attack on Gonyeti increases the likelihood that she'll have continued freedom after speech. Her new affiliations with domestic Zimbabwean activist groups and Western organizations provide another type of protective wall. At the very least, BUSTOP TV has backers at home and abroad that will sound the alarm if its players are ever mistreated.

Then again, even if Gonyeti didn't have this protection, she'd likely keep making jokes in both the "before" and the "after." "I was abducted because of comedy, because of satire," she remarked after the kidnapping. "But I still need to work. Comedy is my job. It's my life."[77]

NINE

The Interview

COMEDIC WAR GAMES

> Apparently, the use of a pseudonym was part of the original plan, but was scotched after a "team of comedians and actors including Jonah Hill and Sacha Baron Cohen" proposed using Kim Jong-un's real name.
>
> TONY SHAW AND TRICIA JENKINS
> "An Act of War? *The Interview* Affair, the Sony Hack, and the Hollywood-Washington Power Nexus Today" (2019)

"YOU KNOW WHAT'S MORE DESTRUCTIVE than a nuclear bomb?" a drunk and pensive Kim Jong-un (played by Randall Park) asks his entourage in the 2014 film *The Interview*. His answer: "words."[1]

It's really quite funny and a profound dig. It implies that for the Supreme Leader, or *Suryong*, of North Korea (DPRK), being criticized is far worse than nuking a few million people into oblivion.[2] The rest of the movie delivers very little in the way of such profundity. It does, however, relentlessly, and recklessly, provoke its subject (the same Supreme Leader), as comedians are wont to do.

The Interview (originally titled *Kill Kim Jong-un*) is about two newsmen, the B-List celebrity journalist Dave Skylark (James Franco) and his underachieving producer, Aaron Rapoport (Seth Rogen).[3] The middling duo gain sudden notoriety after the rapper Eminem comes out as gay to Skylark and the interview goes viral (the artist, known for using homophobic slurs in his music, plays himself in an ingenious bit of autofiction).[4] Producer Rapoport is eventually contacted by a North Korean agent who offers Skylark an opportunity to interview Kim Jong-un.

Soon thereafter, the CIA hijacks their scoop and deputizes the two (willing) journos to assassinate their subject in his palace.

In November 2014, just a few weeks before the Christmas Eve release of *The Interview*, Sony Pictures Entertainment reported a massive hack of their IT infrastructure. Some 38 million files were stolen, ultimately costing the company a hundred million dollars. Over the next few weeks five full-length movies from Sony's digital vaults were illegally downloaded to the internet, along with thousands of social security numbers.[5] Embarrassing private emails were leaked (one called actress Angelina Jolie a "spoiled brat," and the head of the studio made racially offensive jokes about Barack Obama's taste in movies).[6] A hacker group calling itself the Guardians of Peace claimed responsibility for the cyberattacks. American security officials later identified them as North Korean operatives.[7]

This assault on the Japanese company was followed by a series of threats on U.S. targets. A North Korean foreign ministry spokesman likened *The Interview* to "an act of war."[8] The Guardians of Peace, invoking 9/11 and threatening to launch attacks on theaters (presumably those screening *The Interview*), demanded Sony not release the film. In characteristically convoluted prose they warned: "Stop immediately showing the movie of terrorism which can break the regional peace and cause the War!"[9] Pretty soon President Barack Obama entered the fray, seemingly on behalf of what I call the Pre-Digital Liberal Free Speech Consensus. Meanwhile, South Korea, Japan, and China monitored the unfolding events with considerable concern.

Much about the controversy surrounding *The Interview* is a tad more complicated than it initially appears to be—or not what it appears to be at all. My analysis will lead me to nuance the claim that the DPRK was driven to malice because of the comedic vitriol heaped on Kim Jong-un. I will also suggest that Barack Obama's intervention in this crisis was not necessarily the pure and principled defense of expressive liberty that it sounds like.

Nuances aside, the controversy surrounding *The Interview*, I contend, unwittingly posed a question about the relation between art, free speech, and national security. "Never ask a question," goes an old Washington, DC, adage, "when you know you won't like the answer." I'm afraid the answer to the question I will ask about The Consensus reveals an answer many won't like.

THE TRAILER

The original plot for *The Interview* concerned an assassination attempt not on Kim Jong-un but on his father, Kim Jong-il.[10] When the latter died in 2011 the project was tabled. Two years later, inspired by the fanfare surrounding NBA star Dennis Rodman's trip to North Korea, the creative team of Seth Rogen and Evan Goldberg revived their old idea.[11] With a budget of thirty million dollars, *The Interview* began filming in October 2013 and wrapped two months later.[12] A release date of December 2014 was set.

What is often forgotten—and is relevant to my analysis—is that this comedic controversy began well *before* the movie came out. It wasn't the full-length feature film that sparked a massive geopolitical crisis; rather, the ordeal commenced when a ninety-second "teaser trailer" was dropped on June 11, 2014, half a year before the film's scheduled rollout.[13] This "coming attraction" was the stimulus that spurred the Pyongyang regime into action.

What was it about the trailer that led Kim Jong-un to sow chaos? Perhaps it reminded him of earlier Hollywood takedowns of North Korea, such as *Team America: World Police* (2004) and *Die Another Day* (2002).[14] Then there's the reverence that North Korean culture accords cinema. The Kim dynasty is obsessed with this art form. As film scholar Steve Erickson notes, "Kim Jong-il famously published a book on cinema, which promotes the idea that film must represent the goals of the regime and uphold its *Juche* philosophy" (North Korea's national ethos of self-reliance).[15]

In the Hermit Kingdom moviemaking is associated with the celebration of patriotic themes.[16] The purpose of film, in the regime's view, is not to entertain, but to extol the virtues of the country's struggle against American imperialism.[17] The idea that movies should celebrate the regime's heroic confrontations with capitalist invaders may seem unusual to Westerners. Though if this was part of the regime's worldview, *The Interview* would certainly be seen as an act of symbolic violence.

If that wasn't enough to irk Kim Jong-un, then perhaps the trailer's contents did the trick. *The Interview*'s plotline was made clear by the breathless headings: "THIS DECEMBER . . . JAMES FRANCO . . . and SETH ROGEN . . . WILL ATTEMPT TO ASSASSINATE . . . KIM JONG-UN."[18] Commentators have noted how unusual it was for a major motion picture to refer to murdering *an actual living person*.[19] I find it even stranger that the clip personalized the conflict by mentioning *Franco and Rogen* as the assassins, not Skylark and Rapoport from the storyworld.[20]

Among the trailer's other provocations, there was a scene in which CIA Agent Lacey (Lizzy Caplan) informs Skylark and Rapoport that "Kim Jong-un's people believe anything he tells them. Including that he can speak to dolphins or he doesn't urinate or defecate." To which Skylark responds, "You're telling me my man doesn't pee or poop?" The regime might also have taken exception to a cutaway of the leader disrobing from behind.[21]

The June trailer did *not* feature what Sony executives considered perhaps the most incendiary moment of the film.[22] That would be the climactic slow-motion close-up of Kim Jong-un's face bursting into flames.[23]

A "lengthy [and] bizarre" internal correspondence about this scene had already consumed the studio.[24] Sony, especially its Japanese divisions, understood the volatility of the image and begged Rogen to cut it out. Rogen, for his part, stood up for The Consensus, or artistic principle, or some such thing, and pushed back. "This is now," he complained in a leaked email, "a story of Americans changing their movie to make North Koreans happy . . . that is a very damning story."[25]

Rogen's displeasure may have been stoked by (bad) advice he was receiving. Like others who worked on the film, he was assured that its content would have no geopolitical repercussions. Dan Sterling, whom we will meet below and who co-wrote *The Interview*, told *Esquire:* "I . . . had the script looked at by a very high-level person who was in Hillary Clinton's State Department."[26] That "very high-level person," apparently, raised no red flags.

The CEO of Sony Entertainment, Michael Lynton, sat on the board of the RAND Corporation, the very inside-the-Beltway global affairs think tank.[27] His consultation with RAND experts yielded the same conclusion: *The Interview*'s contents posed no concerns.[28] Lynton was similarly assured by the U.S. assistant secretary of state for East Asian and Pacific affairs that releasing *The Interview* would not create any problems.[29]

This whole episode exposed an oddity: experts trained in international affairs, from the state department to RAND, completely misassessed the situation. In each case, the conclusion was the same: the movie posed little if any risk to the United States or Sony. Some even posited that the film might destabilize the Pyongyang regime, thereby helping the United States achieve one of its core foreign policy goals.[30] Interestingly, the nervous studio executives seemed to have a better grasp on the dangers of their film than the international relations professionals who were consulted to aid with the release.

Soon after the trailer dropped, a sequence of events was set in motion that would doom the movie's box office release. An ominous sign occurred when on June 25, two weeks after the trailer was issued, North Korea's foreign minister sent a melodramatically worded communique through the Korean Central News Agency:

> A preview of a film on insulting and assassinating the supreme leadership of the DPRK is floating in broad daylight in the U.S., a kingpin of international terrorism and its cesspool, shocking the world community. . . . Those who defamed our supreme leadership and committed the hostile acts against the DPRK can never escape the stern punishment to be meted out according to a law wherever they might be in the world. If the U.S. administration connives at and patronizes the screening of the film, it will invite a strong and merciless countermeasure.[31]

A few months later said "countermeasure" was launched as the Guardians of Peace conducted their Sony hack and issued their threats.

OUTRAGE AND ITS NUANCES

In this book we've concentrated on the responses of offended audiences to comedic materials of which they strongly disapprove. In some instances, the aggrieved parties were sovereign nation-states. France was troubled by the anti-Semitic humor of Dieudonné and tried to prosecute him for contravening their hate speech and memory laws (chapter 6). Various Muslim-majority nations condemned *Jyllands-Posten* and *Charlie Hebdo* for cartoons about Muhammad (chapter 5). They avenged the blasphemy by inflicting diplomatic and economic hardship on various European countries. North Korea provides another example of a government playing the role of the actively outraged.

One obvious, and simplistic, way of looking at Pyongyang's hostile response to *The Interview* goes like this: Kim Jong-un got wind of the trailer and was furious. *Furious!* He did not appreciate that a multinational conglomerate headquartered in Japan (another country with a tortured relationship to his own) had made a movie about him being killed, and by two imbeciles no less. He failed to interpret the film as "entertainment," "art," or "political satire." Instead, he construed it as an existential threat that modeled the demise of his regime at the hands of his nemesis, the United States. Unencumbered by any respect for The Consensus, his "histrionic" response was perfectly calibrated to the level of rage that was consuming him.[32]

Kim Jong-un would have come to this place of anger *prior* to actually seeing *The Interview* in full. Had he screened the movie—as opposed to just the trailer—he conceivably would have been a lot angrier. He would have learned that he was a superfan of pop singer Katy Perry. He would have learned that he was afflicted by all manner of resentment for his father and was an insecure homicidal sociopath to boot.[33]

He would also have learned that among his trusted subordinates were some who were plotting his overthrow. Sook-yin Park (Diana Bang) is the secretary of communications for the DPRK.[34] Initially loyal, she ultimately recognizes herself as "a terrible person . . . I'm the propagandist of a totalitarian dictatorship." Of her boss she sighs, "He's as cruel as the father and the grandfather before him. . . . How do you prove to 24 million people that their god is a murderer and a liar?"[35] Given the regime's longstanding obsession with "national unity," this plotline would surely have sent Kim over the edge, had he seen the entire movie—which he hadn't done when he first unleashed anarchy.[36]

Now let's explore a less obvious and simplistic explanation for why Kim Jong-un reacted to that trailer as he did. It doesn't invalidate our previous hunch; rather, it adds some texture to our understanding of the Supreme Leader's motivations. In this second reading, North Korea's response to *The Interview* had a pragmatic dimension. Yes, Pyongyang was insulted by the film. But it also saw the controversy as a golden opportunity to pursue concrete strategic interests—interests that, in the words of one analyst, are "rational, meticulously calculated, and essential to the survival of the regime."[37]

Although North Korea's leaders are often perceived as unhinged actors propelled by ideological extremism and magical thinking, many observers of the country have suggested otherwise. Pyongyang's foreign policy moves, according to one specialist, "are most likely based on a deliberate calculus of its needs."[38] Another concludes that Kim Jong-un "is rational, not suicidal," and while he might be aggressive, "he is not reckless or a madman."[39]

These opinions harmonize to make the same point: Kim Jong-un is a cunning operator on the geopolitical scene. He is skilled at defending and advancing his regime's policy priorities, strange though they might be. If this is indeed the case, we might construe North Korea's response to the trailer as an act not merely of passionate rage, but of canny opportunism. Put differently, the regime was not about to let a good crisis go to waste.

Sony's misstep provided Pyongyang with what some refer to as a "propaganda coup."[40] It introduced the world not only to the recently elevated Kim Jong-un, but it let him showcase his new capacities for disruption. Prior to 2014, the regime was infamous for using its nuclear potential as a deterrent. In recent years, however, it had been experimenting with another deterrent: cyber-warfare.[41] The twinning of nuclear and digital weaponry is, some argue, part of an "offset strategy" meant to counterbalance the country's many vulnerabilities.[42] The Sony hack represented "one of only a few instances in history of an attempt by a nation state to use cyberspace for explicitly coercive purposes."[43] By hacking a major Hollywood studio, North Korea put the world on notice: its new leader had arrived and he meant business.

Another explanation for North Korea's intervention might have to do with its ongoing tensions with Japan, South Korea, and China. We needn't explore each case here. What we should note is that its threats reverberated differently, and concerningly, for each government. Ultimately, it's no coincidence that *The Interview* was not released in those countries.[44] As one journalist concluded, "*The Interview* is just an excuse, and Sony just collateral damage, in yet another random act of North Korean violence made to perpetuate international tensions that Kim Jong Un sees as serving his larger strategic interests."[45]

We have framed Kim Jong-un's actions as an admixture of rage and reason. If there is any truth to our second scenario regarding North Korea, we might apply the same insight to the other cases we've encountered in this book. In every chapter of this study, we've met the "actively outraged." They're always really angry about this or that joke. But maybe their involvement in comedic controversies is informed by more than just anger. Maybe the "inexcusable" joke is a mere pretext.

OBAMA: CONTEXT. PRETEXT.

With each passing day in November and December of 2014 the crisis engulfing *The Interview* intensified. In dribs and drabs, damning leaks of Sony content were being made available to a curious public. North Korean threats were ratcheting up. Theaters in the United States were announcing they would not screen the film due to security concerns.[46] Sony itself decided to pull *The Interview* from theatrical release in the United States (only to reverse itself days later).[47] It was amid this tumult that the president of the United States of America made his thoughts known.

During his year-end meeting with the White House Press Corps, President Obama delivered a textbook recitation of the Pre-Digital Liberal Free Speech Consensus:

> We cannot have a society in which some dictator someplace can start imposing censorship here in the United States. Because if somebody is able to intimidate folks out of releasing a satirical movie, imagine what they start doing when they see a documentary that they don't like, or news reports that they don't like. Or even worse, imagine if producers and distributors and others start engaging in self-censorship because they don't want to offend the sensibilities of somebody whose sensibilities probably need to be offended. That's not who we are. That's not what America's about.[48]

A few weeks later Obama slapped sanctions on North Korea, putatively as punishment for the chaos unleashed by the Guardians of Peace.[49] In retrospect, Obama's heavy hand with the DPRK stands in stark contrast to his successor, Donald J. Trump. The 45th/47th president of the United States once revealed that Kim Jong-un wrote him "beautiful letters," and the two leaders "fell in love."[50]

Obama's unloving intervention was launched, it would seem, on behalf of vaunted American ideals of free speech. Yet some have viewed his actions more skeptically. The national-security rationale for his engagement with *The Interview* was always somewhat fuzzy. The likelihood of a North Korean attack on American soil seemed low. Also, why was the leader of the free world taking such a bold stance on behalf of intellectual property produced by two Canadians (Goldberg and Rogen) and owned by a private media conglomerate headquartered in Japan?

This wasn't the first time the president had weighed in on a global free speech controversy. Two years earlier, in July 2012, trailers for a film eventually titled *The Innocence of Muslims* were posted to YouTube.[51] Some affiliated with the project were fundamentalist Christians with long histories of anti-Muslim agitation. One figure who promoted the film was Pastor Terry Jones, who in 2011 triggered deadly riots in Muslim countries by vowing to burn copies of the Quran in public.[52]

In 2012, the *Innocence of Muslims* trailers sparked outrage throughout the Muslim world. Protests in Benghazi, Libya, led to the murder of U.S. Ambassador J. Christopher Stevens and three embassy personnel.[53] Al-Qaeda claimed responsibility for the attack as payback for the Quran burnings led by Pastor Terry Jones(though the group's precise role in the violence, and their true motivations, remain unclear).[54]

On September 25, 2012, Obama tried to calm tensions with Islamic governments by explaining America's rich free speech tradition. In an address to the General Assembly of the United Nations he again gave a master class in The Consensus: "I know there are some who ask why we don't just ban such a video. And the answer is enshrined in our laws: Our Constitution protects the right to practice free speech. Here in the United States, countless publications provoke offense. Like me, the majority of Americans are Christian, and yet we do not ban blasphemy against our most sacred beliefs." The pro-Consensus rhetoric soared even higher as the president invoked the counter-speech doctrine mentioned in our introduction: "The strongest weapon against hateful speech," he affirmed, "is not repression; it is more speech."[55] This was in 2012 and let it be noted that the president gave as full-throated defense of free speech as he did in 2014 when he voiced his support for what he called "a satirical movie."[56]

Obama's robust endorsement of expressive liberty in 2012 and 2014 needs to be contextualized. For in the days and months that followed the tragic 2012 attack in Benghazi, a few data points emerged that led some to charge that Obama had not, in fact, defended free speech. These critics, almost all on the right, contended that the president caved to Muslim fundamentalists and engaged in an act of censorship, thereby betraying The Consensus.[57]

The first and most damning data point was the revelation that the White House, via the State Department, had asked YouTube to review *The Innocence of Muslims* to determine whether it was in compliance with the platform's guidelines.[58] This request was made *before* Obama's grand September 2012 First Amendment oration at the UN. Given that his administration believed American lives were endangered by *The Innocence of Muslims*, his actions are understandable. They do, however, make Obama's celebration of the counter-speech doctrine seem somewhat disingenuous.

The second data point, which also belied Obama's UN speech, concerned a communique published by American diplomats in Cairo prior to the Libya attacks. It read: "The Embassy of the United States in Cairo condemns the continuing efforts by misguided individuals to hurt the religious feelings of Muslims—as we condemn efforts to offend believers of all religions." In light of American norms, the message was problematic. The White House soon repudiated the statement, saying that it did not "reflect the views of the United States Government."[59]

The third data point was the arrest in Los Angeles of the director of *The Innocence of Muslims*, Nakoula Basseley Nakoula, an Egyptian American, for probation violations stemming from a 2010 fraud conviction.[60] The timing of the arrest struck one *Wall Street Journal* op-ed writer as suspicious.[61] So did the subsequent one-year prison sentence handed down to the filmmaker, which some viewed as unusually harsh.[62] Critics alleged that authorities had used the infraction as an excuse to mute a troubling voice.

The non-comedic controversy triggered by *The Innocence of Muslims* is instructive for comedic controversies. It teaches us that the actors in free speech disputes may not be entirely motivated by pure free speech commitments. When Obama charged into the fracas surrounding *The Interview* in 2014, he may have been driven by reasons having little to do with The Consensus. Perhaps it helped him reburnish his free speech credentials, which had been called into question two years earlier. Perhaps the controversy surrounding *The Interview* provided him with the pretext *he* needed to penalize North Korea.

Because of the international incidents following the trailer release, *The Interview* is remembered as a political satire. Genre-wise, however, the film is really more of a comedic stoner bromance with multiple action-adventure sequences. Toward its finale, it suddenly lurches into a gross-out spectacle in which DPRK soldiers die in droves and people bite off one another's fingers.

Stylistically and thematically, all of this tracks with the previous oeuvre of Seth Rogen and Evan Goldberg. Their earlier works (including *Superbad, Neighbors, Pineapple Express, This Is the End)* are all genetic precursors of *The Interview*, except in one regard: little in their filmography equipped the duo to write about an enigmatic autocratic state like North Korea with a dismal human rights record. So a third writer, Dan Sterling, was recruited "to add political relevance and satirical bite."[63] His background in political humor came mostly from working for *The Daily Show*.[64]

Sterling, who eventually became known as "the guy who brought down Sony," later conceded, "I was quite naive going into this."[65] In early drafts he "put more weight on the political stuff, on getting out facts and attending to the people in North Korea who were suffering." Commercial constraints, he intimated, prevented him from going deeper: "It was a difficult balance because this is not a political film, ultimately. This is a Seth Rogen film. This is a big comedy that is obviously in a political setting and all that, but that isn't the point of the film."[66]

Whether *The Interview* was good political satire—or political satire at all—made no difference to Kim Jong-un. When his regime likened the movie to "an act of war," the question of genre was not a consideration. Nor did the Supreme Leader care whether the film was good art or bad art. Movie critics mostly rendered the latter verdict.[67]

For purposes of better comprehending the stakes of this comedic controversy, let's conduct a thought experiment—a little war game. Let's imagine that the movie was critically acclaimed as a seminal work of cinematic art. Let's imagine that, genre-wise, *The Interview* is to political satire what François Truffaut's *The 400 Blows* is to the bildungsroman genre.

Now let's imagine that it's June 2014 and President Obama receives an urgent message from his national security advisor. He is told that Kim Jong-un has just screened *The Interview*—not the trailer, but the full movie. And he is furious.

Given that he is a "madman" (a description we nuanced above, but please recall this is a hypothetical exercise), Kim Jong-un has trained his nuclear missiles on three targets. The first nuke is pointed at downtown Seoul. The second is trained on "Washington" (though no one can figure out if the threat is directed at Washington state, which North Korean missiles could plausibly reach, or Washington, DC). The third is aimed at the Jewish Community Center of Vancouver, British Columbia, where Rogen and Goldberg met during childhood karate lessons.[68] The Supreme Leader has given Obama twenty-four hours to halt distribution of the film indefinitely or face nuclear retribution. The threat is deemed to be credible.

Farfetched though it may be, the scenario poses some unpleasant questions for The Consensus—ones that, sooner or later, will need to be addressed in real life. For starters, how far can or should a liberal democracy go to defend artistic freedom? In the above scenario, clearly, the United States would bend to the Supreme Leader's will. Human lives take precedence over art, even a "masterpiece" like *The Interview*. The president blinks, and screenings of the film become impossible.

As we continue to game this out, let's posit a wild card: the comedians themselves. We've learned in this book that no disincentive, or threat, or punishment will stop comics from making their jokes. This bravado lends a new twist to our war game. Let's imagine that Rogen and Goldberg refuse to desist, just as *Charlie Hebdo*, Dieudonné, Bassem Youssef, and Gonyeti refused to desist. They continue to post scripts, outtakes, and bootlegged scenes from the movie on the internet. The government commands them to stop, searches their homes, tases them, and eventually incarcerates them.

This unhappy exercise reminds us that no country, the United States included, posits an absolute right to free speech. Considerations of "public safety" will always override guarantees of expressive liberty. France, a liberal democracy, shut down Dieudonné's *Le Mur* in 2013 in the name of public order. India tried (but failed) to use sedition laws to punish Vir Das. In our scenario, Obama would try to find a way (via executive order or the National Emergencies Act, say) to prohibit screenings and streaming of *The Interview*.

The implications of this thought experiment are unsettling. The nation would effectively grant tyrants a veto over art they dislike. The (velvety) Consensus is, and was, always underwritten by the iron fist of liberal governments. Enemies, domestic or foreign, who threatened free speech ultimately had to fear the coercive power of the state—not its words, but its laws, law enforcement, armies, and even, potentially, nuclear bombs.

The real Obama of 2014 had the will and the means to protect free speech. The hypothetical Obama of our war game only had the former. President Trump in his second term might only have the latter. Given the relationship he has developed with Kim Jong-un, and given his own rather selective defense of "free speech," it stands to reason that when confronted by the scenario we've just imagined, he might be disinclined to defend The Consensus.

Conclusion

TROLL YOUR OWN?

PRESENTLY, HUNDREDS OF COMEDIC CONTROVERSIES are raging across the world.

The Chinese stand-up Yang Li is involved in an ongoing dispute over her seemingly banal quip "How can [men] look so average and still have so much confidence?"[1] In 2021, the Israeli comic Noam Shuster-Eliassi proposed marriage to the Crown Prince of Saudi Arabia (in Arabic) on television. Naturally, it went viral. "I have never experienced something on this scale," Shuster-Eliassi sighed as she contemplated the difficulties the joke has created for her among Arabs, Iranians, and Israelis.[2] The American stand-up Matt Rife has infuriated multitudes by mocking violence against women.[3] He also joins not one, not two, but *four* others in four different countries who have sparked outrage for making Down syndrome jokes.[4] Comedians traffic in provocation like musicians traffic in tempo.[5]

Because of the surge of interest in comedy, and the related hegemony of digital media, I predict that these cultural flashpoints will only increase and intensify in the decades to come. To that end I've tried to offer a collection of concepts to help readers make sense of what I called "comedic controversies." Although there is some variance, these episodes follow a strikingly similar pattern. In each case it is helpful to identify *The Coalition of the Outraged; The Coalition of the Entertained;* the reactionary communication pattern that is *The Loop;* the practice of *Meta* (also known as the *Lenny Bruce Maneuver*); the *Persona Drop* technique; the state of *Cancellation;* the strategic uses of *Apology;* and the predictable accusations of *Punching Up* and *Punching Down*. I've also referred to *The Hasmukh Complex* as a way of describing comedians' tendency to view their work as salvific (which may explain the mindset that leads them to double down, rather than back down, in the face of collective rage).

Hopefully, these conceptual tools—each of which can certainly be refined and improved upon—will help us to better understand and contextualize forthcoming controversies. In what follows, I'll review the findings yielded by my "sociology of comedy." Along the way, I'll flag oddities or dilemmas raised by our case studies. I'll close with a few predictions, as well as an ambivalent, perhaps dour final meditation on the Pre-Digital Liberal Free Speech Consensus.

AUDIENCES AND THE H-SCALE

A sociology of comedy, I have argued, must take great interest in audiences. The snag is that it is difficult to comprehend something as large, amorphous, and often unworded as a bunch of people reacting to a joke. I focused on the subset of *irate* audiences—agitated publics that tend to leave footprints behind.

I can now draw a few preliminary conclusions about those I call the "actively outraged." Is it the case that conservatives or liberals are "touchier" or more thin-skinned when they are the butt of the joke? *Initially*, I see no stark correlation between political orientation and a feeling of affront. Liberal and leftist audiences complain about jokes that target them (like the LBGTQ community in their encounter with Dave Chappelle), and so do conservative audiences (like the Catholic Church, India's BJP party, and various Islamic state and non-state actors).

The case of Bassem Youssef (chapter 7) illustrates this point. The brave Egyptian news parodist had the unique misfortune of living through consecutive anti-democratic regimes, each with different ideological investments. He criticized the rule of Islamist Mohammad Morsi and Anti-Islamist Abdel al-Sisi—and was assailed by all of their supporters.

A valuable lesson was learned: those in power really do not appreciate being roasted, regardless of their ideological bent.

Then again, does anyone actually appreciate being roasted? Roasted by a complete stranger and in front of many other strangers? Those few who do find pleasure in such an ordeal might be described, sociologically speaking, as "People Who Attend a Performance at a Comedy Club and Sit in the Front Row."

In any case, we might sloganize as follows: *Affront knows no political bounds*. I will note below, however, that there is reason to believe that those who subscribe to the Pre-Digital Liberal Free Speech Consensus appear to absorb comedic mocking with much greater patience. It's important to recognize that these subscribers *needn't only be liberals* (though they often are); they can be people of any political conviction who live in societies where The Consensus is robust and rooted. Put differently, American conservatives in the aughts could easily watch *Saturday Night Live*'s mockery of George W. Bush (as performed by Will Ferrell) and just shrug their shoulders and tune it out. When The Consensus is widely viewed as legitimate, most people, regardless of political persuasion, will make peace with comedic content they find offensive.

Still, future researchers might develop a "Humorlessness Scale"—let's call it the H-Scale—which measures how different ideological cohorts react to humor that upsets them. My hunch is that acceptance of The Consensus is the only causal variable that leads people, regardless of ideology, to come to peace with comedic speech acts they do not like. Whether liberals are more *predisposed* to accept The Consensus seems likely to me, but it remains to be demonstrated.

R.I.P. JOKES

As we continue reflecting on audiences, let's try to figure out what types of jokes run the risk of activating the coalition of the outraged, and which do not. On the basis of what we have seen in this study, jokes about religion, identity groups, and the powerful (R.I.P. jokes for short) presently count as "high-risk" comedic behaviors that tend to galvanize publics.

Much to my surprise, however, obscene gags appear to be rather low risk. Consider comedian Ken Jeong, who opens his comedy special *You Complete Me, Ho*, with a bang. As he takes the stage, his audience welcomes him with a standing ovation. In response to their adulation, Jeong mimics a well-known male masturbation gesture. He then pantomimes the act of flinging his imaginary semen outward.[6]

He does so with a huge, gracious, humble-brag smile on his face. He even throws in a few *namastes!* It's as if this is his way of expressing thanks and humility to his fans. Jeong does this repeatedly, making sure to pollinate every row of the theater, including the mezzanine.

This is a teachable moment. Surely, there are cultures today—indeed, since the dawn of time—where a man pretending to shower onlookers with his ejaculate would not get off without pushback. For whatever reasons, the sperm confetti gag did not land Jeong in hot water. It created zero controversy.

Jeong's gesture was "obscene." In the 1960s, when Lenny Bruce held court, such a pantomime would have gotten him arrested. But obscenity does not appear to have the same transgressive power it did when Bruce was being prosecuted for talking about "cocksuckers" or "Eleanor Roosevelt's tits."[7] Obscenity, at least in the West, is not presently a "high-risk" comedic behavior or a trigger for outraged audiences.

Vulgarity did not figure in our case studies, but jokes about religion certainly did. The offended believers in question were usually either conservatives or fundamentalists. Brazilian Christians were incensed by Porta dos Fundos. Hindus in India were incensed by Munawar Faruqi and Vir Das. Islamists were incensed by Bassem Youssef, *Jyllands-Posten*, and *Charlie Hebdo*. On the basis of what we've seen in this book, we might argue that blasphemy, as a cultural and legal category, is poised for a renaissance.

A recent piece in the *Harvard Law Review* suggests that some may want to bring this renaissance to the United States.[8] Its (anonymous) authors argue that there is no First Amendment right to mock religion.

The article's rationale is less rigorous than it is portentous: clearly some jurists on the right are thinking about bringing blasphemy laws back into play. In the anything(-liberal)-goes MAGA era, it would be silly to view such a gambit as far-fetched.

Our next high-risk category is jokes about identity groups *made by people not belonging to those identity groups*. This was evident in our analyses of Dave Chappelle (who mocked the LGBTQ community), Sarah Silverman (who mocked Christian conservatives), and Shane Gillis (who mocked anyone who didn't look like him). These stand-ups, of course, also mocked their own groups. Chappelle chides Blacks, Silverman scores Jews, Gillis razzes White dudes. That created little trouble for each comedian. But when they derided "others," trouble ensued.

We might posit a helpful ground rule for aspiring comics in this conflicted age: a person with one identity should not make cracks about identities they do not share. Conversely, there is less danger when the comedian's identity aligns with their target.[9] The take-home lesson for the controversy-averse: *troll your own*. Whether this is a healthy principle for art or any sort of analytical endeavor is uncertain—even unlikely. Be that as it may, self-trolling is a low-risk comedic behavior.[10]

THE TOUGHEST CROWD: MOCKING THE POWERFUL

Rounding out our trinity of high-risk jokes is any type of comedy mocking the powerful, be they wealthy, politically connected, occupying positions of authority, or some combination thereof. The dangers comedians face for doing this is especially concerning given that speaking truth to power would seem to be one of the most *morally compelling justifications for the legal protection of offensive comedy*. The Consensus, as we saw, sees great social value in directing open criticism at rulers, popes, presidents, CEOs, generals, celebrities, etc.

Kunal Kamra (chapter 4) said it poignantly in his affidavit to the Supreme Court of India: "To believe any institution of power in a democracy is beyond criticism is . . . irrational and undemocratic. Judges of our constitutional courts are amongst the most powerful people in our country."[11] Kamra's intervention rhymes with that of the South African cartoonist Zapiro (Jonathan Shapiro), who became embroiled in a famous controversy with the leader of the African National Congress, Jacob Zuma.

In 2008, Zapiro published a cartoon in a major South African newspaper which depicted Zuma and his political affiliates about to commit a rape of Lady Justice. We can leave aside the fact that Zuma had just been controversially acquitted of rape charges. We can also leave aside the fact that Zapiro is white and appeared to fall back on racist tropes when criticizing a Black leader. For now, let's focus on Zapiro's truth-to-power rationale for his cartoon: "It is in the public interest that cartoonists and other satirists are able to make such robust interventions in public discourse."[12]

The Consensus concurs with Kamra's and Zapiro's punch-up ethics. People in positions of power—unless they are deeply invested in The Consensus—do not. The dangers of ridiculing them were evident in our studies of Kathy Griffin, Vir Das, Bassem Youssef, Samantha Kureya, and the creators of *The Interview*.

Yet some powerful figures *do* accept The Consensus, and they appear to be at peace with political satire. These folks are far less humorless about it all; they would receive a lower score on the aforementioned H-Scale. Emmanuel Macron, though a frequent target of the *Charlie Hebdo* cartoonists, doggedly defended their right to ridicule.[13] Then there's the White House Correspondents' Association (WHCA) Dinner, an American institution at which (until recently) the most powerful leader of the free world is harangued by stand-ups.[14] Memorably, comedian Larry Wilmore deployed the N-word on President Obama in 2016. Obama, whose H-Scale scores were always admirably low, took it in stride.[15]

It's not that leaders of liberal democracies are masochists who enjoy being dinged by ribald clowns. It's just that The Consensus offers them a moral justification for why they should let clowns do their thing. These leaders govern cultures that long ago made their peace with verbal derision. After much trial and error (and many courtroom trials), their societies simply learned to tolerate incredibly offensive speech—and even to recognize its potential benefits.

The Pre-Digital Liberal Free Speech Consensus is predicated on the notion that, unpleasant though mockery might be, it is integral to a functioning democracy. It enjoins all of us to take the joke, or ignore the joke, but only under extreme circumstances (hate speech, imminent lawless action, threats to public order) to silence the joke. It's just a harmless little joke, says The Consensus.

Everything in this book suggests a great swath of humanity feels otherwise—but hats off to The Consensus. It's such a magnanimous thing!

Enjoy it while it lasts. Narendra Modi's BJP, as we saw in chapter 4, did not take well to Vir Das's criticism of *its* India. Donald Trump famously did not attend the WHCA dinner in 2018, preferring to speak at a MAGA rally instead. (Michelle Wolf, who hosted the event that year, quipped that Trump, who couldn't be dragged to the event, "is the one pussy you're not allowed to grab.")[16] In 2025, the WHCA caved: the group canceled the appearance of comedian Amber Ruffin and determined that no comic would perform at the storied event.[17] Trump has never attended these functions as president, so who knows what type of exercise in "pre-compliance" to government threats the WHCA was performing.

If leaders of liberal democracies like Modi and Trump, and press associations like the WHCA, won't support The Consensus, maybe we shouldn't be surprised that private entertainment conglomerates don't either.[18] Netflix, for example, makes all the requisite noises about protecting artistic freedom—except when its own bottom line is threatened. This became evident when comedian Hasan Minhaj, on his show *Patriot Act*, excoriated Saudi Arabia and its crown prince for their role in the killing of journalist Jamal Khashoggi. In 2018, under pressure from the prince's government, Netflix removed that specific episode in Saudi Arabia.[19]

Criticizing religions, identity groups, and powerful people is hazardous, outraging the mighty always a risky ploy. But we should not forget the lesson of *The Interview:* in some cases, the response of "outrage" may be performative and calculated—a pretext. Actors can pretend to be offended by a joke (or more offended than they actually are). Analysis of comedic controversies calls for a great deal of subtlety, as well as a recognition that the true motivations of irate audiences can be hard to discern, even mysterious.

META AND MENTAL HEALTH

Now that we've pondered audiences, let's move to their dialectical partners: the comedians who drive them to distraction. I have conceptualized the relation between irate audiences and humorists in terms of a loop or reactionary communication pattern. Comedians, I argue, often engage in one signature behavior that extends the loop and electrifies it with crackling negative energy. This meta reflex is one of the most important and underappreciated features of comedic controversies. Just as "the coverup is worse than the crime," this Lenny Bruce Maneuver might create more tumult than the initial offending joke.

What's noteworthy is not that comedians clap back at their critics; artists have been doing that for millennia. The novelty is that artists today *use their art* to explicitly engage with their detractors. And because of the internet, it all happens with preternatural speed and ease.

When comedians go meta they collapse the distinction between their persona and their actual self. In chapters 1 and 3, we weren't watching characters called "Dave Chappelle" or "Kathy Griffin," but something approximating the actual Dave and Kathy. Within their performances they were settling scores with those who did not like their previous performances.

This Persona Drop, as we have seen, is fraught with all sorts of dangers. For starters, it impacts the mental health of comedians. This was apparent in the cases of Griffin and Das, both of whom reported contemplating suicide. It seemed evident in Chappelle's increasingly unfocused self-referential sets. Dieudonné M'Bala M'Bala is locked in a pattern of acrimony with France's Jews that is now stretching into its third decade. His dark musings of late suggest, at least to this analyst, that the constant combat has taken a psychic toll.

Another reason comedians should practice meta with caution is the impact it has on their work. Once the loop is in play, the form and content of an artist's material can change dramatically. This was especially evident in the performances of the humorists just mentioned whose comedy seemed to become angrier and more solipsistic (and to me, less funny). Too, I note with concern the tendency of meta techniques to turn audience members into teammates, political allies. This was evident in the work of Chappelle and Griffin. Vir Das took this "audience participation" to a different level, a point I will return to below.

TOO BIG TO FAIL

"Cancellation" has become a metaphor for something akin to professional annihilation. Our findings recommend prudence when using this term. "Canceled" comedians, as we have seen, lose professional opportunities and with that some of their audience as well. But they never "zero out" their fan base. In fact, they often attract new followers who came aboard *because of* all the noise surrounding the artist's ordeal. True, in some cases the net dividend of cancellation is a smaller audience (as in the case of Kathy Griffin). In others, however, a fan base expands after cancellation (as with Shane Gillis and Dieudonné).

We did not encounter any situation where an artist could no longer earn a living because of cancellation. This might be because the comedians we studied are so well established that they are "too big to fail." In the main, our findings indicate that the discourse around "cancel culture" is overhyped. Though I do wonder if non-established artists who get canceled very early in their career have the same staying power.

I also wonder if gender plays a role in cancellation controversies. The chapter on Kathy Griffin raised this possibility. It is also intriguing that in Zimbabwe it was a woman, Samantha Kureya, who was singled out for an extreme form of punishment (chapter 8). Controversial female artists may have more to overcome than their male counterparts.

One way to mitigate the effects of cancellation is through apologies. But saying you're sorry with a straight face is not a salient comedic attribute. Only Sarah Silverman expressed unambiguously sincere contrition. Most humorists, by contrast, tend to want to make their apologies fun and/or funny—a recipe for disaster if ever there was one. We also saw that they often apologize cynically and strategically—a behavior that creates even more controversy.

PUNCHING DOWN

Many alleged cancellations were accompanied by the charge that the comedian "punched down." Our findings suggested that the concept, together with its twin, "punching up," should be employed cautiously.

One problem with "punching down" is that we lack agreed-upon metrics for accurately assessing the "verticality" of any given comedic blow. Dave Chappelle was repeatedly accused of punching down on the LGBTQ community. Chappelle demurred, maintaining that as a Black man in the United States he was *always* punching up. Punching up was in a sense his default setting, insofar as he believed that African American males are consigned to the lowest rung on the social ladder.

Sometimes those accused of punching down are stunned by the charge because they thought they were doing precisely the opposite. *Charlie Hebdo*'s illustrators felt they were attacking something vast, powerful, and dangerous in the form of militant Islamists—as opposed to Muslims generally. Theirs was not an entirely unwarranted assumption given how the episode shook out. In comedy, as in life, it is not always easy to assess who has more power.

Part of this complicated state of affairs is tied to social media. It could plausibly be argued that *Jyllands-Posten* and *Charlie Hebdo* punched down at Muslims in Denmark and France respectively. But once the cartoons migrated, via the internet, to other parts of the world, the relative power positions were reversed. In the Digital Era, comedians telling the same joke might be punching up in one place and down in another.

Punching down, however, is sometimes very real. Jokes about Down syndrome sufferers are one example, in that those in the targeted community often do not have the means to defend themselves. Shane Gillis, who makes such jokes, tried to finesse the situation, pointing out that people in his own family are afflicted by the condition.[20] In other words, he tries to deflect criticism by "trolling his own."

The crucial fact emerging from all this is that the Pre-Digital Liberal Free Speech Consensus is ensnared in a massive contradiction. Liberal political policies (such as political secularism, which aspires to defend the civil rights of religious minorities) manifest a deep concern for the mistreatment that smaller groups may experience at the hands of majorities. This is why liberals tend to recoil at "punching down," with its bullying tendencies. At the same time, however, liberalism abides by a Consensus that urges all and sundry to make peace with "harmless little jokes" in the name of the greater good. So while liberalism would seem to hate punching down, it still loves free speech. The Consensus's defense of vulnerable minorities collides with its defense of expressive liberty.

THE GUILD

So much of our thinking about free speech reflects the logic, ideation, and technological limitations of the Pre-Digital Age. As we transition deeper into the Digital Era, humorists are increasingly standing in the epicenter of debates about what can and cannot be said. They have seized that role from novelists, with whom they shared this task before screens replaced the pages of the analog era. This means that today, comics are the artists most likely to be on the front lines of extremely contentious and even dangerous free speech controversies.

Given their Hasmukh Complex (that is, their sense of moral righteousness, which leads them to refuse to back down, as discussed in chapter 4) and given the technique discussed above of conscripting one's audience into one's battles, the possibility exists that comedy will become far more politicized than it already is. Comedians will become linked with political viewpoints, in much the same way that football teams in Europe have ideologically identifiable cohorts of supporters.

This is why the "audience participation" techniques of Vir Das give me pause. If this technique becomes normative, we can expect some frightening outcomes, and not just in terms of artistic quality. Given the tools that the internet provides to angry publics, comedy risks becoming a vehicle of mass political polarization. It stands to reason that more humorists are going to be threatened, intimidated, sued, and even killed.

For these reasons I wonder if comedians need a guild. It would be run by some adult-in-the-room, thirty-years-sober veteran with no #MeToo skeletons in the closet. This person would be teamed up with a slew of First Amendment lawyers and maybe security specialists. The functions of this professional trade organization would be twofold. First, the Guild would monitor and advise comedians across the world facing legal threats and violence. The Guild might draw attention to far-flung comedic controversies much in the way PEN International does for writers who are censored. (Interestingly, PEN was rent asunder as an organization over *Charlie Hebdo.*)[21]

The Guild may also need to protect comedians *from themselves*. It might warn its members ensnarled in a loop that it's time to stand down. One of the most beguiling findings of this book concerns the indomitability of comedians in the face of danger. Even when their targets had obvious means of retaliation, and a clear willingness to deploy them, our comics persisted in their attack. They are ginned up on what Magi (chapter 8) called "bravado from nowhere." The specter of boycotts, fines, prison, exile, and even death could not stop them from going meta and cracking their controversial jokes.

Perhaps the Guild could offer professional development resources to its rank and file. I envision instructional videos such as "A Guide to Comedic De-escalation," or "When Not to Crack an R.I.P. Joke," or "How to Apologize and Influence People."

Then again, on the basis of what we have seen, it's more likely that the Guild will be as stubborn as the individual comedians it represents. The Guild will defend those who, caressed by "protective" laughter, feel invincible as they mock their detractors. And that's fine! But the Guild will have to compete with other interest groups and, at least in liberal democracies, with the laws of the land.

All of which reminds us of something comedians—understandably, given the beauty of their art form—tend to forget: society isn't made by or for them. Certain considerations outweigh free speech. This was the point of our war game exercise involving North Korea (chapter 9). And it was the grim lesson imparted by the *Charlie Hebdo* affair.

• • •

Jokes now have digital wings. Audiences are boundlessly large. Rage seems to be a human emotion experiencing its own cyber-renaissance. The Consensus, noble and highly imperfect, is coming undone.

Comedians, by joking about Down syndrome, Islam, Jews, Blacks, gays (including gay Jesus), the pope, the president, dictators, etc., are playing their small part in bringing ever larger groups of people around to the same conclusion: there must be more limitations on speech. Comedians *should* be provoking; that's their job and their unique heroism. Yet the more they do it, the more they imperil the free speech protections they claim to revere. That is the paradox that this book cannot resolve—and I wonder if it can ever be resolved.

In sum, the moral arc of the global comedic universe is not necessarily bending toward greater expressive liberty. Humorists are increasingly confronted by those who wish to shut them up and shut them down. The comedians, as we have noted, refuse to accept that fate. Their spirited resistance contributes to the distorted curvature of the aforementioned arc. In these confrontations where comics, their fans, the actively outraged, and the government all square off, no one is completely innocent. Then again, no one ever is.

NOTES

INTRODUCTION

1. Jacques Berlinerblau, "Will Smith and the Function of a Slap—What It Means for Comedy and Comedians," *Salon*, March 29, 2022, https://www.salon.com/2022/03/29/will-smith-and-the-function-of-a-slap-what-it-means-for-comedy-and-comedians/.

2. Matt Stevens, "After Attacks, Comedians Wonder: Can People Still Take a Joke?" *New York Times*, May 12, 2022, https://www.nytimes.com/2022/05/12/arts/comedians-safety-dave-chappelle-chris-rock.html.

3. Mujib Mashal, "After Kunal Kamra's Controversial Gig, Demolition Drive at Mumbai Comedy Club," *Hindustan Times*, March 24, 2025, https://www.hindustantimes.com/india-news/kunal-kamra-mumbai-the-habitat-studio-at-unicontinental-hotel-bmc-demolition-eknath-shinde-joke-101742804483405.html.

4. These cases are discussed in Kliph Nesteroff, *Outrageous: A History of Showbiz and the Culture Wars* (New York: Abrams, 2023), 145–153.

5. See Victor Navasky, *The Art of Controversy: Political Cartoons and Their Enduring Power* (New York: Alfred A. Knopf, 2013), 69–72, 73–75; and Haydn Mason, *Candide: Optimism Demolished* (New York: Twayne, 1992), 13.

6. William J. Brady, Molly J. Crockett, and Jay Joseph Van Bavel, "The MAD Model of Moral Contagion: The Role of Motivation, Attention, and Design in the Spread of Moralized Content Online," *Perspectives on Psychological Science* 15, no. 4 (2020): 978–1010, https://doi.org/10.1177/1745691620917336.

7. Jesse David Fox, *Comedy Book: How Comedy Conquered Culture—and the Magic That Makes It Work* (New York: Farrar, Straus & Giroux, 2023); Ken Jennings, *Planet Funny: How Comedy Took over Our Culture* (New York: Scribner, 2018), 1–10.

8. Chas Danner and Margaret Hartmann, "The Complete Guide to Will Smith Slap Takes," *New York Magazine*, April 1, 2022, https://nymag.com/intelligencer/2022/03/the-complete-guide-to-will-smith-slap-takes.html.

9. For some comprehensive (i.e., global) histories of free speech, see Jacob Mchangama, *Free Speech: A History from Socrates to Social Media* (New York: Basic Books, 2022); Robert Hargreaves, *The First Freedom: A History of Free Speech* (Thrupp, UK: Sutton, 2002). On Lenny Bruce, see Edward de Grazia, *Girls Lean Back Everywhere* (New York: Random House, 1992). Also see Barry Spunt, *Heroin, Acting, and Comedy in New York City* (New York: Palgrave Macmillan, 2014), 142–145.

10. Emile Durkheim, *The Rules of Sociological Method and Selected Texts on Sociology and Its Method*, ed. Steven Lukes (New York: Free Press, 1982), 102; Jacques Berlinerblau, "Toward a Sociology of Heresy, Orthodoxy, and Doxa," *History of Religions* 40, no. 4 (2001): 327–351, http://www.jstor.org/stable/3176370.

11. John Stuart Mill, *On Liberty* (New York: Pearson Longman, 2007), 77, 80.

12. Nat Hentoff, *Free Speech for Me—but Not for Thee: How the American Left and Right Relentlessly Censor Each Other* (New York: HarperCollins, 1992).

13. On obscenity, see de Grazia, *Girls Lean Back Everywhere*. On blasphemy and free speech, see Helen Pringle, "Are We Capable of Offending God? Taking Blasphemy Seriously," in *Negotiating the Sacred: Blasphemy and Sacrilege in a Multicultural Society*, ed. Elizabeth Burns Coleman and Kevin White (Canberra: ANU Press, 2006), 31–42, https://www.jstor.org/stable/j.ctt2jbjjq.7; Maja Munivrana Vajda, "The Right to Mock, Ridicule, and Criticize Religion—Exploring the Limits of Free Speech in a Democratic and Just Society," *Gonzaga Journal of International Law* 55, no. 2 (2019): 274–289, https://gjil.scholasticahq.com/article/12332-the-right-to-mock-ridicule-and-criticize-religion-exploring-the-limits-of-free-speech-in-a-democratic-and-just-society. An anonymous piece of interest makes the controversial claim that blasphemy is not constitutionally protected in the United States: "Blasphemy and the Original Meaning of the First Amendment," *Harvard Law Review* 135 (2021): 690–710, https://harvardlawreview.org/print/vol-135/blasphemy-and-the-original-meaning-of-the-first-amendment.

14. *Brandenburg v. Ohio*, 395 U.S. 444 (1969), https://supreme.justia.com/cases/federal/us/395/444; Samuel Walker, *Hate Speech: The History of an American Controversy* (Lincoln: University of Nebraska Press, 1994); Jacques Berlinerblau, *Secularism: The Basics*, 2nd ed. (New York: Routledge, 2024); Jacques Berlinerblau, "Cheat Sheet for Political Secularism and Secular Studies," *Secular Studies* 5, no. 1 (2023): 53–82, https://doi.org/10.1163/25892525-bja10046.

15. Ronald Dworkin, "The Right to Ridicule," *New York Review of Books*, March 23, 2006, https://www.nybooks.com/articles/2006/03/23/the-right-to-ridicule.

16. *Whitney v. California*, 227 U.S. 377 (1927), https://supreme.justia.com/cases/federal/us/274/357/#T4; David Hudson, "Counterspeech Doctrine," *Free Speech Center*, January 1, 2009 (updated July 2, 2024), https://firstamendment.mtsu.edu/article/counterspeech-doctrine.

17. Stephan Haggard and Jon R. Lindsay, "North Korea and the Sony Hack: Exporting Instability through Cyberspace," *East-West Center*, no. 117 (May 2015), http://www.jstor.org/stable/resrep06456.

18. "'Yes, I Think They Made a Mistake': President Obama on Sony Hack," *C-SPAN*, December 19, 2014, https://www.youtube.com/watch?v=y59yyxpgAUI.

19. Matt Sienkiewicz and Nick Marx, *That's Not Funny: How the Right Makes Comedy Work for Them* (Oakland: University of California Press, 2022).

20. "Greg Gutfield: Colleges Are Going to Hell!" *Fox News*, November 21, 2024, https://www.youtube.com/watch?v=x7PyzVa6ueg, 0:00–2:35; "Tony Hinchcliffe Calls Puerto Rico 'Floating Island of Garbage' at Trump Rally," *ABC7*, October 28, 2024, https://www.youtube.com/watch?v=LNBdYplmKcI.

21. Sienkiewicz and Marx, *That's Not Funny*, 173.

22. Other than the study of Sienkiewicz and Marx, peer-reviewed scholarship on *Murdoch Murdoch* is hard to identify. For studies of the use of comedy by right-wing extremists, see Keith Scott, "Ha Ha Only Serious: Irony in Information Warfare and the Comedy-Cloaked Extremism," in *16th International Conference on Cyber Warfare and Security (ICCWS 2021)*, ed. Juan Lopez Jr., Ambareen Siraj, and Kalyan Perumalla (Reading, UK: Academic Conferences International Limited, 2021), https://www.proceedings.com/content/058/058552webtoc.pdf; Jordan McSwiney and Kurt Sengul, "Humor, Ridicule, and the Far Right: Mainstreaming Exclusion through Online Animation," *Television and News Media* 25, no. 4 (2024): 315–333, https://doi.org/10.1177/15274764231213816.

23. "Waiting for the Superman," *Murdoch Murdoch*, 2020, https://www.murdochmurdoch.net/murdoch/waiting-for-the-superman/, 9:20–9:33.

24. "Waiting for the Superman," 9:37–10:14.

25. See Harry Robertson, "Murdoch Murdoch—the Alt-Right's Very Own Sitcom," *Medium*, December 10, 2021, https://medium.com/tales-from-the-alt-right/murdoch-murdoch-the-alt-rights-sitcom-6c033d30d2ae. One of my research assistants has identified alternative metrics to measure the series' popularity,

including search engine performance and number of links to the archives of the series. The tool used for this investigation was Spyfu, though similar SEO research tools yielded similar results; see "murdochmurdoch.net SEO Overview," *SpyFu*, https://www.spyfu.com/seo/kombat?query=murdochmurdoch.net.

26. According to the social media statistics site SocialBlade, the group had 18.3 million subscribers on YouTube as of November 2024, ranking as the 32nd most popular channel in Brazil. "Porta dos Fundos," *SocialBlade*, https://socialblade.com/youtube/user/portadosfundos.

27. "Oh, meu Deus!," *Porta dos Fundos*, August 19, 2013, 0:00–0:27 and 0:51–1:05, https://www.youtube.com/watch?v=AYiSqyiVaA4.

28. Simon Romero, "On YouTube, Comedy Troupe Tickles Brazil and Ruffles Feathers," *New York Times*, August 31, 2013, https://www.nytimes.com/2013/09/01/world/americas/on-youtube-comedy-troupe-tickles-brazil-and-ruffles-feathers.html.

29. LaTesha Harris, "Netflix Facing Backlash over Comedy Special with Gay Jesus," *Variety*, December 16, 2019, https://variety.com/2019/film/news/netflix-gay-jesus-movie-controversy-1203439807/.

30. Jake Spring and Gabriela Mello, "Brazilian Far-Right Group Claims Attack on 'Gay Jesus' Comedy Troupe," *Reuters*, December 26, 2019, https://www.reuters.com/article/world/brazilian-far-right-group-claims-attack-on-gay-jesus-comedy-troupe-idUSKBN1YU0WX/; "Brazil's Supreme Court Overturns Ban on Netflix's Gay Jesus film," *NBC News*, January 10, 2020, https://www.nbcnews.com/feature/nbc-out/brazil-s-supreme-court-overturns-ban-netflix-s-gay-jesus-n1113521.

31. "Jesus hétero," *Porta dos Fundos*, December 24, 2020, 0:00–0:37, https://www.youtube.com/watch?v=y2mccgB3XIk.

32. "Jesus hétero," 0:35–0:50, 1:05–1:11, 2:38–2:48, 2:47–2:50.

33. A parallel insight is offered by Chris Gilbert, who speaks of "being comical at the expense of comedy." For more, see Christopher J. Gilbert, *When Comedy Goes Wrong* (Bloomington: Indiana University Press, 2025).

34. George Paton, "In Search of Literature on the Sociology of Humour: A Sociobibliographical Afterword," in *Humour in Society: Resistance and Contro*l, ed. Chris Powell and George Paton (New York: St. Martin's Press, 1988), 260–271; Sharon Lockyer and Simon Weaver, "On the Importance of the Dynamics of Humour and Comedy for Constructionism and Reflexivity in Social Science Research Methodology," *International Journal of Social Research Methodology* 25, no. 5 (2022): 645–657, https://www.tandfonline.com/doi/full/10.1080/13645579.2021.1926050; Sharon Lockyer and Michael Pickering, "You Must be Joking: The Sociological Critique of Humour and Comic

Media," *Sociology Compass* 2, no. 3 (2008): 808–820, http://dx.doi.org/10.1111/j.1751-9020.2008.00108.x.

35. Jason Robert Allan Hughes, "Norbert Elias and the Habits of Good Sociology," University of Leicester, 2013, https://hdl.handle.net/2381/28043.

36. William Cameron, *Informal Sociology: A Casual Introduction to Sociological Thinking* (New York: Random House, 1967), 81.

37. Invoking Durkheim's notion of "social facts" to make this point is Giselinde Kuipers, *Good Humor, Bad Taste: A Sociology of the Joke* (The Hague: Mouton de Gruyter, 2006), 6–7.

38. Kavyta Kay has looked at comments on Facebook and YouTube in her work on Indian comedians in the digital age; see Kavyta Kay, *New Indian Nuttahs: Comedy and Cultural Critique in Millennial India* (Cham, Switzerland: Palgrave MacMillan, 2018), 3. Rebecca Johnson has scrutinized comments left on the *Guardian*'s website regarding a story about the fearless comedy troupe Al-Taseh, which has the brazen audacity to troll the terrorist group ISIS; see Rebecca Johnson, "The Clash of Articulations: Aesthetic Shock, Multivalent Narratives, and Islam in the Post-9/11 Era," PhD thesis, University of Manchester, 2017, https://pure.manchester.ac.uk/ws/portalfiles/portal/59811426/full_text.pdf, 80, 175–181. Amanda Källstig has spoken to audience members after shows in her fieldwork studying the Zimbabwean stand-up scene; see Amanda Källstig, "Humouring the State? Zimbabwean Stand-Up Comedians as Political Actors," PhD thesis, University of Manchester, 2021, https://pure.manchester.ac.uk/ws/portalfiles/portal/205621734/full_text.pdf, 26.

39. Jacques Berlinerblau, "The Productive Obscene: Philip Roth and the Profanity Loop," in *Profane: Sacrilegious Expression in a Multicultural Age*, ed. Christopher S. Grenada et al. (Berkeley: University of California Press, 2014), 59, https://www.jstor.org/stable/10.1525/j.ctt7zw3fb.7. On "dislike" as a variable in the study of culture, see Jonathan Gray, *Dislike-Minded: Media, Audiences, and the Dynamics of Taste* (New York: New York University Press, 2021).

40. Ronald Collins and David Skover, *The Trials of Lenny Bruce: The Fall and Rise of an American Icon* (Naperville, IL: Sourcebooks MediaFusion, 2002), 50–51; Spunt, *Heroin, Acting, and Comedy*, 144.

41. Bridget Haina, "The Language of Outrage: Defining and Communicating Outrage and Incivility via Social Media during the Charlottesville Protests," *Journal of Social Media in Society* 10, no. 2 (2021): 67.

42. Eve Ng, *Cancel Culture: A Critical Analysis* (Cham, Switzerland: Palgrave Macmillan, 2023), 5–6.

CHAPTER ONE

1. *The Closer*, directed by Stan Lathan, featuring Dave Chappelle (Netflix Worldwide Entertainment, 2021), 0:36:30, https://www.netflix.com/title/81228510.

2. Josh Wolk, "EW Investigates the Disappearance of Dave Chappelle," *EW*, May 16, 2005, https://ew.com/article/2005/05/16/ew-investigates-disappearance-dave-chappelle/.

3. *Dave Chappelle: Sticks and Stones*, directed by Stan Lathan, featuring Dave Chappelle (Pilot Boy Productions, 2019), 0:21:50, https://www.netflix.com/title/81140577.

4. Naledi Ushe, "Dave Chappelle's Alleged Attacker Speaks out on Incident: 'What He Said Was Triggering'" *USA Today*, May 23, 2022, https://www.usatoday.com/story/entertainment/celebrities/2022/05/23/dave-chappelle-alleged-attacker-motive-isaiah-lee-triggering-jokes/9890771002/.

5. *The Age of Spin: Dave Chappelle Live at the Hollywood Palladium*, directed by Stan Lathan, featuring Dave Chappelle (Netflix Worldwide Entertainment, 2017), 0:37:00, https://www.netflix.com/watch/80161055.

6. *Dave Chappelle: The Dreamer*, directed by Stan Lathan, featuring Dave Chappelle (Netflix Worldwide Entertainment, 2023), 0:10:15–0:10:46, https://www.netflix.com/title/81665820.

7. *Dave Chappelle: Sticks and Stones*, 0:22:54

8. Daphne Dorman [@DaphneDorman], *X*, August 29, 2019, https://x.com/DaphneDorman/status/1166937728681791488; *Dave Chappelle: The Closer*, 1:05:54.

9. *Dave Chappelle: The Closer*, 1:04:55. See the counter-narrative presented by Michael Hobbes, "Dave Chappelle's 'Some of My Best Friends Are Trans' Story Doesn't Hold Up," *Confirm My Choices*, November 17, 2021, https://michaelhobbes.substack.com/p/dave-chappelles-some-of-my-best-friends.

10. *Dave Chappelle: The Closer*, 1:05:30.

11. Lucas Grindley, "Dave Chappelle Has Some Problem with LGBT Activists," *Advocate*, November 6, 2016, https://www.advocate.com/media/2016/11/06/dave-chappelle-has-some-problem-lgbt-activists; Eric Sasson, "What Is Dave Chappelle's Problem with Gay People?" *New Republic*, March 23, 2017, https://newrepublic.com/article/141550/dave-chappelles-problem-gay-people; Tiq Milan, "Dave Chappelle's Jokes about Trans People Haven't Aged Well," *BuzzFeed*, March 25, 2017, https://www.buzzfeed.com/tiqmilan/dave-chappelles-anti-trans-jokes-reveal-how-fragile.

12. "Dave Chappelle's brand has become synonymous with ridiculing trans people and other marginalized communities. Negative reviews and viewers

loudly condemning his latest special is a message to the industry that audiences don't support platforming anti-LGBTQ diatribes. We agree." GLAAD [@glaad], *X*, October 6, 2021, https://x.com/glaad/status/1445870767548231685.

13. "I'm not 'triggered' by Chappelle's views on trans people. It is what it is, and he's entitled to his opinion. But he's one note, now. 'Look at me, I'm pressing people's buttons." biggamax, *Reddit*, January 2, 2024, https://www.reddit.com/r/netflix/comments/18wssnf/comment/kgoec4n/.

14. Novotny Lawrence, "Comic Genius or Con Man? Deconstructing the Comedy of Dave Chappelle," in *The Comedy of Dave Chappelle: Critical Essays*, ed. K. A. Wisniewski (Jefferson, NC: McFarland & Co., 2009), 31, 38.

15. *Dave Chappelle: Killin' Them Softly*, directed by Stan Lathan, featuring Dave Chappelle (HBO, 2000), https://www.max.com/movies/dave-chappelle-killin-them-softly/b302305e-5e05-4ed9-9b3e-daad57bf9d21; *Dave Chappelle: For What It's Worth*, directed by Stan Lathan, featuring Dave Chappelle (Showtime, 2000), 0:1:49, 21:50, https://www.youtube.com/watch?v=B-hynjEdTaY.

16. In season 1 there was "Ask a Gay Dude: With Mario Cantone," *Chappelle's Show*, season 1, episode 6, "Mad Real World & Ask a Gay Dude," written by Dave Chappelle and Neal Brennan (Comedy Central, March 31, 2004), 6:02, https://www.cc.com/episodes/b2r05u/chappelle-s-show-mad-real-world-ask-a-gay-dude-season-1-ep-6. Also see *Chappelle's Show*, season 2, episode 10, "Mandela Boot Camp & The Time Haters," written by Dave Chappelle and Neal Brennan (Comedy Central, March 31, 2004), 6:35, https://www.netflix.com/watch/70138035; *Chappelle's Show*, season 2, episode 9, "Kneehigh Park & Making da Band," written by Dave Chappelle and Neal Brennan (Comedy Central, March 24, 2004), 8:50, https://www.netflix.com/watch/70138034; *Chappelle's Show*, season 2, episode 12, "Lil Jon on Lil Jon & Black Bush," written by Dave Chappelle and Neal Brennan (Comedy Central, April 14, 2004), 16:35, https://www.netflix.com/watch/70138037.

17. *The Closer*, 42:00.

18. Aurora Grajeda [@Tranny], "Dave Chappelle's Homo/Transphobia Hate Speech @ New Parish Oakland," *Daily Kos*, March 4, 2010, https://www.dailykos.com/stories/2010/3/4/843117/-.

19. *Chappelle's Show*, season 1, episode 1, "Pop Copy & Clayton Bigsby," written by Dave Chappelle and Neal Brennan (Comedy Central, January 22, 2003), 12:05, https://www.netflix.com/watch/70138013.

20. Richard Gray II and Michael Putnam, "Exploring Niggerdom: Racial Inversion in Language Taboos," in Wisniewski, ed., *Comedy of Dave Chappelle*, 24–25.

21. See Bambi Haggins, "In the Wake of the 'Nigger Pixie': Dave Chappelle and the Politics of Crossover Comedy," in *Satire TV: Politics and Comedy in the Post-Network Era*, ed. Jonathan Gray, Jeffrey P. Jones, and Ethan Thompson (New York: New York University Press, 2009), 237; Janine Bradbury, "Parodying Racial Passing in *Chappelle's Show* and *Key & Peele*," in *Comedy and the Politics of Representation: Mocking the Weak*, ed. Helen Davies and Sarah Ilott (London: Palgrave Macmillan, 2018), 79–97.

22. David Gillota, *Ethnic Humor in Multiethnic America* (New Brunswick, NJ: Rutgers, 2013), 33.

23. Douglas Dowie, "Everybody's Not Laughing at Eddie Murphy," *UPI*, January 14, 1984, https://www.upi.com/Archives/1984/01/14/Everybodys-not-laughing-at-Eddie-Murphy/2002442904400/.

24. Molly J. Crockett, "Moral Outrage in the Digital Age," *Nature Human Behaviour* 1, no. 11 (2017): 769–770, https://doi.org/10.1038/s41562-017-0213-3.

25. William Brady and Killian McLoughlin, "How Social Media Contexts Affect the Expression of Moral Emotions," in *The Psychology of Technology: Social Science Research in the Age of Big Data*, ed. S. C. Matz (Washington, DC: American Psychological Association, 2022), 239–265, https://doi.org/10.1037/0000290-008. Also see William Brady et al., "How Social Learning Amplifies Moral Outrage Expression in Online Social Networks," *Science Advances* 7, no. 33 (2021): 239–265, https://doi.org/10.1126/sciadv.abe5641.

26. William J. Brady et al., "Overperception of Moral Outrage in Online Social Networks Inflates Beliefs about Intergroup Hostility," *Nature Human Behaviour* 7, no. 6 (2023): 917–27, https://doi.org/10.1038/s41562-023-01582-0.

27. Emphasis mine. Bridget Haina, "The Language of Outrage: Defining and Communicating Outrage and Incivility via Social Media during the Charlottesville Protests," *Journal of Social Media in Society* 10, no. 2 (2021): 58–75.

28. *Deep in the Heart of Texas: Dave Chappelle Live at Austin City Limits*, directed by Stan Lathan, featuring Dave Chappelle (Netflix Worldwide Entertainment, 2017), 38:30, 38:35, and 39:20, https://www.netflix.com/title/80161054. Despite best efforts, I was unable to locate the blog post Chappelle refers to in this segment.

29. For a detailed recent discussion of the comic persona, see Sarah Balkin and Marc Mierowsky, *Comedy and Controversy: Scripting Public Speech* (Cambridge: Cambridge University Press, 2025).

30. "Dave Chappelle," *The Actors Studio*, uploaded April 25, 2022, 21:26, https://www.youtube.com/watch?v=vARB88Y3wmE&t=4221s.

31. *Dave Chappelle: Equanimity*, directed by Stan Lathan, featuring Dave Chappelle (Netflix Worldwide Entertainment, 2017), 23:40 and 24:15, https://www.netflix.com/watch/80171759.

32. *Dave Chappelle: Sticks and Stones*, 21:47.

33. Jacques Berlinerblau, "Dave Chappelle Can't Stop Punching Down. And That's Not the Worst Part," *MSNBC*, January 2, 2024, https://www.msnbc.com/opinion/msnbc-opinion/dave-chappelle-the-dreamer-anti-trans-rcna131931.

34. *Dave Chappelle: The Dreamer*, 5:57–6:16.

35. Dave Chappelle, "Stunted," October 25, 2021, https://www.youtube.com/watch?v=g4vle2df-34.

36. Zoe Christen Jones, "Netflix Employees Stage Walkout over Dave Chappelle Special," *CBS News*, October 25, 2021, https://www.cbsnews.com/news/dave-chappelle-netflix-employees-walkout/.

37. "Stunted," 1:06, 0:56–1:06, and 1:26.

38. "Stunted," 4:05. Hannah Gadsby is a gender non-conforming comedian.

39. *Dave Chappelle: Live in Real Life*, directed by Steven Bognar and Julia Reichert, featuring Dave Chappelle (Pilot Boy Productions, 2021).

40. "Stunted," 2:52 and 2:55–3:00.

41. "Stunted," 4:38 and 4:50.

CHAPTER TWO

Epigraph: Helen Davies and Sarah Ilott, "Mocking the Weak? Contexts, Theories, Politics," in *Comedy and the Politics of Representation: Mocking the Weak*, ed. Helen Davies and Sarah Ilott (London: Palgrave Macmillain, 2018).

1. Andy DeYoung, dir., "Bernie Sanders Is the One for Me: Sarah Silverman Explains," *YouTube*, posted by Sarah Silverman, March 28, 2016, https://www.youtube.com/watch?v=1dh78xoPr1s.

2. Liam Lynch, dir., *Sarah Silverman: Jesus Is Magic* (Showtime, 2005), https://www.youtube.com/watch?v=1qYxTC4UED8.

3. *Sarah Silverman: A Speck of Dust* (Netflix, 2017).

4. Jonathan Krisel, dir., *Sarah Silverman: Someone You Love* (HBO Max, 2023).

5. Amy York Rubin, dir., "An Indecent Proposal from Sarah Silverman (Explicit)," *YouTube*, posted by SchlepLabs, July 16, 2012, https://www.youtube.com/watch?v=2B506-qNk6Q.

6. "The Great Schlep (NSFW)—Starring Sarah Silverman," *YouTube*, posted by SchlepLabs, April 9, 2015, https://www.youtube.com/watch?v=AEGFQR1u-Mk.

7. Sarah Silverman, *The Bedwetter: Stories of Courage, Redemption, and Pee* (New York: Harper, 2010), 192–193.

8. Nardine Saad, "How a 2005 Sarah Silverman Joke Sparked Death Wishes from Two Baptist Pastors," *Los Angeles Times*, August 9, 2019, https://www.latimes.com/entertainment-arts/tv/story/2019-08-09/sarah-silverman-baptist-pastor-death-clip.

9. Sarah Silverman [@SarahKSilverman], *Twitter*, August 8, 2019, https://x.com/SarahKSilverman/status/1159559200210468864.

10. Paul Lewis, "Beyond Empathy: Sarah Silverman and the Limits of Comedy," *Tikkun* 22, no. 5 (Sept./Oct. 2007): 88–89, https://muse.jhu.edu/article/592711/pdf.

11. All of these slights can be found in Silverman's *Jesus Is Magic* as well as many of her other performances.

12. "Sarah Silverman Interview—7/11/2001," *YouTube*, posted by Conan Fanatic, February 22, 2018, https://www.youtube.com/watch?v=7dhl1t7SwrI.

13. Alexandra Jacobs, "Saving Silverman," *Observer*, August 6, 2001, https://observer.com/2001/08/saving-silverman/.

14. Silverman, *Bedwetter*, 147.

15. Silverman, *Bedwetter*, 148.

16. "Politically Incorrect—'Racist' Jokes—David Spade Sarah Silverman Bill Maher," *YouTube*, posted by AmetReloads, May 2, 2015, https://www.youtube.com/watch?v=WiCEaLHZp24.

17. "Politically Incorrect." That this was not an oversight is indicated by the fact that Silverman repeated the joke years later in *Jesus Is Magic*.

18. *Sarah Silverman: Jesus Is Magic*.

19. Guy Aoki, "Bill Maher Called Me a Chink, but He Apologized for Using the N-Word," *NextShark*, June 15, 2017, https://nextshark.com/guy-aoki-bill-maher-apologized-for-saying-the-n-word-yet-called-me-a-chink.

20. For a discussion of Silverman's use of persona, see Lacy Lowrey, Valerie R. Renegar, and Charles E. Goehring, "'When God Gives You AIDS . . . Make Lemon-AIDS': Ironic Persona and Perspective by Incongruity in Sarah Silverman's 'Jesus Is Magic,'" *Western Journal of Communication* 78, no. 1 (August 2, 2013): 58–77, https://doi.org/10.1080/10570314.2013.792387.

21. Lowrey et al., "'When God Gives You AIDS . . .,'' referred to this persona somewhat differently as "the kid" (65).

22. Silverman, *Bedwetter*, 157. See *I Love You, America, with Sarah Silverman*, season 1, episode 3, directed by Allan Kartun, featuring Sarah Silverman

and Don Cheadle, aired October 26, 2017, on Hulu, https://www.hulu.com/series/i-love-you-america-with-sarah-silverman-1501fdad-75d2-4748-80ae-e63d95ff44f6.

23. Silverman, *Bedwetter*, 146.

24. Sam Anderson, "Irony Maiden: How Sarah Silverman Is Raping American Comedy," *Slate*, November 10, 2005, https://slate.com/culture/2005/11/sarah-silverman-rapes-american-comedy.html.

25. Will Leitch, "Animal Magnetism," *New York Magazine*, April 8, 2010, https://nymag.com/arts/books/features/65351/.

26. Lowrey et al., "'When God Gives You AIDS . . .,'" 74.

27. Silverman, *Bedwetter*, 157. Also making this point are Debra Aarons and Marc Mierowsky, "Public Conscience of 'The Chosen People': Sarah Silverman in the Wake of Lenny Bruce," *Comedy Studies* 8, no. 2 (July 21, 2017): 154–66, https://doi.org/10.1080/2040610x.2017.1343272.

28. *Jesus Is Magic*, 50:16–50:28 and 50:36–51:03.

29. *Jesus Is Magic*, 51:05, 51:13–51:33, 51:55–52:02, and 52:04.

30. *Jesus Is Magic*, 52:50.

31. "Sarah Silverman German Cars," *YouTube*, 0:00–2:30, uploaded by scott left, December 12, 2016, https://www.youtube.com/watch?v=d8hGR1ZpUPw.

32. Sarah Silverman, "Chappelle, B*Face, Anything Goes," *Sarah Silverman Podcast*, December 1, 2022, https://open.spotify.com/episode/50exJfsfXrmN5j2Apfw5nT?si=045a03a7c2bf451e.

33. Kevin Hart, "Sarah Silverman," *Comedy Gold Minds with Kevin Hart*, April 15, 2021, https://podcasts.apple.com/us/podcast/gold-minds-with-kevin-hart/id1549388085?i=1000517217711. See also Bill Simmons, "Sarah Silverman on 'Funny' in 2019, Cancel Culture, 'Big Mouth,' Death Threats, the 2020 Election, and 'Big Little Lies,'" *Bill Simmons Podcast*, August 8, 2019, https://podcasts.apple.com/us/podcast/the-bill-simmons-podcast/id1043699613?i=1000446485582; Silverman, "Chappelle, B*Face, Anything Goes."

34. Rob Picheta, "Sarah Silverman Says She Was Fired from a Movie for an Old Blackface Sketch," *CNN*, August 12, 2019, https://www.cnn.com/2019/08/12/entertainment/sarah-silverman-blackface-scli-intl/index.html.

35. Silverman elaborated on the definition of "Jewface" in "Jewface, Iron Dome, Mr. Mom," *Sarah Silverman Podcast*, September 30, 2021, https://podcasts.apple.com/us/podcast/the-sarah-silverman-podcast/id1533130572?i=1000537086147.

36. Sadaf Ahsan, "'It's Racist out of Context': Sarah Silverman Kind of Regrets Wearing Blackface," *National Post*, October 30, 2015, https://

nationalpost.com/entertainment/celebrity/its-racist-out-of-context-sarah-silverman-kind-of-regrets-wearing-blackface.

37. A review of the Himes can be found at https://www.commentary.org/articles/milton-klonsky/lonely-crusade-by-chester-himes/; and the Malamud story can be found at https://faculty.history.umd.edu/BCooperman/NewCity/AngelLevine.html.

38. David Gillota, *Ethnic Humor in Multiethnic America* (New Brunswick, NJ: Rutgers University Press, 2013), 58. Also see Terrence L. Johnson and Jacques Berlinerblau, *Blacks and Jews in America: An Invitation to Dialogue* (Washington, DC: Georgetown University Press, 2022).

39. Robert Lloyd, "Sarah Silverman Defends Dave Chappelle and Humor that Offends: 'That's Comedy. You Overstep,'" *Los Angeles Times*, September 16, 2019, https://www.latimes.com/entertainment-arts/tv/story/2019-09-16/emmys-sarah-silverman-i-love-you-america-hulu. For more on cancel culture see Osita Nwanevu, "The 'Cancel Culture' Con," *New Republic*, September 23, 2019, https://newrepublic.com/article/155141/cancel-culture-con-dave-chappelle-shane-gillis.

40. Simmons, "Sarah Silverman on 'Funny.'"

41. Ligaya Mishan, "The Long and Tortured History of Cancel Culture," *New York Times*, December 3, 2020, https://www.nytimes.com/2020/12/03/t-magazine/cancel-culture-history.html.

42. Kevin Hart, "Wanda Sykes," on the podcast *Comedy Gold Minds with Kevin Hart*, November 18, 2021, https://podcasts.apple.com/us/podcast/gold-minds-with-kevin-hart/id1549388085?i=1000542310350.

43. Nwanevu, "'Cancel Culture' Con."

44. Cara Buckley, Jodi Kantor, and Melena Ryzik, "Louis C.K. Is Accused by 5 Women of Sexual Misconduct," *New York Times*, November 9, 2017, https://www.nytimes.com/2017/11/09/arts/television/louis-ck-sexual-misconduct.html; Marc Burrows, "Louis C.K.'s Sold-out Show at Madison Square Garden Proves There's No Such Thing as Cancel Culture," *Big Issue*, January 30, 2023, https://www.bigissue.com/culture/louis-cks-sold-out-show-at-madison-square-garden-proves-theres-no-such-thing-as-cancel-culture/.

45. Dustin Jones, "Louis C.K. Cancels His Cancellation, Wins a Grammy, and Triggers a Backlash," *NPR*, April 4, 2022, https://www.npr.org/2022/04/04/1090743278/louis-c-k-crawls-out-of-cancellation-wins-a-grammy-and-triggers-a-backlash; Abbey White, "Louis C.K.'s Latest Comeback an Oddly Normal Night of Off-Color Comedy," *Hollywood Reporter*, August 14, 2021, https://www.hollywoodreporter.com/news/general-news/louis-ck-madison-square-garden-new-york-national-tour-1234997761/.

46. Mona Khalifeh, "Sarah Silverman Apologizes to Paris Hilton for Jail Joke at 2007 MTV Movie Awards," *ET*, March 4, 2021, https://www.etonline.com/sarah-silverman-apologizes-to-paris-hilton-for-jail-joke-at-2007-mtv-movie-awards-161713.

47. Callum Henderson, "Sarah Silverman Apologizes to Paris Hilton for 2007 Joke: 'I Can't Imagine What You Were Going Through,'" *VT*, March 5, 2021, https://vt.co/news/entertainment-news/sarah-silverman-apologizes-to-paris-hilton-for-2007-joke-i-cant-imagine-what-you-were-going-through. A recording of her apology can be found at https://www.instagram.com/tv/CMAsEoCAYxc.

48. Alexia Fernandez, "Sarah Silverman Responds to Nick Cannon Sharing an Old Tweet Where She Used Homophobic Language," *People*, December 10, 2018, https://people.com/movies/sarah-silverman-addresses-nick-cannon-accusation-homophobic-tweets/.

49. Sophie Heawood, "Sarah Silverman: 'There Are Jokes I Made 15 Years Ago I Would Absolutely Not Make Today,'" *Guardian*, November 19, 2017, https://www.theguardian.com/global/2017/nov/19/sarah-silverman-interview-jokes-i-made-15-years-ago-i-wouldnt-make-today.

50. *I Love You, America, with Sarah Silverman*, season 1, episode 3.

51. Silverman, "Chappelle, B*Face, Anything Goes"; Kevin Hart, "Sarah Silverman," *Comedy Gold Minds with Kevin Hart*, April 15, 2021, https://podcasts.apple.com/us/podcast/gold-minds-with-kevin-hart/id1549388085?i=1000517217711; Simmons, "Sarah Silverman on 'Funny.'"

52. Quoted in Randall Colburn, "Sarah Silverman Reveals She Was Just Recently Fired from a Movie over 2007 Blackface Sketch," *AV Club*, August 12, 2019, https://www.avclub.com/sarah-silverman-reveals-she-was-just-recently-fired-fro-1837175090.

53. Jacques Berlinerblau, "Sarah Silverman and the Secret to Successful Comedy," *MSNBC*, May 30, 2023, https://www.msnbc.com/opinion/msnbc-opinion/sarah-silverman-max-comedy-special-review-rcna86792.

CHAPTER THREE

1. "Kathy Griffin Beheads Donald Trump in Shocking Photo Shoot," *TMZ*, May 30, 2017, https://www.tmz.com/2017/05/30/kathy-griffin-beheads-donald-trump-photo-tyler-shields/; @MarqMarti, "Why did you delete this?," *Twitter*, May 30, 2017, https://x.com/MarqMarti/status/869704152309522432.

2. Jonathan Martin and Maggie Haberman, "Hand-Wringing in G.O.P. after Donald Trump's Remarks on Megyn Kelly," *New York Times*, August 8, 2015, https://www.nytimes.com/2015/08/09/us/politics/donald-trump-disinvited-from-conservative-event-over-remark-on-megyn-kelly.html.

3. "Kathy Griffin Beheads Donald Trump."

4. Coleman Spilde, "There'll Never Be Another Show Like Kathy Griffin's 'My Life on the D-List,'" *Daily Beast*, May 14, 2024, https://www.thedailybeast.com/obsessed/there-will-never-be-another-show-like-kathy-griffins-my-life-on-the-d-list.

5. Chris Rovzar, "Kathy Griffin Will Knock Those Pesky D's out of Your Mouth," *New York Magazine*, January 2, 2009, https://nymag.com/intelligencer/2009/01/kathy_griffin_will_knock_those.html; Nellie Andreeva, "Kathy Griffin Kisses Anderson Cooper's Private Parts on Live TV: Video," *Deadline*, January 1, 2013, https://deadline.com/2013/01/kathy-griffin-kisses-anderson-coopers-crotch-on-live-tv-395180/.

6. Gary Susman, "E! Apologizes for Dakota Fanning Rehab Joke," *Entertainment Weekly*, January 19, 2005, https://ew.com/article/2005/01/19/e-apologizes-dakota-fanning-rehab-joke/.

7. "Kathy Griffin's Jesus Remark Cut from Emmy Show," *Reuters*, September 11, 2007, https://www.reuters.com/article/lifestyle/kathy-griffins-jesus-remark-cut-from-emmy-show-idUSN11445129/.

8. Bruce Fessier, "Mother of Alt Comedy Brings UnCabaret Stars to Palm Springs," *Desert Sun*, November 22, 2016, https://www.desertsun.com/story/life/entertainment/arts/2016/11/22/ace-alt-comedy-deigns-play-palm-springs/93260414/; Kathy Griffin, "Love Letter to the LGBTQ Community," *Billboard*, June 18, 2018, https://www.billboard.com/culture/pride/kathy-griffin-love-letter-lgbtq-community-8461242/.

9. Nicholas Denysenko, "An Appeal to Mary: An Analysis of Pussy Riot's Punk Performance in Moscow," *Journal of the American Academy of Religion* 81, no. 4 (December 2013): 1062, http://www.jstor.org/stable/24488115.

10. Maria Puente, "'I Went Way Too Far': Kathy Griffin Apologizes for Trump 'Beheaded' Photos," *USA Today*, May 30, 2017, https://www.usatoday.com/story/life/tv/2017/05/30/kathy-griffin-stirs-fury-pic-holding-mock-decapitated-head-donald-trump/102321134/.

11. Kate Bennett and Allie Malloy, "Melania Trump's Strong Words about That Kathy Griffin Photo," *CNN*, May 31, 2017, https://www.cnn.com/2017/05/31/politics/melania-trump-kathy-griffin-photo/index.html.

12. Jenna Ellis, "Why Kathy Griffin Has the Right to Grotesquely Mock Donald Trump," *Time*, May 31, 2017, https://time.com/4800018/kathy-griffin-free-speech/.

13. Morgan Gstalter, "Kathy Griffin Says She Faced Potential 'Conspiracy to Assassinate the President' Charge over Trump Head Photo," *The Hill*, December 8, 2018, https://thehill.com/thehill.com/blogs/in-the-know/in-the-know/420406-kathy-griffin-says-she-faced-potential-conspiracy-to/.

14. GITMO KAG2020 [@President1Trump], *Twitter*, June 18, 2018, https://x.com/President1Trump/status/1008674774472646656.

15. James Woods [@RealJamesWoods], *Twitter*, June 3, 2017, https://x.com/RealJamesWoods/status/871091541082726400.

16. Robert J. Kohn [@BobsNewsToday], *Twitter*, June 4, 2017, https://x.com/BobsNewsToday/status/871418879452557312.

17. Zack Budryk, "Kathy Griffin Says She Still Gets Death Threats over Beheaded Trump Picture," *The Hill*, March 24, 2019, https://thehill.com/homenews/news/435522-kathy-griffin-says-she-still-gets-death-threats-over-beheaded-trump-picture/; Allie Yang, Ashley Louszko, and Jake Lefferman, "Kathy Griffin Battles Lung Cancer, Shares about Dark Chapter of Addiction," *ABC News*, August 2, 2021, https://abcnews.go.com/US/kathy-griffin-shes-recovering-addict-now-hopes-beat/story?id=79173454.

18. Maeve Mcdermott, "Kathy Griffin Reveals Why She 'Felt Guilty' after Trump Photo, How the FBI Saved Her Life," *USA Today*, July 31, 2019, https://www.usatoday.com/story/entertainment/celebrities/2019/07/31/kathy-griffin-says-the-fbi-saved-my-life-when-she-kill-list/1875599001/.

19. Anderson Cooper [@andersoncooper], *Twitter*, May 30, 2017, https://x.com/andersoncooper/status/869726823306887169.

20. Chelsea Clinton [@ChelseaClinton], *Twitter*, May 30, 2017, https://x.com/ChelseaClinton/status/869660019016466432.

21. Jonathan Bernstein, "Kathy Griffin: 'Trump Went for Me Because I Was an Easy Target,'" *Guardian*, September 23, 2017, https://www.theguardian.com/culture/2017/sep/23/kathy-griffin-trump-went-for-me-easy-target.

22. Maria Puente, "'I Went Way Too Far': Kathy Griffin Apologizes for Trump 'Beheaded' Photos," *USA Today*, May 30, 2017, https://www.usatoday.com/story/life/tv/2017/05/30/kathy-griffin-stirs-fury-pic-holding-mock-decapitated-head-donald-trump/102321134/.

23. "Kathy Griffin Retracts Apology for Decapitated Trump Photo: 'I Am No Longer Sorry, the Whole Outrage Was BS,'" *ABC News*, August 30, 2017, https://abcnews.go.com/Politics/kathy-griffin-retracts-apology-decapitated-trump-photo-longer/story?id=49506224; for the *Guardian* interview, see Bernstein, "Kathy Griffin."

24. "21. Kathy Griffin—A Hell of a Story (2019)," *YouTube*, 43:37, posted by Kathy Forever, November 23, 2023, https://www.youtube.com/watch?v=oZI2f1ShOoE.

25. Katherine Rosman, "Kathy Griffin Is Trying to Get Back on the D-List," *New York Times*, June 22, 2023, https://www.nytimes.com/2022/01/19/arts/television/kathy-griffin.html.

26. Rosman, "Kathy Griffin Is Trying"; "Kathy Griffin Tells All, Including Feud with Elon Musk and Trump," *YouTube*, 21:00, posted by Howie Mandel Does Stuff, January 2, 2024, https://www.youtube.com/watch?v=mGo3kCJ7CoQ.

27. "Kathy Griffin Net Worth: How Much Does Kathy Griffin Make Per Show?," *Marca*, March 27, 2024, https://www.marca.com/en/lifestyle/celebrity-net-worth/2024/03/27/660460b8e2704e38928b45b0.htm; Esther Povitsky and Khalyla Kuhn, "Kathy Griffin's Life on the PTSD List," on the podcast *Trash Tuesday*, March 26, 2024, 24:00 and 28:15, https://open.spotify.com/episode/2zlXHjwZdUYhGmtfoYTT7K?si=MUnrjo7ST3WD1e23s_LqDg; Ryan Smith, "Kathy Griffin Begs People to Buy Tour Tickets—'Not Selling Well,'" *Newsweek*, January 26, 2024, https://www.newsweek.com/kathy-griffin-my-life-ptsd-list-comedy-tour-tickets-video-1864204.

28. Rosman, "Kathy Griffin Is Trying"; Smith, "Kathy Griffin Begs People."

29. Not Shane Gillis, "Dave Chappelle Requests a Joke from Shane Gillis," *YouTube*, 00:00–00:09, uploaded July 24, 2023, https://www.youtube.com/watch?v=DHIddmyowZo.

30. See "Shane Gillis Net Worth," Celebrity Net Worth, posted March 22, 2024, https://www.celebritynetworth.com/richest-celebrities/richest-comedians/shane-gillis-net-worth/.

31. Rick Porter, "'Saturday Night Live' Adds Trio to Season 45 Cast," *Hollywood Reporter*, September 24, 2019, https://www.hollywoodreporter.com/tv/tv-news/saturday-night-live-adds-chloe-fineman-shane-gillis-bowen-yang-1239167/.

32. See commentary from Stacey Prussman [@StaceyPrussman], "I would like to dig through @sasimons past and find out where all the self righteousness comes from," *Twitter*, October 30, 2019, https://x.com/StaceyPrussman/status/1189649072468172800.

33. Doha Madani, "Video Surfaces of New 'SNL' Cast Member Using Asian Slur on Same Day Show Casts Asian American," *NBC News*, September 13, 2019, https://www.nbcnews.com/news/asian-america/video-surfaces-new-snl-cast-member-using-asian-slur-same-n1053746.

34. Jeff Yang [@originalspin], "Yeah if you want to know what being a person of color is like," *Twitter*, September 12, 2019, https://x.com/originalspin/status/1172290374942912512.

35. Jomny Failsunn, "Shane Gillis Chinatown," *YouTube*, 02:01, 0:00–0:05, and 01:06–01:19, uploaded September 13, 2019, http://www.youtube.com/watch?v=NLFuap1U3P4.

36. Theo Von Clips, "Shane Gillis on Getting Canceled and Fired from SNL," *YouTube*, 06:54–06:57, uploaded August 18, 2021, https://www.youtube.com/watch?v=DRIbT5ouYYs.

37. Tommy Pope and Shane Gillis, "A Fair One 011," *Compound Media*, 11:29–11:43, https://www.compoundmedia.com/on-demand/a-fair-one. (Note that since I wrote this chapter, this and the following *Compound Media* resources have been deleted from the internet.)

38. Tommy Pope and Shane Gillis, "A Fair One 004," *Compound Media on Demand*, 8:49–9:01, https://www.compoundmedia.com/on-demand/a-fair-one.

39. Tommy Pope and Shane Gillis, "A Fair One 017," *Compound Media on Demand*, 1:07:37–1:07:53, https://www.compoundmedia.com/on-demand/a-fair-one.

40. Tommy Pope and Shane Gillis, "A Fair One 012," *Compound Media on Demand*, https://www.compoundmedia.com/on-demand/a-fair-one.

41. For ableist jokes see Pope and Gillis, "A Fair One 012," 05:18–05:28; for pro-white jokes see "A Fair One 004," 08:49–09:01; for concerned fans on Reddit, see thread within "Shane Is Going to SNL," https://www.reddit.com/r/MSsEcReTPoDcAsT/comments/d3az8g/shane_is_going_to_snl/.

42. Nancy Wang Yuen [@nancywyuen], "Woke up thinking about how great we have Bowen Yang on #SNL," *Twitter*, September 13, 2019, https://x.com/nancywyuen/status/1172497797909639168.

43. Padma Lakshmi [@PadmaLakshmi], "A great way to not get fired for making lame racist jokes is to not do that," *Twitter*, September 16, 2019, https://x.com/PadmaLakshmi/status/1173700414396674048.

44. Audrey Cleo Yap, "Comedians Condemn Shane Gillis over Slurs," *Variety*, September 15, 2019, https://variety.com/2019/tv/news/comedians-condemn-snl-shane-gillis-over-slurs-1203335929/.

45. Theo Von Clips, "Shane Gillis on Getting Canceled"; "Andrew Yang Sits Down with Comedian Shane Gillis," *YouTube*, 10:50–10:57, July 11, 2022, https://www.youtube.com/watch?v=QRF7PgHF1Oc.

46. Shane Gillis [@Shanemgillis], "I'm a comedian who pushes boundaries," *Twitter*, September 13, 2019, https://x.com/Shanemgillis/status/1172340437752807424?s=20.

47. Doha Madani, "'SNL' Fires Shane Gillis after Video Surfaces of Comedian Using Asian Slur," *NBC News*, September 16, 2019, https://www.nbcnews

.com/pop-culture/pop-culture-news/snl-drops-shane-gillis-after-video-surfaces-comedian-using-asian-n1055076.

48. Marlow Stern, "Shane Gillis Is Hosting SNL. It's a Controversial Choice," *Rolling Stone*, February 11, 2024, https://www.rollingstone.com/tv-movies/tv-movie-features/shane-gillis-snl-host-racism-homophobia-bowen-yang-nikki-haley-dave-chappelle-1234966171/.

49. "Andrew Yang Sits Down with Comedian Shane Gillis," 06:40–06:16.

50. "Joe Rogan Experience #1685—Shane Gillis,'" *YouTube*, 43:36–43:37 and 47:24, uploaded by Powerful JRE, June 27, 2024, https://www.youtube.com/watch?v=bQtP7p7Q99U.

51. "Andrew Yang Sits Down with Comedian Shane Gillis," 06:55–07:03.

52. "2019 Comedy Awards! Here Are Your Winners (as Voted for by You!) for the Sixth Annual Comedy Awards," *TheInterrobang*, January 7, 2020, https://theinterrobang.com/2019-comedy-awards-here-are-your-winners-as-voted-for-by-you-for-the-sixth-annual-comedy-awards/; John McKeever and Shane Gillis, *Gilly and Keeves, YouTube* site, https://www.youtube.com/@GillyandKeeves.

53. Gilly and Keeves, *Shane Gillis Live in Austin, YouTube*, September 7, 2021, https://www.youtube.com/watch?v=zKUpf1Vxovs; Lynette Rice, "Shane Gillis to Make Netflix Comedy Debut in September," *Deadline*, August 22, 2023, https://deadline.com/2023/08/shane-gillis-netflix-comedy-special-september-1235525264/.

54. Gilly and Keeves, *Shane Gillis Live in Austin*, 04:24 and 15:32–15:40.

55. *Saturday Night Live*, "Shane Gillis Stand-Up Monologue—SNL," *YouTube*, 00:36–01:07 and 02:52–03:27, February 25, 2024, https://www.youtube.com/watch?v=2YnonYf463s.

56. Gilly and Keeves, "The Last White Football Team," *YouTube*, 00:14–00:15, April 27, 2021, https://www.youtube.com/watch?v=HotDJ2FhB84.

57. *The Tim Dillon Show*, "#173—Shane Gillis," *YouTube*, 33:44–33:45, November 10, 2019, https://www.youtube.com/watch?v=KcNMljjsqGg.

58. Bernstein, "Kathy Griffin."

59. For a detailed account of O'Connor's *SNL* appearance and *SNL*'s reaction, see Jack Whatley, "The Infamous Moment Sinéad O'Connor Was Banned from *SNL*," *Far Out Magazine*, July 26, 2023, https://faroutmagazine.co.uk/sinead-o-connor-banned-reason-snl-1992/. For more on the Irish Magdalene Laundries, where tens of thousands of "fallen women" were trapped and forced

to work under the purview of the Catholic Church, and where O'Connor herself spent time in her teenage years, see Erin Blakemore, "How Ireland Turned 'Fallen Women' into Slaves," *History*, March 12, 2018, https://www.history.com/news/magdalene-laundry-ireland-asylum-abuse.

60. The Chicks (formerly the Dixie Chicks) changed their name after the murder of George Floyd. See Jacob Uitti, "Behind the Career Altering Band Name Change The Dixie Chicks to The Chicks," *American Songwriter*, May 16, 2023, https://americansongwriter.com/behind-the-career-altering-band-name-change-the-dixie-chicks-to-the-chicks.

61. Jada Watson and Lori Burns, "Resisting Exile and Asserting Musical Voice: The Dixie Chicks Are 'Not Ready to Make Nice,'" *Popular Music* 29 (October, 2010): 327–328, http://www.jstor.org/stable/40926939.

62. Johns Hopkins University School of Advanced International Studies, "Blocked: Censorship at the Intersection of Gender, Race, and the Media," lecture, March 24, 2021, https://sais.jhu.edu/news-press/event-recap/blocked-censorship-intersection-gender-race-and-media.

63. Emma Alice Jane, "'Back to the Kitchen, Cunt': Speaking the Unspeakable about Online Misogyny," *Continuum*, June 17, 2014, https://doi.org/10.1080/10304312.2014.924479, also available at https://www.collegesidekick.com/study-docs/24175217.

64. For more on discrimination against women online, see Mary Anne Franks, "Censoring Women," *Boston University Law Review*, 95, annex 61 (2015): 61–66, https://www.bu.edu/bulawreview/bulronline/franks-censoring-women/; Audun Fladmoe and Marjan Nadim, "Silencing Women? Gender and Online Harassment," *Social Science Computer Review* 39, no. 2 (2019): 246–247, https://doi.org/10.1177/0894439319865518; Jessica Megarry, "Online Incivility or Sexual Harassment? Conceptualising Women's Experiences in the Digital Age," *Women's Studies International Forum* 47 (2014): 49–50, https://doi.org/10.1016/j.wsif.2014.07.012.

65. Dave Itzkoff, "Bill Maher Apologizes for Use of Racial Slur on 'Real Time,'" *New York Times*, June 3, 2017, https://www.nytimes.com/2017/06/03/arts/television/bill-maher-n-word.html.

66. Brian Welk, "Kathy Griffin Says She Was Detained at Every Airport on Her World Tour," *TheWrap*, April 3, 2018, https://www.thewrap.com/kathy-griffin-detained-airport-world-tour/.

67. Steve Bennett, "'I Had to Get Metal Detectors at My Gigs after Death Threats,'" *Chortle*, June 1, 2017, https://www.chortle.co.uk/news/2017/06/01/36680/i_had_to_get_metal_detectors_at_my_gigs_after_death_threats.

CHAPTER FOUR

1. Vir Das, "I Come From Two Indias," *YouTube*, 00:13-00:17, uploaded by Vir Das Comedy, November 15, 2021, https://www.youtube.com/watch?v=5A-F9qu6c_4.

2. "MP Home Minister Threatens to Ban Vir Das from Performing in State," *Telegraph*, November 19, 2021, https://www.telegraphindia.com/india/madhya-pradesh-narottam-mishra-ban-threat-to-vir-das/cid/1839575.

3. Das mentioned the proposed revocation of citizenship in *Landing*, directed by Vir Das, written by Vir Das (Netflix, 2022), 11:36–11:45. Other penalties were suggested. See Garima Satija, "Ashoke Pandit Wants Vir Das to Be 'Tried under Terror Laws,' Raza Murad Demands Legal Action," *India Times*, November 17, 2021, https://www.indiatimes.com/entertainment/celebs/ashoke-pandit-wants-vir-das-to-be-tried-under-terror-laws-raza-murad-demands-legal-action-554476.html; Daniel Russo, "Comedy and Tolerance: Vir Das, Standup Comedy and Religious Tolerance in India," *Mediální Studia* 14, no. 2 (2020): 242–256.

4. Jacques Berlinerblau, "The Productive Obscene: Philip Roth and the Profanity Loop," in *Profane: Sacrilegious Expression in a Multicultural Age* (Berkeley: University of California Press, 2014), 57–81.

5. Ashwathy Nair, "Creating Contact Zones via Stand-up Comedy and Defamiliarising the Construct of 'India': A Study of Vir Das's *For India,"* in *Politics of Recognition and Representation in Indian Stand-up Comedy*, ed. Richa Chilana and Rashi Bhargava (Cham, Switzerland: Palgrave Macmillan, 2024), 71–94.

6. Marc Myers, "Vir Das Made His Way from India to America TV via National Lampoon," *Wall Street Journal*, February 26, 2019, https://www.wsj.com/articles/vir-das-made-his-way-from-india-to-american-tv-via-national-lampoon-11551195036.

7. *Losing It*, directed by Vir Das, written by Vir Das (Netflix, 2018), 7:39–7:53.

8. Myers, "Vir Das Made His Way"; Marc Maron, interview with Vir Das, *WTF with Marc Maron*, 33:13–33:19, May 29, 2023, https://www.wtfpod.com/podcast/episode-1439-vir-das.

9. Das's background is outlined in Priyanka Pereira, "Vir Das: No Laughing Matter," *OPEN*, November 16, 2016, https://openthemagazine.com/cinema/vir-das-no-laughing-matter/.

10. Maron, interview with Vir Das, 52:47–54:25. See also "Vir Das: Bollywood, Drugs, Journalism, India, a Loose Rant," *YouTube*, uploaded by Vir Das

Comedy, October 5, 2020, https://www.youtube.com/watch?v=JOd9_H4Wlmo.

11. Maron, interview with Vir Das, 1:12:12–1:12:49.

12. Maron, interview with Vir Das.

13. For online channels, see Kavyta Kay, *New Indian Nuttahs: Comedy and Cultural Critique in Millennial India* (Palgrave Macmillian, 2018), 5; for decentering, 80.

14. Vir Das, "IS the West More Privileged? | #TenOnTen | Vir Das—Ep. 3," *YouTube*, uploaded by Vir Das Comedy, March 10, 2021, https://www.youtube.com/watch?v=qhTufX7qGsw; Sanjoy Majumder, "Narendra Modi 'Allowed' Gujarat 2002 Anti-Muslim Riots," *BBC*, April 22, 2011, https://www.bbc.com/news/world-south-asia-13170914.

15. "Religion vs. Comedy | #TenOnTen | Vir Das[—Ep. 1]," *YouTube*, uploaded by Vir Das Comedy, January 11, 2021, https://www.youtube.com/watch?v=u5hS8vzmQXI.

16. "How to Unite Social Media—Vir Das—Stand Up Comedy," *YouTube*, uploaded by Vir Das Comedy, July 11, 2022, https://www.youtube.com/watch?v=QdNuwZHDiM8.

17. "Who Has Freedom of Speech? | #TenOnTen | Vir Das—Ep. 2," *YouTube*, uploaded by Vir Das Comedy, February 10, 2021, https://www.youtube.com/watch?v=CQbm8XKi_xw.

18. "Jokes for the Dead | #TenOnTen | Vir Das—Ep 4," *YouTube*, uploaded by Vir Das Comedy, March 10, 2021, https://www.youtube.com/watch?v=gDkFz36OF8s.

19. Neha Mahrotra and Ashok Sharma, "Pressure Rises for India Lockdown; Surge Breaks Record Again," *Associated Press*, May 7, 2021, https://apnews.com/article/coronavirus-india-modi-4b84e957a87139ac6bd90390f2d08b42.

20. Vir Das, "Manic Man: World Tour," stand-up performance at Kennedy Center, Washington, DC, November 12, 2021, https://www.kennedy-center.org/whats-on/digital-programs/concert-hall/concert-hall-archive/.

21. Maron, interview with Vir Das, 1:04:49–1:05:05.

22. "I Come from Two Indias," 4:45–4:56 and 3:49–3:52.

23. "I Come from Two Indias," 2:09–2:19.

24. "I Come from Two Indias," 1:06–1:09.

25. For crime statistics see Ministry of Home Affairs, *IPC Crimes (Crime Head-Wise):* 2019–2021, National Crime Records Bureau, 2021, https://ncrb.gov.in/uploads/nationalcrimerecordsbureau/post/1679649431TABLE12.pdf; Manveena Suri, Vedika Sud, and Rhea Mogul, "Deadly Rape of Indian Woman Has 'Shaken the Nation Once Again,'" *CNN*, September 13, 2021, https://

www.cnn.com/2021/09/13/india/sakinaka-rape-and-murder-intl-hnk/index.html.

26. "I Come from Two Indias," 3:07–3:14.

27. Sumit Ganguly and Navyug Gill, "The Indian Farmer Protests," transcription of lecture, *Council for Foreign Relations*, March 9, 2021, https://www.cfr.org/event/indian-farmer-protests.

28. "India Farmers' Protests: Punjab Families Grieve Their Dead," *BBC*, December 8, 2021, https://www.bbc.com/news/world-asia-india-59574938; Bilal Kuchay, "India Farmers Killed after Violence Erupts during Protest," *Al-Jazeera*, October 3, 2021, https://www.aljazeera.com/news/2021/10/3/eight-including-four-farmers-killed-in-uttar-pradesh.

29. "I Come from Two Indias," 5:37–6:07.

30. Rhoda Kwan, "He's A Hit in the US, but Comedian Stirs Fury at Home with 'Two Indias' Speech," *NBC News*, November 18, 2021, https://www.nbcnews.com/news/world/s-hit-us-comedian-vir-das-stirs-fury-home-two-indias-speech-rcna5983.

31. Maron, interview with Vir Das, 1:10:07–1:10:14.

32. *Landing*, 18:05–18:26.

33. "I Come from Two Indias," 3:54–3:56.

34. For both quotes see Gerry Shih and Niha Masih, "Indian Comedian Causes Stir with Kennedy Center Monologue," *Washington Post*, November 19, 2021 https://www.washingtonpost.com/world/2021/11/17/india-comedian-rape-complaint/.

35. Aditya Jha [@adityajhadelhi], *Twitter*, November 16, 2021, https://x.com/adityajhadelhi/status/1460592063167156227.

36. Ashoke Pandit [@ashokepandit], in excerpt from *India Today*, November 16, 2021, https://www.indiatoday.in/movies/celebrities/story/courageous-to-terrorist-vir-das-divides-bollywood-1877655-2021-11-17.

37. "Kangana Ranaut Calls Vir Das a 'Criminal,' Says Controversial 'I Come from Two Indias' Video Amounts to 'Soft Terrorism,'" *Indian Express*, November 17, 2021, https://indianexpress.com/article/entertainment/bollywood/kangana-ranaut-calls-vir-das-a-criminal-says-controversial-i-come-from-two-indias-video-amounts-to-soft-terrorism-7626965/.

38. Ayesha Pattanik, "Loyalty, Liberty, and the Law: Analyzing the Juxtaposition of Nation and Citizen in the Indian Sedition Law," *Social and Legal Studies* 31, no. 6 (2022), https://doi.org/10.1177/09646639221086859.

39. "Section 124A in The Indian Penal Code, 1860," *Kanoon*, https://indiankanoon.org/doc/1641007/.

40. "Who Has Freedom of Speech? 12:15–13:22.

41. Shashi Tharoor [@ShashiTharoor], *Twitter*, November 16, 2021, https://x.com/ShashiTharoor/status/1460661164002582534.

42. Abhishek Singhvi [@DrAMSinghvi], *Twitter*, November 16, 2021, https://x.com/DrAMSinghvi/status/1460650443122495490.

43. Ziad Buchh and A. Martinez, "His Poem Polarized India. Now Comedian Vir Das Is Telling His Side," *WRVO Public Media*, January 10, 2023, https://www.wrvo.org/2023-01-10/his-poem-polarized-india-now-comedian-vir-das-is-telling-his-side.

44. *Landing*, 51:29–52:16 and 57:13–57:44.

45. *Landing*, 10:12–10:35. Rishita Roy Chowdhury, "Courageous to Terrorist, Vir Das' 2 Indias Monologue Divides Bollywood," *India Today*, November 21, 2021, https://www.indiatoday.in/movies/celebrities/story/courageous-to-terrorist-vir-das-divides-bollywood-1877655-2021-11-17.

46. *Landing*, 29:53–30:03 and 30:16–30:27.

47. *Landing*, 58:30–59:10

48. Vineet Bhalla and Shreyam Sharma, "Right to Offend and Hurt: What We Can Learn from Vir Das, Kangana Ranaut, and the Film 'Jai Bhim,'" *The Leaflet*, November 21, 2021, https://theleaflet.in/right-to-offend-and-hurt-what-we-can-learn-from-vir-das-kangana-ranaut-and-the-film-jai-bhim/.

49. Shivangi Nanda, "Comedian Vir Das Takes His 'Mind Fool Tour' across the Globe," *Case Western Observer*, November 3, 2023, https://observer.case.edu/35775-2/.

50. Reporters without Borders, "World Press Freedom Index—India," Data set, n.d., https://rsf.org/en/index?year=2024.

51. Tripurdaman Singh, "The Authoritarian Roots of India's Democracy," *Journal of Democracy* 34, no. 3 (2023): 136.

52. Tara Subramaniam, "Indian Author Arundhati Roy Faces Sedition Charges over 2010 Remarks on Kashmir," *CNN*, October 12, 2023, https://www.cnn.com/2023/10/12/india/india-author-arundhati-roy-sedition-case-intl-hnk/index.html; Kunal Purohit, "Our New Database Reveals Rise in Sedition," *A14*, February 2, 2021, https://www.article-14.com/post/our-new-database-reveals-rise-in-sedition-cases-in-the-modi-era.

53. Jack M. Balkin, "How Rights Change: Freedom of Speech in the Digital Era," *Sydney Law Review* 26 (2004), https://openyls.law.yale.edu/bitstream/handle/20.500.13051/1734/How_Rights_Change_Freedom_of_Speech_in_the_Digital_Era.pdf.

54. For details see "Challenge to the IT Rules 2023, *Kunal Kamra v. Union of India*," *Supreme Court Observer*, March 21, 2024, https://www.scobserver.in

/cases/challenge-to-the-it-rules-2023/. See also Press Information Bureau, "PIB Fact Check Unit," *Government of India*, https://pib.gov.in/aboutfactchecke.aspx.

55. Suhit Kelkar. "Kunal Kamra: Indian Comedian Riles Ruling Party with Edgy Humour," *Al-Jazeera*, June 21, 2018, https://www.aljazeera.com/features/2018/6/21/kunal-kamra-indian-comedian-riles-ruling-party-with-edgy-humour.

56. "Challenge to the IT Rules 2023."

57. "Why No Political Comedy? | BE LIKE Part 3 | Kunal Kamra | Standup Comedy 2022," *YouTube*, April 24, 2022, https://www.youtube.com/watch?v=9PtIjicaTKE. For more on India's Supreme Cout and its take on potential comic dissent, see Mihir S. Asolekar, "Cartoons and Comedy in India: How Far Should the Supreme Court Go?," *Supremo Amicus* 26 (2021): 284–301.

58. "'Country of Incarcerated Artists & Flourishing Lapdogs' Is Where India Is Headed,' Kamra Tells SC," *The Wire*, January 29, 2021, https://thewire.in/law/kunal-kamra-supreme-court-contempt-affidavit.

59. Sonia Faleiro, "How an Indian Stand Up Comic Found Himself Arrested for a Joke He Didn't Tell," *Time*, February 10, 2021, https://time.com/5938047/munawar-iqbal-faruqui-comedian-india/.

60. Mujib Mashal, "Mob Descends on a Comedy Club after a Comic Jokes about a Politician," *New York Times*, March 25, 2025, https://www.nytimes.com/2025/03/25/world/asia/india-habitat-mumbai-comedy.html.

61. Mashal, "Mob Descends"; "Munawar Faruqui Leaving Comedy," *YouTube*, uploaded by Munawar Faruqui, February 13, 2021, https://www.youtube.com/watch?v=I6ShaTlyzZQ&t=562s.

62. Faleiro, "How an Indian Stand Up Comic Found Himself Arrested."

63. Ross Ibbetson, "Indian Comedian Is Beaten by Mob and Arrested for Making 'Indecent Comments' about Hindu Gods in His Stand Up Routine," *Daily Mail*, January 4, 2021, https://www.dailymail.co.uk/news/article-9110989/Indian-comedian-beaten-mob-arrested-making-indecent-comments-Hindu-gods.html; "Details of IPC Sections 153A, 295 & 295A," *Association for Democratic Reforms*, https://adrindia.org/sites/default/files/Details%20of%20IPC%20Sections%20153A,%20295%20&%20295A.pdf.

64. Faleiro, "How an Indian Stand Up Comic Found Himself Arrested."

65. Joe Wallen and Mohammad Sartaj Alam, "'Hate Won': Top Indian Comedian Quits after Receiving Death Threats from Nationalists," *Telegraph*, December 7, 2021, https://www.telegraph.co.uk/global-health/terror-and-security/hate-won-top-indian-comedian-quits-receiving-death-threats-nationalists/.

66. Falerio, "How an Indian Stand Up Comic Found Himself Arrested."

67. Arundhati Rajput, "Stand-Up Comics and the Imbroglio of Criminal Complaints," *Criminal Law Blog of National Law University, Jodhpur*, January 26, 2022, https://criminallawstudiesnluj.wordpress.com/2022/01/26/stand-up-comics-the-imbroglio-of-criminal-complaints/.

68. "I Come from Two Indias," 4:18–4:25.

CHAPTER FIVE

1. For a full detailing of the Rushie case, which I can only discuss in passing, see Steven Erlanger, "Rushdie Has Lived under an Iranian Death Sentence since 1989," *New York Times*, August 12, 2022, https://www.nytimes.com/2022/08/12/nyregion/salman-rushdie-fatwa-satanic-verses.html.

2. Jytte Klausen, *The Cartoons That Shook the World* (New Haven, CT: Yale University Press, 2009), 2.

3. According to Yale University Press, the decision not to include them "rested solely on the experts' assessments that there existed a substantial likelihood of violence that might take the lives of innocent victims." See "The Controversy Regarding 'The Cartoons That Shook the World,'" *YaleNews*, September19,2011,https://news.yale.edu/2009/12/02/controversy-regarding-cartoons-shook-world.

4. Klausen, *Cartoons That Shook the World*, 14. The author was Kåre Bluitgen.

5. Klausen (*Cartoons That Shook the World*, 131–146) argues that Muslim prohibitions on representing the Prophet have never been consistently applied by Muslims themselves. Also see Marc Wagner, "The Problem of Non-Muslims Who Insult the Prophet Muhammad," *Journal of the American Oriental Society* 135 (2015), available at https://www.thefreelibrary.com/The+problem+of+non-Muslims+who+insult+the+prophet+Muhammad.-a0437059032. Reflecting on the laxness of this prohibition is Mohamed Sifaoui, *L'affaire des caricatures: Dessins et manipulations* ([Paris]: Privé, 2006), 53–58.

6. These concerns continue to the present day. See Joshua Goodman, "Author Salman Rushdie Stabbed on Lecture Stage in New York," *AP News*, October 2, 2023, https://apnews.com/article/salman-rushdie-attacked-9eae99aea82cb0d39628851ecd42227a.

7. Lucinda Creighton, "Eye on Blasphemy: Cartoon Wars—the Case of *Jyllands-Posten*," *Fighting Terror*, November 2, 2023, 12:26–12:30, https://www.buzzsprout.com/1118519/13871006.

8. Klausen, *Cartoons That Shook the World*, 14.

9. Flemming Rose, "Why I Published Those Cartoons," I*slamic Studies* 45, no. 1 (2006): 131, http://www.jstor.org/stable/20839006.

10. Rose, "Why I Published," 131.

11. Klausen, *Cartoons That Shook the World*, 14–15.

12. "Danish *Jyllands-Posten* Muhammad Cartoons," December 11, 2010, https://www.atour.com/news/international/20101211a.html.

13. Matthias Wivel, "Westergaard and the World's Most Notorious Cartoon," *Comics Journal*, January 19, 2022, https://www.tcj.com/westergaard-and-the-worlds-most-notorious-cartoon/.

14. The political scientist Paul Sniderman and his team argued that "Danes impressively lined up in support of the civil rights of Muslims." Paul M. Sniderman et al., *Paradoxes of Liberal Democracy: Islam, Western Europe, and the Danish Cartoon Crisis* (Princeton, NJ: Princeton University Press, 2014), 11.

15. Klausen, *Cartoons That Shook the World*, 4, 27, 55.

16. Klausen, *Cartoons That Shook the World*, 89–92; Sifaoui, *L'affaire des caricatures*, 74–76.

17. Klausen, *Cartoons That Shook the World*, 186.

18. Klausen, *Cartoons That Shook the World*, 189.

19. Carsten Juste, "Honourable Fellow Citizens of the Muslim World," *Jyllands-Posten*, February 8, 2006, https://jyllands-posten.dk/international/ECE4771289/Honourable-Fellow-Citizens-of-the-Muslim-World/.

20. See Klausen, *Cartoons That Shook the World*, 191–194, 192, 107. Victor Navasky cites a higher number of five hundred dead, though he does not document the claim; *The Art of Controversy: Political Cartoons and Their Enduring Power* (New York: Alfred A. Knopf, 2013), xiv.

21. Klausen, *Cartoons That Shook the World*, 113.

22. Associated Press, "Bin Laden Accuses Pope of 'Crusade' in New Tape," *NBCNews*, March 19, 2008, https://www.nbcnews.com/id/wbna23714855.

23. Hilary Rhodes, "'Sanctae Terre' and Sacred Warfare: The Construction of Crusading and Cultures of Violence in the Euro-American Historical Narrative," *Academia*, June 2014, https://www.academia.edu/13159902/_Sanctae_Terre_and_Sacred_Warfare_The_Construction_of_Crusading_and_Cultures_of_Violence_in_the_Euro_American_Historical_Narrative.

24. Sylvia Poggioli, "Pope's Remarks on Islam, Violence Spur Anger," *NPR*, September 15, 2006, https://www.npr.org/2006/09/15/6084194/popes-remarks-on-islam-violence-spur-anger.

25. Klausen, *Cartoons That Shook the World*, 51.

26. Charb, *Open Letter: On Blasphemy, Islamophobia, and the True Enemies of Free Expression* (New York: Little, Brown, 2016), 22–23.

27. Jane Weston Vauclair and David Vauclair, *De Charlie Hebdo à #Charlie: Enjeux, histoire, perspectives* (Paris: Eyrolles, 2016), 12. Also see Jane Weston, "*Bête et méchant:* Politics, Editorial Cartoons, and *Bande Dessinée* in the French Satirical Newspaper *Charlie Hebdo*," *European Comic Art* 2, no. 1 (2009): 116, https://doi.org/10.3828/eca.2.1.7.

28. Cited in Vauclair and Vauclair, *De Charlie Hebdo*, 81.

29. See Weston, "*Bête et méchant*," 110, 121, and 109.

30. Céline Goffette and Jean-François Mignot, "Non, 'Charlie Hebdo' n'est pas obsédé par l'islam," *Le Monde*, February 23, 2015, https://www.lemonde.fr/idees/article/2015/02/24/non-charlie-hebdo-n-est-pas-obsede-par-l-islam_4582419_3232.html. Also see Damien Boone and Lucile Ruault, "Chiffrer les 'unes' de 'Charlie Hebdo' ne dit pas tout," *Le Monde*, March 5, 2015, https://www.lemonde.fr/idees/article/2015/03/05/oui-charlie-hebdo-est-obsede-par-l-islam_4588297_3232.html.

31. Vauclair and Vauclair, *De Charlie Hebdo*, 35.

32. Jonathan Ervine, *Humour in Contemporary France: Controversy, Consensus, and Contradictions* (Liverpool: Liverpool University Press, 2019), 20, 54, https://doi.org/10.2307/j.ctvsn3n23. See also Vauclair and Vauclair, *De Charlie Hebdo*, 51.

33. Vauclair and Vauclair, *De Charlie Hebdo*, 26. This point is reiterated by the widow of one of the slain illustrators; see Maryse Wolinski, *Darling, I'm Going to Charlie: A Memoir*, trans. H. J. Stone (New York: Atria, 2017), 3–4.

34. Vauclair and Vauclair, *De Charlie Hebdo*, 40.

35. Vauclair and Vauclair, *De Charlie Hebdo*, 40; James Joyner, "Catholic League President Blames *Charlie Hebdo* Publisher for Own Death," *Outside the Beltway*, January 9, 2015, https://outsidethebeltway.com/catholic-league-president-blames-charlie-hebdo-publisher-for-own-death/.

36. On the French media's response to the Danish cartoons see Carolina Sanchez Boe, "From *Jyllands-Posten* to *Charlie Hebdo:* Domesticating the Mohammed Cartoons," in *After Charlie Hebdo: Terror, Racism and Free Speech*, ed. Gavan Titley et al. (London: Zed Books, 2017), 166–179.

37. Ervine, *Humour in Contemporary France*, 24, 36; James Joyner, "Danish Muslim Cartoons Republished by French and German Papers," *Outside the Beltway*, February 1, 2006, https://outsidethebeltway.com/french_paper_publishes_danish_muslim_cartoons/.

38. Navasky, *Art of Controversy*, 180; Craig S. Smith and Ian Fisher, "Temperatures Rise over Cartoons Mocking Muhammad," *New York Times*, February 3, 2006, https://www.nytimes.com/2006/02/03/international/europe/03cartoons.html.

39. Ervine, *Humour in Contemporary France*, 24.

40. Ervine, *Humour in Contemporary France*, 25. The cover can be seen in an article by Mark Liberman, "It's Hard Being Loved by Jerks," *Language Log*, January 10, 2015, https://languagelog.ldc.upenn.edu/nll/?p=17059.

41. Ervine, *Humour in Contemporary France*, 28–30.

42. Christian Guimelli, Grégory Lo Monaco, and Jean-Claude Deschamps, "The Lawsuit against 'Charlie Hebdo' and Its Effects on the Social Representations of the Muslim Community," *Cairn.info*, January 1, 2011, https://www.cairn.info/revue-internationale-de-psychologie-sociale-2010-4-page-5.htm.

43. Lars Binderup and Eva Lassen, "The Blasphemy Ban in Denmark," in *Blasphemy and Freedom of Expression: Comparative, Theoretical, and Historical Reflections after the Charlie Hebdo Massacre*, ed. Jeroen Temperman and András Koltay (Cambridge: Cambridge University Press, 2017), 431–455.

44. "Loi du 29 juillet 1881 sur la liberté de la presse," *Légifrance*, December 31, 2004, https://www.legifrance.gouv.fr/loda/id/LEGIARTI000006419745/2004-12-31/#LEGIARTI000006419745.

45. Tom Heneghan, "Cartoon Row Goes to French Court," *Independent Online*, February 2, 2007, https://www.iol.co.za/news/world/cartoon-row-goes-to-french-court-313615.

46. "French Cartoons Editor Acquitted," *BBC News*, March 22, 2007, http://news.bbc.co.uk/2/hi/europe/6479673.stm.

47. Charb, *Open Letter*, 16.

48. Heneghan, "Cartoon Row."

49. Charb, *Open Letter*, 32–33.

50. "French Cartoons Editor Acquitted."

51. Vauclair and Vauclair, *De Charlie Hebdo*, 38. For a translation of the verdict, see Craig S. Smith, "French Court Rules for Newspaper That Printed Muhammad Cartoons," *New York Times*, March 23, 2007, https://www.nytimes.com/2007/03/23/world/europe/23france.html.

52. Vauclair and Vauclair, *De Charlie Hebdo*, 67; "French Cartoons Editor Acquitted."

53. Amanda Taub, "Charlie Hebdo and Its Biting Satire, Explained in 9 of Its Most Iconic Covers," *Vox*, January 7, 2015, https://www.vox.com/2015/1/7/7507883/charlie-hebdo-explained-covers.

54. "French Satirical Paper *Charlie Hebdo* Attacked in Paris," *BBC News*, November 2, 2011, https://www.bbc.com/news/world-europe-15550350.

55. "Charlie Hebdo and Its Place in French Journalism," *BBC News*, January 8, 2015, https://www.bbc.com/news/world-europe-15551998.

56. Harrison Jacobs, "16 Bold Covers from the Satirical Paris Magazine That Was Attacked on Wednesday," *Business Insider*, January 7, 2015, https://www.businessinsider.com/16-bold-covers-from-the-satirical-paris-magazine-that-was-attacked-today-2015-1#this-may-2011-cover-came-on-the-heels-of-the-us-announcement-of-bin-ladens-death-12.

57. "Charlie Hebdo Attack: Three Days of Terror," *BBC News*, January 14, 2015, https://www.bbc.com/news/world-europe-30708237.

58. Associated Press, "Paris Terror Attack: Suspects in Charlie Hebdo Attack Possibly Spotted Near Forest," *ABC News*, January 8, 2015, https://abcnews.go.com/International/manhunt-suspects-charlie-hebdo-attack/story?id=28077252. For eyewitness testimony in the following trial, see "Charlie Hebdo Attack Survivor Recalls 'Horror' at Trial," *France* 24, September 8, 2020, https://www.france24.com/en/20200908-charlie-hebdo-attack-survivor-recalls-horror-at-trial.

59. Griff Witte, "In a Kosher Grocery Store in Paris, Terror Takes a Deadly Toll," *Washington Post*, January 9, 2015, https://www.washingtonpost.com/world/europe/paris-kosher-market-seized-in-second-hostage-drama-in-nervous-france/2015/01/09/f171b97e-97ff-11e4-8005-1924ede3e54a_story.html.

60. Abdellali Hajjat, "A Double-Bind Situation? The Depoliticisation of Violence and the Politics of Compensation," in Titley et al., eds., *After Charlie Hebdo*, 79.;Ministère de l'Europe et des affaires étrangères, "Terrorism: France's International Action," *France Diplomacy*, n.d., https://www.diplomatie.gouv.fr/en/french-foreign-policy/security-disarmament-and-non-proliferation/terrorism-france-s-international-action/; Dustin Byrd, *Unfashionable Objections to Islamophobic Cartoons* (Newcastle upon Tyne: Cambridge Scholars Publishing, 2017), 2–3.

61. Gary K. Busch, "The French in Syria—A Long and Tortured History," *Lima Charlie World*, April 20, 2018, https://limacharlienews.com/foreign-policy/french-in-syria/; John Irish and Dominique Vidalon, "France Launches Air Strikes against Islamic State in Syria," *Reuters*, September 27, 2015, https://www.reuters.com/article/us-mideast-crisis-france-syria-idUSKCN0RR07Y20150927/.

62. Associated Press, "20 Men Are Convicted in the 2015 Paris Terror Attacks; One Sentenced to Life in Prison," *NPR*, June 29, 2022, https://www.npr.org/2022/06/29/1108715478/paris-attacks-2015-conviction-life-sentence. For more on the Bataclan attack, see "What We Know about the Paris Attacks and the Hunt for the Attackers," *Washington Post*, March 18, 2016, https://www.washingtonpost.com/graphics/world/paris-attacks/.

63. "Nice Attack: At Least 84 Killed by Lorry at Bastille Day Celebrations," *BBC News*, July 15, 2016, https://www.bbc.com/news/world-europe-36800730.

64. Robert Danin, "Hostile Middle East Reactions to Today's Charlie Hebdo Cover," *Council on Foreign Relations*, January 14, 2015, https://www.cfr.org/blog/hostile-middle-east-reactions-todays-charlie-hebdo-cover; Atlantic Council, "As Charlie Hebdo Ups Print Run, Egypt to Ban Foreign Publications Insulting Religion," *Atlantic Council*, August 15, 2019, https://www.atlanticcouncil.org/blogs/menasource/as-charlie-hebdo-ups-print-run-egypt-to-ban-foreign-publications-insulting-religion/; JT Agencies Desk, "Muslims Unite in Anger over New Charlie Cartoons," *Jordan Times*, January 14, 2015, https://www.jordantimes.com/news/local/muslims-unite-anger-over-new-charlie-cartoons.

65. For Pakistan see "Pakistan Clashes over Charlie Hebdo Cartoon," *BBC News*, January 16, 2015, https://www.bbc.com/news/world-asia-30848689. For Iran see Antoine Blua, "Hacked off: Islamic Republic's Angry Retaliation for Charlie Hebdo's 'Sacrilegious' Cartoons," *IranWire*, January 14, 2023, https://iranwire.com/en/khameneicom/112595-hacked-off-islamic-republics-angry-retaliation-for-charlie-hebdos-sacrilegious-cartoons/. For Mauritania see Naharnet Newsdesk, "Thousands Protest in Mauritania against Charlie Hebdo Cartoon," *Naharnet*, January 16, 2015, https://m.naharnet.com/stories/en/163726-anti-charlie-hebdo-protesters-burn-french-flag-in-afghanistan. As for Saudi Arabia's role in all of this, see Tarek Osman, "The Charlie Hebdo Dilemma and Islamic Institutions," *Cairo Review of Global Affairs*, January 7, 2016, https://www.thecairoreview.com/tahrir-forum/the-charlie-hebdo-dilemma-and-islamic-institutions/.

66. For Al-Qaeda see "Al Qaeda Gave Charlie Hebdo Killers $20K," *ABC News*, January 14, 2015, https://abcnews.go.com/International/al-qaeda-laid-plan-charlie-hebdo-massacre-video/story?id=28213640. For ISIS/ISIL see "Charlie Hebdo Reprints Offensive Prophet Muhammad Caricatures," *Al-Jazeera*, September 2, 2020, https://www.aljazeera.com/news/2020/9/2/charlie-hebdo-reprints-offensive-prophet-muhammad-caricatures. For Boko Haram see Alexander Smith, "Boko Haram Boss Abubakar Shekau Hails Paris Terror Attacks," *NBCNews*, January 14, 2015, https://www.nbcnews.com/storyline/missing-nigeria-schoolgirls/boko-haram-boss-abubakar-shekau-hails-paris-terror-attacks-n286086. For protests led by Hizb ut-Tahrir (supported by Palestinian Islamic Jihad), see Maayan Lubell, "Thousands of Palestinians Protest Charlie Hebdo Mohammad Cartoon," *Reuters*, January 24, 2015, https://www.reuters.com/article/france-shooting-palestinians-idINKBN0KX0MH20150124.

67. Joyner, "Catholic League President Blames"; Elizabeth Dias, "Pope Francis on 'Charlie Hebdo': 'One Cannot Make Fun of Faith,'" *Time*, January 15, 2015, https://time.com/3668875/pope-francis-charlie-hebdo/.

68. See Simon Dawes, "#JeSuisCharlie, #JeNeSuisPasCharlie, and Ad Hoc Publics," in Titley et al., eds., *After Charlie Hebdo*, 180–191.

69. An analysis of this shift can be found in Blair Taylor, "Ruthless Critique or Selective Apologia? The Postcolonial Left in Theory and Practice," *American Studies* 62, no. 4 (2017): 649–661. Also see Jacques Berlinerblau, "The Crisis in Secular Studies," *Chronicle of Higher Education* 8 (2014); Jacques Berlinerblau, "Let the Study of American Secularisms Begin!" *Critical Research on Religion* 2 (2013): 225–232, https://doi.org/10.1177/2050303213490101b; Jacques Berlinerblau, "Political Secularism," in *The Oxford Handbook of Secularism*, ed. Phil Zuckerman and John R. Shook (New York: Oxford University Press, 2017), 85–102.

70. The term is used in a book about the *Jyllands-Posten* controversy; see Anshuman Mondal, *Islam and Controversy: The Politics of Free Speech after Rushdie* (New York: Palgrave Macmillan, 2014), 150.

71. See, for example, Aurélien Mondon and Aaron Winter, "Charlie Hebdo, Republican Secularism, and Islamophobia," in Titley et al., eds., *After Charlie Hebdo*, 31–45; Nicholas de Genova, "The Whiteness of Innocence: *Charlie Hebdo* and the Metaphysics of Anti-terrorism in Europe," in Titley et al., eds., *After Charlie Hebdo*, 108.

72. Knut Rio, "The *Barbariat* and Democratic Tolerance," in *The Event of Charlie Hebdo: Imaginaries of Freedom and Control*, ed. Alessandro Zagato (New York: Berghahn, 2015), 21.

73. Paul A. Silverstein, *Postcolonial France: Race, Islam, and the Future of the Republic* (London: Pluto Press, 2018), 87.

74. Theodoros Rakopoulos, "On Blasphemy: The Paradoxes of Protecting and Mocking God," in Zagato, ed., *Event of Charlie Hebdo*, 88.

75. Emmanuel Todd, *Who Is Charlie? Xenophobia and the New Middle Class*, trans. Andrew Brown (Cambridge: Polity Press, 2015), 39–45, 68.

76. Vauclair and Vauclair, *De Charlie Hebdo*, 69, 92.

77. Bjørn Enge Bertelsen and Alessandro Zagato, "Introduction: The Event of *Charlie Hebdo*–Imaginaries of Freedom and Control," in Zagato, ed., *Event of Charlie Hebdo*, 8.

78. Axel Rudi, "The West and the Sacred," in Zagato, ed., *Event of Charlie Hebdo*, 27; Taylor, "Ruthless Critique," 652.

79. Saba Mahmood, "Religious Reason and Secular Affect: An Incommensurable Divide?" *Critical Inquiry* 35, no. 4 (2009): 836–62, https://doi.org/10.1086/599592.

80. Mahmood, "Religious Reason," 848–849.

81. A final illustration of the left/liberal split I have been describing might be seen in the schism that developed between figures associated with PEN

when it awarded *Charlie Hebdo* the "Freedom of Expression Courage Award." See "Charlie Hebdo Receives Disputed Pen Award in New York," *BBC News*, May 6, 2015, https://www.bbc.com/news/world-us-canada-32601549.

82. Grant Julin, "What's the Punch Line? Punching Up and Down in the Comic Thunderdome," in *It's Funny 'Cause It's True: The Lighthearted Philosophers' Society's Introduction to Philosophy through Humor*, ed. Jennifer Marra Henrigillis and Steven Gimbel (N.p.: Lighthearted Philosophers' Society, 2021), 156–167, https://cupola.gettysburg.edu/cgi/viewcontent.cgi?article=1009&=&context=oer.

83. A similar point is made in Taylor, "Ruthless Critique," 651.

84. "French Satirical Paper Charlie Hebdo Attacked."

85. Klausen, *Cartoons That Shook the World*, 4, 55. For the French case see Susan Benesch, "Charlie the Freethinker: Religion, Blasphemy, and Decent Controversy," *Religion and Human Rights* 10, no. 3 (2015): 244–254, https://doi.org/10.1163/18710328-12341291.

86. Philip Dodd, "Slavoj Žižek, Camille Paglia, Flemming Rose," *Arts and Ideas* podcast, 45:40, September 26, 2018, https://www.bbc.co.uk/sounds/play/p06m8l28.

87. "Tout est pardonné" [All is forgiven], cartoon by Luz [Rénald Luzier], *Charlie Hebdo*, January 14, 2015, https://www.researchgate.net/figure/Je-Suis-Charlie-Tout-est-Pardone-All-is-Forgiven-Cartoon-by-Luz-Charlie-Hebdo-14_fig2_339434742.

88. "*Charlie Hebdo*'s Luz Quits Muhammad Cartoons," *BBC News*, April 29, 2015, https://www.bbc.com/news/world-europe-32520563.

89. Anne Laffeter, "Luz : 'J'avais un bout de cerveau qui cognait contre les murs,'" *Les Inrockuptibles*, April 28, 2015, https://www.lesinrocks.com/actu/luz-javais-un-bout-de-cerveau-qui-cognait-contre-les-murs-100047-28-04-2015/.

90. Translation from Vauclair and Vauclair, *De Charlie Hebdo*, 25.

91. "*Charlie Hebdo*'s Luz Quits"; Vauclair and Vauclair, *De Charlie Hebdo*, 167.

92. Pascale Santi, "Charb, le rire d'abord," *Le Monde*, January 8, 2015, https://www.lemonde.fr/actualite-medias/article/2015/01/07/charb-je-prefere-mourir-debout-que-vivre-a-genoux_4550759_3236.html.

93. Gérard Biard, editor-in-chief of *Charlie Hebdo*, quoted in Xavier Ternisien, "Archive : A 'Charlie Hebdo', on n'a 'pas l'impression d'égorger quelqu'un avec un feutre,'" *Le Monde*, September 20, 2012, https://www.lemonde.fr/actualite-medias/article/2012/09/20/je-n-ai-pas-l-impression-d-egorger-quelqu-un-avec-un-feutre_1762748_3236.html.

94. See Eric Barendt, "Foreword," in *Blasphemy and Freedom of Expression: Comparative, Theoretical, and Historical Reflections after the Charlie Hebdo Massacre*, ed. Jeroen Temperman and András Koltay (Cambridge: Cambridge University Press, 2017), xvii.

95. Robert Corn-Revere, "Hate Speech Laws: Ratifying the Assassin's Veto," *Cato*, March 24, 2016, https://www.cato.org/policy-analysis/hate-speech-laws-ratifying-assassins-veto; Rodney A. Smolla, "25. Heckler's Veto," in *Confessions of a Free Speech Lawyer: Charlottesville and the Politics of Hate* (Ithaca, NY: Cornell University Press, 2021), 220–232, https://doi.org/10.1515/9781501749674-026; Daniel Ortner, "The Terrorist's Veto: Why the First Amendment Must Protect Provocative Portrayals of the Prophet Muhammad," *Northwestern Journal of Law and Social Policy* 1 (2016): 1–44, http://scholarlycommons.law.northwestern.edu/njlsp/vol12/iss1/1.

96. Siddharth Narrain, "Hate Speech, Hurt Sentiment, and the (Im)Possibility of Free Speech," *Economic and Political Weekly* 51, no. 17 (2016): 119, http://www.jstor.org/stable/44003415.

97. Narrain, "Hate Speech," 119.

98. Smolla, "Heckler's Veto," 220, 222.

99. Berlinerblau, *How to Be Secular*.

100. Elise Harris, "Vatican Paper Blasts Charlie Hebdo Cover as 'Insulting' to All Faiths," *Catholic News Agency*, January 7, 2016, https://www.catholicnewsagency.com/news/33212/vatican-paper-blasts-charlie-hebdo-cover-as-insulting-to-all-faiths;

101. Charb, *Open Letter*, 63.

102. John Villasenor, "Views Among College Students Regarding the First Amendment: Results from a New Survey," *Brookings*, September 18, 2017, https://www.brookings.edu/articles/views-among-college-students-regarding-the-first-amendment-results-from-a-new-survey/; Jean M. Twenge, "Young Liberals Used to Be the Most Supportive of Free Speech. Now They're the Least," *Generation Tech*, January 18, 2024, https://www.generationtechblog.com/p/young-liberals-used-to-be-the-most.

103. Krishnadev Calamur, "'Charlie Hebdo,' a Magazine of Satire, Mocks Politics, Religion," *NPR*, January 7, 2015, https://www.npr.org/sections/thetwo-way/2015/01/07/375599183/charlie-hebdo-a-magazine-of-satire-mocks-politics-religion.

104. National Assembly of France, *Declaration of the Rights of Man and of the Citizen*, 1789, https://avalon.law.yale.edu/18th_century/rightsof.asp.

105. Larry Dietrich, "Je Suis Charlie," *Syracuse New Times*, January 13, 2015, https://syracusenewtimes.com/je-suis-charlie; "Imams Say British Muslims

'Will Inevitably Be Hurt by Republication of the Cartoons' as Charlie Hebdo Sells Out," *Press Gazette*, January 14, 2015, https://pressgazette.co.uk/publishers/magazines/imams-say-british-muslims-will-muslims-will-inevitably-be-hurt-republication-cartoons-charlie-hebdo/.

106. "Flemming Rose, 'Violence Works'—No to Hebdo Reprint," *Hardtalk*, January 13, 2015, https://www.bbc.co.uk/programmes/p02gwz1r (clip no longer available; accessed August 13, 2024).

107. Quoted in Timothy Garton Ash, "Defying the Assassin's Veto," *New York Review of Books*, July 22, 2020, https://www.nybooks.com/articles/2015/02/19/defying-assassins-veto/.

108. "Flemming Rose, 'Violence Works.'"

CHAPTER SIX

Epigraph: This phrase, cited in Anne-Sophie Mercier, *La vérité sur Dieudonné* (Paris Plon, 2005), 53, is essentially untranslatable. I'd approximate it as "Liberty, equality, fraternity, blah blah blah [or maybe, tra la la], up my ass," though that doesn't really do it justice. All translations below, unless otherwise specified, are my own. See the study of Bruno Chaouat, "Postscript: Theorizing Antisemitic Laughter," in *Is Theory Good for the Jews?* (Liverpool: Liverpool University Press, 2016), 224–225, http://www.jstor.org/stable/j.ctt1ps3368.11.

1. He later took down the comment; "Visé par une enquête pour apologie du terrorisme, Dieudonné répond au parquet," *La Tribune*, January 12, 2015, https://www.latribune.fr/actualites/economie/france/20150112tribbf4e03a24/vise-par-enquete-pour-apologie-du-terrorisme-dieudonne-repond-au-parquet.html. Also see Agnes Callamard, "Religion, Terrorism, and Speech in a 'Post–Charlie Hebdo' World," *Religion and Human Rights* 10, no. 3 (2015): 217–218, https://brill.com/view/journals/rhrs/10/3/article-p207_2.xml.

2. For discussions of the hashtag, see Brian Klug, "In the Heat of the Moment: Bringing 'Je Suis Charlie' into Focus," *French Cultural Studies* 27, no. 3 (2016): 223–232; Simon Dawes, "#JeSuisCharlie, #JeNeSuisPasCharlie, and Ad Hoc Publics," in *After Charlie Hebdo: Terror, Racism, and Free Speech*, ed. Gavan Titley et al. (London: Zed Books, 2017), 180–191; Sorin Petrof, "The Dialectics of Media Representation: *Je Suis Charlie* as Fetishization of an Image," *Journal for Communication Studies* 8, no. 2 (2015): 207–225; Emmanuel Todd, *Who Is Charlie? Xenophobia and the New Middle Class*, trans. Andrew Brown (Cambridge: Polity Press, 2015).

3. Andrew Higgins, "French Police Say Suspect in Attack Evolved from Petty Criminal to Terrorist," *New York Times*, January 10, 2015, https://www.nytimes.com/2015/01/11/world/europe/neighbors-say-suspect-in-french-attacks-and-his-companion-lived-quiet-lives.html.

4. "Dieudonné Arrested over Facebook Post on Paris Gunman," *Guardian*, January 14, 2015, https://www.theguardian.com/world/2015/jan/14/Dieudonné-arrest-facebook-post-charlie-coulibaly-paris-gunman.

5. There are a variety of studies about this artist, some highly polemical, others more balanced: Michel Briganti, André Déchot, and Jean-Paul Gautier, *La galaxie Dieudonné: Pour en finir avec les impostures* (Paris: Syllepse, 2011); Frédéric Haziza, *Vol au-dessus d'un nid de fachos: Dieudonné, Soral, Ayoub et les autres* (Paris, Fayard, 2014); Anne-Sophie Mercier, *Dieudonné démasqué* (Paris: Éditions du Seuil, 2009); Anne-Sophie Mercier, *La vérité sur Dieudonné* (Paris: Plon, 2005); Olivier Mukuna, *Egalité zéro! Enquête sur le procès médiatique de Dieudonné* (Paris: Éditions Blanche, 2005).

6. Paul A. Silverstein, *Postcolonial France: Race, Islam, and the Future of the Republic* (London: Pluto Press, 2018), 91. For some studies of his relationship to anti-Semitism specifically, see Jonathan Ervine, *Humour in Contemporary France: Controversy, Consensus, and Contradictions* (Liverpool: Liverpool University Press, 2019), 57–94, https://doi.org/10.2307/j.ctvsn3n23.6; Deborah Paci, "Hate Speech in France: From Drumont to Dieudonné," *Antisemitism Studies* 6, no. 2 (2022): 260–298, https://doi.org/10.2979/antistud.6.2.04; Günther Jikeli, "A Framework for Assessing Antisemitism: Three Case Studies (Dieudonné, Erdoğan, and Hamas)," in *Deciphering the New Antisemitism*, ed. Alvin H. Rosenfeld (Bloomington: Indiana University Press, 2015), 43–76, http://www.jstor.org/stable/j.ctt18crxz7.7; Michelle Mazel, "French Jewry and the Dieudonné Affair," *Jewish Political Studies Review* 26, no. 1 (2014): 70–78, http://www.jstor.org/stable/44289825; Jean Robin, *Soral et Dieudonné: La tentation antisémite* (Paris, Tatamis, 2014).

7. Silverstein, *Postcolonial France*, 96; Mercier, *La Vérité*, 12; Vivienne Walt, "No Laughing Matter," *Time*, August 28, 2014, https://time.com/3206308/no-laughing-matter/.

8. Emmanuel Berretta, "Dieudonné vu par sa mère," *Le Point*, February 3, 2014, https://www.lepoint.fr/politique/emmanuel-berretta/dieudonne-vu-par-sa-mere-03-02-2014-1787233_1897.php.

9. "Je n'en ai jamais vraiment souffert. Je suis parfaitement intégré," quoted in Michel Holtz, "Dieudonné, nom de Dreux," *Libération*, April 29, 1999, https://www.liberation.fr/france/1999/04/29/dieudonne-33-ans-a-l-affiche-au-cinema-et-a-l-olympia-installe-dans-l-eure-et-loir-le-comique-s-y-es_271856/.

10. Berretta, "Dieudonné vu par sa mère."

11. "Elie et Dieudonné—Les bouchers," *YouTube*, uploaded by Auteuil92, April 8, 2009, https://www.youtube.com/watch?v=AwBDttQRm34; "Le jeu de la tatane," *YouTube*, uploaded by Nicolas Martin, August 19, 2006, https://www.youtube.com/watch?v=8eq4fYRelHc.

12. See, for example, "Elie et Dieudonné—Une certaine idée de la France," *YouTube*, uploaded by Pablo44300, April 1, 2013, https://www.youtube.com/watch?v=KnvQ_eOM1x.

13. "Elie & Dieudonné—Cohen et Bokassa," *YouTube*, uploaded by Nix872, June 16, 2013, https://www.youtube.com/watch?v=nj2cuAa-Z-4.

14. Eventually their association would devolve into public recriminations and the exchange of manifesto-like "diss tracks." See Ervine, *Humour in Contemporary France*, 58. An extremely uncomfortable reunion can be found in "Les retrouvailles d'Elie Semoun et de Dieudonné chez Thierry Ardisson," *YouTube*, uploaded by INA Arditube, November 2, 2021, https://www.youtube.com/watch?v=VRH9bDc1q_Q. At the end of the following video (a response to Semoun's takedown of his former colleague) the two were compelled to speak by phone, and their conversation was predictably unpleasant for all and sundry: "Droit de réponse légal: Dieudonné répond à Élie Semoun," *YouTube*, uploaded by LEGEND, September 1, 2024, https://www.youtube.com/watch?v=qFk_8btS1VU.

15. Michel Holtz, "Dieudonné, nom de Dreux."

16. Michel Holtz, "Dieudonné, nom de Dreux."

17. "Dieudonné—l'humour en campagne (1997)," *YouTube*, 2:50–3:05, uploaded by Les archives de la RTS, August 23, 2019, https://www.youtube.com/watch?v=wGvd7Qg3NP8.

18. Michel Holtz, "Dieudonné, nom de Dreux."

19. Stéphanie Binet and Blandine Grosjean, "La nébuleuse Dieudonné," *Libération*, November 10, 2005, https://www.liberation.fr/grand-angle/2005/11/10/la-nebuleuse-Dieudonné_538535/.

20. Pierre-André Taguieff, *La nouvelle judéophobie* (Paris: Fayard/Mille et Une Nuits, 2002), 11. Also see Phillipe Blanchard, "Les grands médias français face au conflit israélo-palestinien depuis la seconde intifada: Difficile neutralité," *Annuaire français des relations internationales* 4 (2003): 864–83; Nonna Mayer, "Nouvelle judéophobie ou vieil antisémitisme?" *Raisons politiques* 4, no. 16 (2004): 91–103.

21. Taguieff, *La nouvelle judéophobie*, 16; Eric Hazan and Alain Badiou, *L'antisémitisme partout: Aujourd'hui en Franc*e (Paris: La Fabrique, 2011).

22. Mayer, "Nouvelle judéophobie ou vieil antisémitisme?" 91–92.

23. His collaborator was political philosopher Louis Sala-Molins. See Stéphanie Binet et Blandine Grosjean, "La nébuleuse Dieudonné"; "La dernière interview tendue de Dieudonné par Thierry Ardisson," *YouTube*, 30:30-33:00, uploaded by INA Arditube, December 18, 2020, https://www.youtube.com/watch?v=Hu3lfjIspKM.

24. Dieudonné made this claim in an interview uploaded to the website *BlackMap* on October 22, 2002, but since taken down; see Ervine, *Humour in Contemporary France*, 63, 71. During the 1980s and 1990s white Jewish Americans and non-Jewish Black Americans watched their storied "Grand Alliance" of the Civil Rights era collapse. A common flash point was the posing of an unusual question, to wit: which was worse, the slave trade and its consequences or the Holocaust? See Terrence L. Johnson and Jacques Berlinerblau, *Blacks and Jews in America: An Invitation to Dialogue* (Washington, DC: Georgetown University Press, 2022).

25. He stresses these themes in Olivier Mukuna, *Dieudonné: Entretien à cœur ouvert* (Anvers: EPO, 2005), 76–80.

26. See note 26.

27. The episode is carefully reconstructed by Ervine, *Humour in Contemporary France*, 57–94.

28. Ervine, *Humour in Contemporary France*, 59.

29. "#209 Dieudonné—Hors système," *YouTube*, 34:40, uploaded by Biomécanique, January 1, 2024, https://www.youtube.com/watch?v=bRWlQo6XUec

30. "Dieudonné renonce à faire appel de sa condamnation pour diffamation envers Arthur," *La Dépêche*, September 20, 2007, https://www.ladepeche.fr/article/2007/09/20/18512-Dieudonné-renonce-faire-appel-condamnation-diffamation-envers-arthur.html.

31. Ervine, *Humour in Contemporary France*, 59–60.

32. Chaouat, "Postscript," 224.

33. "Dieudonné: 'Je ne suis ni nazi ni antisémite'—11/01," *YouTube*, 0:10, uploaded by BFMTV, January 11, 2014, https://www.youtube.com/watch?v=40tQ2aMiTBg&lc=Ugjx1Dwu6apY3ngCoAEC. Also see Ervine, *Humour in Contemporary France*, 58.

34. Often he will speak of the Jewish mafia and immediately add that he does not mean all Jews. See, e.g., "Le choc des dernières confessions," *YouTube*, 1:24:00, uploaded by Les funérailles des Tabous, June 16, 2024, https://www.youtube.com/watch?v=1tzg7DKLAkI; "Dieudonné Speaks about DSK English Subtitles," *YouTube*, 7:30, uploaded by Morgan Baleston, February 26, 2015, https://www.youtube.com/watch?v=nSG7BPTvut8; "#209 Dieudonné—Hors système," 1:15:00.

35. "Droit de réponse légal," 11:35.

36. Benoît Hopquin, "Dieudonné: La posture de paria, un ascenseur pour son succès," *Le Monde*, December 28, 2013, https://www.lemonde.fr/societe/article/2013/12/28/dieudonne-la-posture-de-paria-un-ascenseur-pour-son-succes_4340971_3224.html.

37. John Eligon, "Strauss-Kahn Drama Ends with Short Final Scene," *New York Times*, August 23, 2011, https://www.nytimes.com/2011/08/24/nyregion/charges-against-strauss-kahn-dismissed.html.

38. "Dieudonné speaks about DSK," 3:50-4:05.

39. Craig S. Smith, "Torture and Death of Jew Deepen Fears in France," *New York Times*, March 5, 2006, https://www.nytimes.com/2006/03/05/world/europe/torture-and-death-of-jew-deepen-fears-in-france.html.

40. The entire appalling story is told by Marc Weitzmann, "Ilan Halimi's Tortured Ghost Will Continue Haunting France," *Tablet Magazine*, September 2, 2014, https://www.tabletmag.com/sections/news/articles/frances-toxic-hate-5.

41. Ari Soffer, "Dieudonné Mocks Murder of Ilan Halimi," *Israel National News*, July 7, 2014, https://www.israelnationalnews.com/news/182616.

42. "Gang Leader Receives Life in Prison for Killing," *NBC News*, July 10, 2009, https://www.nbcnews.com/id/wbna31854942; Dieudonné Cleared of Spreading Anti-Semitic Video Online," *France* 24, July 2, 2014, https://www.france24.com/en/20140207-dieudonne-cleared-spreading-anti-semitic-video-online-france. Years later, he conceded that the Halimi joke was an instance in which he went too far: "#209 Dieudonné—Hors système," 1:48:25–1:48:45.

43. "Comedian Fined for Inciting Racial Hatred," *Guardian*, March 10, 2006, https://www.theguardian.com/world/2006/mar/11/france.mainsection; also see Ervine, *Humour in Contemporary France*, 64–65.

44. "L'ITW dans Lyon Capitale qui a fait condamner," *Lyon Capitale*, January 3, 2014, https://www.lyoncapitale.fr/actualite/l-itw-dans-lyon-capitale-qui-a-fait-condamner-Dieudonné.

45. Hugh Schofield, "Dieudonné: The Bizarre Journey of a Controversial Comic," *BBC News, Paris*, December 31, 2013, https://www.bbc.com/news/magazine-25563233.

46. Andrew Hussey, "Meet the Anti-Semitic French Comedian Who Invented the Quenelle," *New Republic*, January 31, 2014, https://newrepublic.com/article/116444/dieudonne-mbala-frances-most-anti-semitic-comedian.

47. These figures include Alain Soral and Robert Faurisson. A documentary about his network is "Au coeur du réseau Dieudonné," *YouTube*, uploaded by Investigations, February 3, 2023, https://www.youtube.com/watch?v=iiIn2tgT9Wk.

48. Aaron Blake, "The Dangerous Game Tucker Carlson Is Playing on Vaccines," *Washington Post*, March 16, 2021, https://www.washingtonpost.com/politics/2021/03/16/dangerous-game-tucker-carlson-is-playing-vaccines/.

49. "French Court Orders Comic Dieudonné to Remove Parts of YouTube Video," *France* 24, February 12, 2014, https://www.france24.com/en/20140212-Dieudonné-youtube-video-remove-court.

50. Michel Dreyfus, "L'antisémitisme de Dieudonné ou le négationnisme à l'ère des masses," *Le Monde*, January 10, 2014, https://www.lemonde.fr/idees/article/2014/01/10/l-antisemitisme-de-dieudonne-ou-le-negationnisme-a-l-ere-des-masses_4345899_3232.html.

51. Matthieu Pechberty, "Dieudonné tient sa liste," *Journal du Dimanche*, September 5, 2009, https://www.lejdd.fr/Politique/Dieudonne-tient-sa-liste-38643-3073949; John Lichfield, "What Is the 'Quenelle'? Nicolas Anelka Banned for Five Matches for Performing Gesture in Premier League Match," *Independent*, February 27, 2014, https://www.the-independent.com/sport/football/news/what-is-the-quenelle-nicolas-anelka-banned-for-fivematches-for-performing-gesture-in-premier-league-match-9158322.html; Scott Sayare, "Concern over an Increasingly Seen Gesture Grows in France," *New York Times*, January 2, 2014, https://www.nytimes.com/2014/01/03/world/europe/concern-over-quenelle-gesture-grows-in-france.html; Sandrine Boudana, "Not Just a Joke: The 'Quenelle' as a Running Gag Masking Anti-Semitic Communication," *European Journal of Cultural Studies* 21, no. 2 (2018): 189–206, https://doi.org/10.1177/1367549415603374.

52. "Dieudonné Shoananas," *YouTube*, uploaded by adytom88, June 9, 2015, https://www.youtube.com/watch?v=80QQogFbwR0.

53. Jessica Elgot, "Iran Funds Comic's 'Anti-Zionist' Film," *Jewish Chronicle*, November 30, 2009, https://www.thejc.com/news/world/iran-funds-comics-anti-zionist-film-tqdlqqcu.

54. Elgot, "Iran Funds Comic's 'Anti-Zionist' Film."

55. Ann Jouan, "Dieudonné, du rire à la nausée," *L'Express*, September 8, 2018, https://www.lexpress.fr/societe/dieudonne-du-rire-a-la-nausee_2033680.html.

56. Walt, "No Laughing Matter"; Sam Ball, "Dieudonné: From Anti-Racist to Anti-Semitic Zealot," *France* 24, January 21, 2014, https://www.france24.com/en/20140104-dieudonne-anti-racist-anti-semitic-zealot.

57. Tom Reiss, "Laugh Riots," *New Yorker*, November 19, 2007, https://www.newyorker.com/magazine/2007/11/19/laugh-riots.

58. "Dieudonné—Palestine," *YouTube*, uploaded by Polo Chon, March 28, 2013, https://www.youtube.com/watch?v=l2tqaI-gWjE.

59. Ali Saad, "The French Paradox and the Dieudonné Affair," *Al-Jazeera*, May 24, 2014, https://www.aljazeera.com/opinions/2014/5/24/the-french-paradox-and-the-dieudonne-affair; Olivier Bertrand, "Dieudonné chahuté à Lyon," *Libération*, February 7, 2004, https://www.liberation.fr/societe/2004/02/07/dieudonne-chahute-a-lyon_468167/; Olivier Mukuna, *Dieudonné: Entretien à cœur ouvert*, 43.

60. Amiram Barkat, "Four Israelis Held for Allegedly Attacking French Comedian," *Haaretz*, March 3, 2005, https://www.haaretz.com/2005-03-03/ty-article/four-israelis-held-for-allegedly-attacking-french-comedian/0000017f-e9e6-dc91-a17f-fdef43260000.

61. "Dieudonné 1905 fête ainsi les 100 ans de Laïcité | Réal Hilaci Attia | Spectacle Complet," *YouTube*, 1:03:30–end, uploaded by ass Ben-Attia, November 18, 2017, https://www.youtube.com/watch?v=UAEFicu-8m8.

62. Silverstein, *Postcolonial France*, 91; Ervine, *Humour in Contemporary France*, 73.

63. Kim Willsher, "Dieudonné M'bala M'bala: French 'Quenelle' Comedian Banned from UK," *Guardian*, February 3, 2014, https://www.theguardian.com/world/2014/feb/03/Dieudonné-banned-uk-nicolas-anelka-quenelle.

64. "Moroccan Authorities Stop Dieudonné's Casablanca Show," *Times of Israel*, April 17, 2015, https://www.timesofisrael.com/moroccan-authorities-stop-Dieudonnés-casablanca-show/.

65. Benjamin Shingler, "Dieudonné Isn't Welcome in Montreal, Mayor Denis Coderre Says," *CBC*, April 22, 2016, https://www.cbc.ca/news/canada/montreal/Dieudonné-comedian-coderre-1.3548122.

66. "French Comedian Dieudonné Guilty of Racial Discrimination, Top Court Confirms," *SWI*, April 14, 2023, https://www.swissinfo.ch/eng/society/french-comedian-dieudonn%C3%A9-guilty-of-racial-discrimination-top-court-confirms/48436296; Tim Hume and Pierre-Eliott Buet, "Controversial French Comic Dieudonné Sentenced for 'Inciting Hatred' in Show," *CNN*, November 27, 2015, https://www.cnn.com/2015/11/26/europe/belgium-france-comedian-Dieudonné-sentenced/index.html.

67. Eugene Volokh, "One-to-One Speech vs. One-to-Many Speech, Criminal Harassment Laws, and 'Cyberstalking,'" *Northwestern University Law Review* 107, no. 2 (2013), https://scholarlycommons.law.northwestern.edu/cgi/viewcontent.cgi?article=1068&context=nulr.

68. Karen Bird, "Racist Speech or Free Speech? A Comparison of the Law in France and the United States," *Comparative Politics* 32, no. 4 (2000): 411, https://doi.org/10.2307/422386.

69. Joseph Bamat, "Anti-Semitic Comic Backs Down, to Unveil New Routine," *France* 24, January 21, 2014, https://www.france24.com/en/20140112-dieudonne-show-cancelled-anti-semitic-france; "France May Ban French Comic's Show for 'Anti-Semitism,'" *France* 24, December 27, 2013, https://www.france24.com/en/20131227-Dieudonné-france-famous-french-comic-show-could-be-banned-anti-semitic-content; Vincent Bouquet, "Dieudonné regrette les chambres à gaz, Radio France attaque," *Nouvel Obs*, December 20, 2013, https://www.nouvelobs.com/societe/20131220.OBS0356/dieudonne-regrette-les-chambres-a-gaz-radio-france-attaque.html.

70. "France May Ban French Comic's Show for 'Anti-Semitism.'"

71. Bird, "Racist Speech or Free Speech?" 408; "Lois et décrets (version papier numérisée) n° 0154 du 02/07/1972," *République Française*, July 2, 1972, https://www.legifrance.gouv.fr/jorf/jo/id/JORFCONT000000020730.

72. Schofield, "Dieudonné: The Bizarre Journey."

73. "Dieudonné, star de la semaine judiciaire," *Le Figaro*, June 26, 2008, https://www.lefigaro.fr/actualite-france/2008/06/26/01016-20080626ARTFIG00373-dieudonne-star-de-la-semaine-judiciaire.php.

74. Reuters, "Paris Court Fines French Comic for Comparing Jews to Slave Traders," *Haaretz*, March 10, 2006, https://www.haaretz.com/2006-03-10/ty-article/paris-court-fines-french-comic-for-comparing-jews-to-slave-traders/0000017f-e2ee-d568-ad7f-f3efb8680000.

75. "Loi n° 90-615 du 13 juillet 1990 tendant à réprimer tout acte raciste, antisémite ou xénophobe," *Gouvernement Français*, https://www.legifrance.gouv.fr/loda/id/JORFTEXT000000532990.

76. Julie Suk, "Denying Experience: Holocaust Denial and the Free-Speech Theory of the State," in *The Content and Context of Hate Speech*, ed. Michael Herz and Peter Molnar (Cambridge: Cambridge University Press, 2012), 144–163, https://www.cambridge.org/core/books/abs/content-and-context-of-hate-speech/denying-experience/EB7420FAB0BE5EC372D30B1642E014CC; Michel Troper, "La loi Gayssot et la constitution," *Annales. Histoire, Sciences Sociales* 54, no. 6 (1999): 1239–1255, https://www.jstor.org/stable/27586025; Yifat Gutman, "Memory Laws: An Escalation in Minority Exclusion or a Testimony to the Limits of State Power?" *Law & Society Review* 50, no. 3 (2016): 575–607, http://doi.org/10.1111/lasr.12221; Michael Whine, "Expanding Holocaust Denial and Legislation against It," *Jewish Political Studies Review* 20, nos. 1/2 (2008): 57–77, https://www.jstor.org/stable/25834777.

77. "French Court Orders Comic Dieudonné to Remove.

78. "French Comedian Dieudonné Denounces Paris Attacks in Court," *Guardian*, February 4, 2015, https://www.theguardian.com/world/2015/feb/04/dieudonne-french-comedian-paris-attacks-court.

79. "French Comedian Dieudonné Denounces."

80. Andrew Hussey, "Dieudonné's War on France: The Holocaust Comedian Who Isn't Funny," *New Statesman*, January 30, 2014, https://www.newstatesman.com/long-reads/2014/01/dieudonne-war-france.

81. On the relationship between *laïcité* and secularism, see Jacques Berlinerblau, *Secularism: The Basics*, 2nd ed. (London: Routledge, 2025); Jacques Berlinerblau, "Cheat Sheet for Political Secularism and Secular Studies," *Secular Studies* 5, no. 1 (2023): 53–82, https://doi.org/10.1163/25892525-bja10046.

82. Blair Taylor, "Ruthless Critique or Selective Apologia? The Postcolonial Left in Theory and Practice," *American Studies* 62, no. 4 (2017): 650.

83. "Dieudonné: Mes excuses," *Spotify*, 14:45–15:20, uploaded by Best of Comédie Française, September 2023, https://open.spotify.com/episode/5yJ45iMraq1haUXPuzaKsx?si=89a1eda5c29042d0; "Ruth Safarti journaliste," *Spotify*, 8:00–8:30, uploaded by Dieudonné, February 4, 2021, https://open.spotify.com/track/3h79ovNlw9QIw79HvZAuB0?si=2c95494cbde7429c. Here the comedian comes very close to approaches that demonstrate the racist underpinnings of Enlightenment heroes. Charles Mills famously conducted this type of analysis on Immanuel Kant; see Charles W. Mills, *Blackness Visible: Essays on Philosophy and Race* (Ithaca, NY: Cornell University Press, 2015), 67–96, https://doi.org/10.7591/9781501702952-005.

84. "Dieudonné—Mes excuses, Spectacle complet," *YouTube*, 37:40–38:00, uploaded by theatre & spectacle, March 5, 2023, https://www.youtube.com/watch?v=6aWl4cG9Kbo (video no longer available; accessed September 22, 2024.)

85. "#226 Dieudonné—Droit dans le mur," *YouTube*, 44:45–45:15, uploaded by Biomécanique, April 29, 2024, https://www.youtube.com/watch?v=AtGzmifA6vY.

86. See Berlinerblau, *Secularism: The Basics* and "Cheat Sheet for Political Secularism."

87. "Dieudonné 1905 fête ainsi les 100 ans de laïcité | Réal Hilaci Attia | Spectacle complet," *YouTube*, 1:28:55–1:29:23, uploaded by Lass Ben-Attia, November 18, 2017, https://www.youtube.com/watch?v=UAEFicu-8m8.

88. "Dieudonné 1905 fête."

89. "DIEUDONNE: L'entretien exclusif | CANCEL #1," *YouTube*, 27:05–27:11, uploaded by Alohanews, September 8, 2023, https://www.youtube.com/watch?v=HH_1PxyS_ic.

90. Chaouat ("Postscript," 236) argues that his conception of history as always written by victors is a popularization of postcolonial approaches.

91. "#209 Dieudonné—Hors système," *YouTube*, 1:19:00, uploaded by Biomécanique, January 1, 2024, https://www.youtube.com/watch?v=

bRWlQo6XUec; Dieudonné, "Nuremberg," *Spotify*, 2:53–3:54, February 2, 2021, https://open.spotify.com/track/4KAhtUQuWOfFaMR4T4bPAp.

92. Silverstein, *Postcolonial France*, 92.

93. Quoted in Charlotte Elliot-Harvey, "Considering Ethnic Group Tensions: The Symptomatic Case of French Comedian Dieudonné," *Open Library of Humanities* 6, no. 2 (2020), https://olh.openlibhums.org/article/id/4648/.

94. "French Comedian Dieudonné Sentenced for Fraud and Money Laundering," *RFI*, May 7, 2019, https://www.rfi.fr/en/france/20190705-french-comedian-dieudonne-sentenced-fraud-and-money-laundering; "French Comedian Dieudonne Given Two-Year Sentence for Tax Fraud," *Times of Israel*, July 5, 2019, https://www.timesofisrael.com/french-comedian-dieudonne-given-two-year-sentence-for-tax-fraud/.

95. "Choc des dernières confessions," 1:51.

96. "Choc des dernières confessions," 2:30.

97. "Choc des dernières confessions," 14:23–14:47.

98. "Choc des dernières confessions," 1:06:28–1:06:50; "DIEUDONNE: L'entretien exclusif | CANCEL #1," 20:00–20:11

99. A news investigation showed he was staging illegal shows during the COVID lockdown (though maybe it was just a swindle to sell nonrefundable tickets for performances he knew would likely never take place?). Codesource, "Dans l'arrière-boutique de Dieudonné, les coulisses de notre enquête," *Spotify*, February 9, 2021, https://open.spotify.com/episode/0FjBWSsxRvL6Kr6AUbp8IP.

100. "#226 Dieudonné—Droit dans le mur," 37:00–37:30.

101. "#226 Dieudonné—Droit dans le mur," 43:00–46:40.

102. "L'homophobie en Afrique," from *Gilets Jaunes*, uploaded to Spotify by Dieudonné, February 4, 2021, https://open.spotify.com/track/589ZWaJ8rQClORjtHew38A?si=7616159473284 47f.

103. "#209 Dieudonné—Hors système," 51:05.

104. "#209 Dieudonné—Hors système," 52:40–53:05, 52:30.

105. "#209 Dieudonné—Hors système," 59:58–1:00:28

106. "#209 Dieudonné—Hors système," 54:30–54:41.

107. "#226 Dieudonné—Droit dans le mur," 31:00–31:45.

108. Dieudonné M'Bala M'Bala, "Je demande pardon. Dieudonné," *Israel Magazine*, January 10, 2023, https://israelmagazine.co.il/je-demande-pardon-dieudonne/.

109. I have taken this translation almost entirely from *MEMRI*, though I changed one or two words according to my own preferences. "French Antisemitic Comedian Dieudonné M'bala M'bala: I Ask for Forgiveness," *MEMRI*, February 8, 2023, https://www.memri.org/reports/french-antisemitic

-comedian-dieudonn%C3%A9-mbala-mbala-i-ask-forgiveness; Dieudonné M'Bala M'Bala, "Je demande pardon."

110. Eléonore Weil, "French Jews Slam 'Apology' from Convicted Antisemite and Holocaust Denier Comedian," *Haaretz*, January 13, 2023, https://www.haaretz.com/world-news/europe/2023-01-13/ty-article/.premium/french-jews-slam-apology-from-convicted-antisemite-and-holocaust-denier-comedian/00000185-aa50-d670-a3b5-ae52b8b30000; Silverstein, *Postcolonial France*, 94.

111. "Kanak, Soral, bracelet électronique, Dieudonné nous dit tout!" *YouTube*, 32:00–32:10, uploaded by Média en 4-4-2, May 30, 2024, https://www.youtube.com/watch?v=f2HKP4_m83w.

112. "Kanak, Soral, bracelet électronique," 31:00–32:04.

113. "Droit de réponse légal," 25:00–25:30.

114. "Kanak, Soral, bracelet électronique," 37:10–37:17

115. Meg Bortin, "Letter from France: Le Pen's Tricky Business," *New York Times*, January 4, 2007, https://www.nytimes.com/2007/01/04/world/europe/04iht-letter.4097286.html; John Lichfield, "Civil War in the Bizarre World of Dieudonné, the Black, Anti-Semitic Comedian at the Centre of the 'Quenelle' Row," *Independent*, December 30, 2014, https://www.independent.co.uk/news/world/europe/dieudonne-m-bala-m-bala-friends-turn-on-france-s-black-antisemitic-comedian-for-forming-political-party-with-farright-activist-9948943.html; John Lichfield, "Only in France: The Black, Anti-Semitic Comedian at a Rally of Le Pen's Far Right," *Independent*, November 19, 2006, https://www.independent.co.uk/news/world/europe/only-in-france-the-black-antisemitic-comedian-at-a-rally-of-le-pen-s-far-right-424947.html.

116. Pierre Birnbaum, *La France aux français: Histoire des haines nationalistes* (Paris: Seuil, 1993).

117. Schofield, "Dieudonné: The Bizarre Journey"; "Jean-Marie Le Pen Fined Again for Dismissing Holocaust as 'Detail,'" *Guardian*, https://www.theguardian.com/world/2016/apr/06/jean-marie-le-pen-fined-again-dismissing-holocaust-detail.

118. For analyses of Dieudonné's constituencies, see Michel Wieviorka, "Derrière l'affaire Dieudonné, l'essor d'un public 'antisystème,'" *Le Monde*, December 31, 2013, https://www.lemonde.fr/idees/article/2013/12/31/affaire-dieudonne-l-essor-d-un-public-antisysteme_4341646_3232.html; Klug, "In the Heat of the Moment"; Silverstein, *Postcolonial France*, 95; Propos recueillis par Paris, "Le nouvel antisémitisme," *Le Temps*, January 9, 2014, https://www.letemps.ch/monde/nouvel-antisemitisme?srsltid=AfmBOoqgfGK9Al7qbUHdIFEhngi9-jCfpiIrxNsFvt80ackW1UDjTURm; Chloé Leprince, "Dans le public de Dieudonné, 'Le seul qui nous fasse rire,'" *Nouvel Obs*, August 11,

2008, https://www.nouvelobs.com/rue89/rue89-rue89-culture/20080811.RUE5266/dans-le-public-de-dieudonne-le-seul-qui-nous-fasse-rire.html.

119. Silverstein, *Postcolonial France*, 95. He can count among his network Black supremacists like Kémi Séba who espouse Nation of Islam rhetoric and White supremacists like Alain Soral; see "Le militant radical panafricain Kémi Séba déchu de la nationalité française," *Libération*, July 10, 2024, https://www.liberation.fr/international/afrique/le-militant-radical-panafricain-kemi-seba-dechu-de-la-nationalite-francaise-20240710_NUCFIALWENAOJOC-Q6S4EZPXYGU/.

CHAPTER SEVEN

1. "The Charity Bazaar," *The Abbott and Costello Show*, season 1, episode 10, directed by Jean Yarbrough, written by Sid Fields, aired February 6, 1953, on CBS, https://www.youtube.com/watch?v=f7pMYHn-1yA. Rebecca Krefting, "Savage New Media: Discursive Campaigns for/against Political Correctness," in *The Joke Is on Us: Political Comedy in (Late) Neoliberal Time*s, ed. Julie Weber (Lanham, MD: Lexington Books, 2019), p. 247.

2. See Geoffrey Baym, "*The Daily Show:* Discursive Integration and the Reinvention of Political Journalism," *Political Communication* 22, no. 1 (2005): 261, https://www.tandfonline.com/doi/epdf/10.1080/10584600591006492; Amber Day, "And Now . . . the News? Mimesis and the Real in *The Daily Show*," in *Satire TV: Politics and Comedy in the Post-Network Era*, ed. Jonathan Gray, Jeffrey Jones, and Ethan Thompson (New York: NYU Press, 2009), 87.

3. Jamie Warner, "Political Culture Jamming: The Dissident Humor of *The Daily Show with Jon Stewart*," *Popular Communication* 5, no. 1 (2007): 23–24, https://nknu.pbworks.com/f/Political+Culture+Jamming.pdf.

4. Jeffrey Jones, *Entertaining Politics: New Political Television and Civic Culture* (Lanham, MD: Rowman & Littlefield, 2005), 57.

5. On "political TV satire," see Geoffrey Baym and J. Jones, "News Parody in Global Perspective: Politics, Power, and Resistance," *Popular Communication* 10, nos. 1–2 (2012): 3; Jay D. Hmielowski, R. Lance Holbert, and Jayeon Lee, "Predicting the Consumption of Political TV Satire: Affinity for Political Humor, *The Daily Show*, and *The Colbert Report*," *Communication Monographs* 78, no. 1 (2011): 97. On "news parody," see Sangeet Kumar, "Transgressing Boundaries as the Hybrid Global: Parody and Postcoloniality on Indian Television," *Popular Communication* 10, no. 1 (2012): 80. On "televised news satire," see Matt Sienkiewicz, "Out of Control: Palestinian News Satire and

Government Power in the Age of Social Media," *Popular Communication* 10, no. 1 (2012): 106. On "satirical news shows," see Katharina Kleinen–von Königslöw and Guido Keel, "Localizing *The Daily Show:* The Heute Show in Germany," *Popular Communication* 10, no. 1 (2012): 76. On "parodic news" and "parodic news shows," see Amber Day, *Satire and Dissent: Interventions in Contemporary Political Debate* (Bloomington: Indiana University Press, 2011), 43–44. For "fake news," see Muyun Zhou, "Satirizing News Media, Changing Taiwan's Feelings: *The Night Night Show with Brian Tseng*'s Adaptation of the American Satire News Format," *Journalism and Media* 4 (2023): 1107. A definition of fake news can be found in Albert Chibuwe, "Fake News as Political Communication: On Fake News, Digital Media, and the Struggle for Hegemony in Post-Mugabe Zimbabwe," *Political Research Quarterly* 77, no. 4 (2024), https://doi.org/10.1177/10659129241262230.

6. Day, "And Now . . . the News?" 85.

7. Kristina Riegert, "Introduction," in *Politicotainment: Television's Take on the Real*, ed. Kristina Riegert (New York: Peter Lang, 2007), 1–19.

8. Baym and Jones, "News Parody in Global Perspective," 6; Day, *Satire and Dissent*, 45–52; Kleinen–von Königslöw and Keel, "Localizing *The Daily Show*," 68. On the Canadian show *This Hour Has Seven Days*, see Day, *Satire and Dissent*, 47–49.

9. Day, "And Now . . . the News?" 98.

10. Day, "And Now . . . the News?" 97; Day, *Satire and Dissent*, 77.

11. Jones, *Entertaining Politics*, 108.

12. Lorraine Ali and Robert Lloyd, "What Made 'The Daily Show' the Most Influential Late-Night Comedy of the Last 25 Years," *Los Angeles Times*, July 22, 2021, https://www.latimes.com/entertainment-arts/tv/story/2021-07-22/the-daily-show-trevor-noah-jon-stewart-craig-kilborn-25th-anniversary-influence.

13. Matt Sienkiewicz and Nick Marx, *That's Not Funny: How the Right Makes Comedy Work for Them* (Oakland: University of California Press, 2022), 35.

14. Baym and Jones, "News Parody in Global Perspective," 8; David Lipson, Mark Boukes, and Samira Khemkhem, "The Glocalization of *The Daily Show*," *Popular Communication* 21, nos. 3–4 (2023): 131–145, https://doi.org/10.1080/15405702.2023.2251961.

15. Baym and Jones, "News Parody in Global Perspective," 5.

16. Baym and Jones, "News Parody in Global Perspective," 5; Dannagal Goldthwaite Young, "*The Daily Show* as the New Journalism: In Their Own Words," in *Laughing Matters: Humor and American Politics in the Media Age*, ed. Jody Baumgartner and Jonathan Morris (New York: Routledge, 2008), 242.

17. Jonathan Morris and Jody Baumgartner, "*The Daily Show* and Attitudes toward the News Media," in Baumgartner and Morris, eds., *Laughing Matters*, 315–331.

18. For a two-pronged definition of politainment, see Kristina Reigert and Sue Collins, "Politainment," *The International Encyclopedia of Political Communication*, ed. Gianpietro Mazzoleni et al. (Hoboken, NJ: Wiley-Blackwell, 2015), 1.

19. "Rep. Ken Buck," *The Daily Show*, season 29, episode 53, performed by Jon Stewart and Ken Buck, aired June 3, 2024, on Comedy Central.

20. This leaves the status of the parody and the parodist a bit ambiguous. See Day, "And Now . . . the News?" 98.

21. Jones, *Entertaining Politics*, 116.

22. Cited in Young, "*The Daily Show* as the New Journalism," 241.

23. Jeffrey Gottfried, Katerina Eva Matsa, and Michael Barthel, "As Jon Stewart Steps Down, 5 Facts about the *The Daily Show*," *Pew Research Center*, August 6, 2015, https://www.pewresearch.org/short-reads/2015/08/06/5-facts-daily-show/.

24. Cited in Jones, *Entertaining Politics*, 55.

25. Cited in Jones, *Entertaining Politics*, 114.

26. "Bassem Youssef," *Harvard Kennedy School Institute of Politics*, Spring 2015, https://iop.harvard.edu/fellows/bassem-youssef.

27. Sharif Paget, "Bassem Youssef: The Wild Story of 'Egypt's Jon Stewart,'" *BBC*, January 10, 2018, https://www.bbc.com/culture/article/20180110-bassem-youssef-the-wild-story-of-egypts-jon-stewart.

28. Joel Gordon and Heba Arafa, "'Stuck with Him': Bassem Youssef and the Egyptian Revolution's Last Laugh," *Review of Middle East Studies* 48, nos. 1/2 (2014): 35.

29. Gordon and Arafa, "'Stuck with Him,'" 35.

30. Bassem Youssef, *Revolution for Dummies: Laughing through the Arab Spring* (New York: Dey Street Books, 2017), 21.

31. Patrick Bet-David et al., "'Jon Stewart of the Nile'—How Bassem Youssef Used the Media to Get Jon Stewart's Attention," *YouTube*, uploaded by PBD Podcast, 2024, https://www.youtube.com/watch?v=hZ70cyWBb_w; Youssef, *Revolution for Dummies*, xi; Judy Kurtz, "Egyptian Comic Known as 'Jon Stewart of the Middle East' Says He Won't Be 'Blackmailed' into Voting for Biden, Hails 'Daily Show' Host's Return," *The Hill*, February 14, 2024, https://thehill.com/blogs/in-the-know/4467340-egyptian-comic-jon-stewart-biden-daily-show/.

32. Gordon and Arafa, "'Stuck with Him,'" 36. Stewart also blurbed Youssef's book *Revolution for Dummies:* "Hilarious and heartbreaking. Comedy shouldn't take courage, but it made an exception for Bassem."

33. Jacques Berlinerblau, "The Cancellation of Stephen Colbert's 'Late Show' Is a Warning for Comedy's Future," *MSNBC*, July 19, 2025, https://www.msnbc.com/opinion/msnbc-opinion/stephen-colbert-late-show-cancelled-trump-rcna219591.

34. Lloyd Vries, "Viacom Buys All Of Comedy Central," *CBS News*, April 22, 2003, https://www.cbsnews.com/news/viacom-buys-all-of-comedy-central/; "Bassem Youssef Biography," *IMDb*, n.d., https://www.imdb.com/name/nm5117997/bio/?ref_=nm_ov_bio_sm.

35. Youssef, *Revolution for Dummies*, 19.

36. Chris Moody, "A Comedian in Exile," *CNN*, April 14, 2017, https://www.cnn.com/2017/04/14/politics/bassem-youssef-egyptian-jon-stewart/index.html; Patrick Bet-David, Adam Sosnick, and Vincent Oshana, "HEATED Israel vs. Palestine Debate w/ Bassem Youssef," *PBD Podcast*, episode 349, January 12, 2024, https://www.youtube.com/live/KE71VcdvpAs, 16:30.

37. Paget, "Bassem Youssef"; Youssef, *Revolution for Dummies*, 24.

38. Paget, "Bassem Youssef"; Youssef, *Revolution for Dummies*, 51–56; Gordon and Arafa, "'Stuck with Him,'" 35.

39. Bet-David, Sosnick, and Oshana, "HEATED Israel," 11:40.

40. "*Al-Bernamig*—Season 1, Episode 2," *Egypt Revolution* 2011, n.d., https://egyptrevolution2011.ac.uk/items/show/123.

41. Ibrahim El Houdaiby, "Islamism in and after Egypt's Revolution," in *Arab Spring in Egypt: Revolution and Beyond*, ed. Bahgat Korany and Rabab El-Mahdi (Cairo: American University in Cairo Press, 2012), 142, http://www.jstor.org/stable/j.ctt15m7mbm.12.

42. "*Al-Bernamig*—Season 1, Episode 2."

43. Youssef, *Revolution for Dummies*, 52, 54.

44. Youssef, *Revolution for Dummies*, 103.

45. *Al-Bernamig*, season 2, episode 4, performed by Bassem Youssef, produced by Amr Ismail, directed by Ahmed Abbas, aired December 14, 2012, https://www.youtube.com/watch?v=Rw45GaGUWfk, see markers 6:10, 7:31, 9:45, 11:10, 12:20, 13:40, 14:50.

46. See David Kenner, "Bassem Youssef Isn't Joking Around," *Foreign Policy*, May 20, 2013, https://foreignpolicy.com/2013/05/20/bassem-youssef-isnt-joking-around/.

47. *Al-Bernamig*, season 2, episode 5, 24:20, performed by Bassem Youssef, produced by Amr Ismail, directed by Ahmed Abbas, aired December 21, 2012, https://www.youtube.com/watch?v=i1_ZVTN8CjE&t=1450s.

48. *Al-Bernamig*, season 2, episode 5, 5:56.

49. Stephen Kalin, "Here Are the Jokes That Got Bassem Youssef, the 'Jon Stewart of Egypt,' Arrested," *QZ*, April 8, 2013, https://qz.com/71678/this-is-what-bassem-youssef-the-jon-stewart-of-egypt-actually-said-to-get-himself-arrested.

50. Justin Monticello, "Bassem Youssef Was 'Egypt's Jon Stewart.' Then He Was Forced to Flee," *Reason*, July 14, 2017, https://reason.com/video/2017/07/14/bassem-youssef-jon-stewart-egypt-censor/.

51. The Tamarod movement was a largely civilian movement funded and supported by the UAE and Intelligence Service to incite opposition to Mohammad Morsi and his regime. The end goal was to overthrow Morsi and have new elections and, though portrayed as a democratic movement, was widely criticized for power centralization. Youssef, *Revolution for Dummies*, 165.

52. Tarek Masoud, "Egyptian Democracy: Smothered in the Cradle, or Stillborn?" *Brown Journal of World Affairs* 20, no. 2 (2014): 3–17, http://www.jstor.org/stable/24590971.

53. *Al-Bernamig*, season 3, episode 1, 56:00, performed by Bassem Youssef, produced by Tarek El Kazzaz, directed by Mahamed Khalifa, aired August 1, 2011, https://www.youtube.com/watch?v=YdrTb4rFrVE.

54. Nervana Mahmoud, "Egypt and Political Satire," *Daily News Egypt*, November 3, 2013, https://www.dailynewsegypt.com/2013/11/03/egypt-and-political-satire/.

55. Jared Malsin, "Bassem Youssef Abruptly Cancels Egyptian Satire Show before Sisi Declared President," *Time*, June 3, 2014, https://time.com/2818306/bassem-youssef-abruptly-cancels-egyptian-satire-show-before-sisi-declared-president/.

56. Tarek Masoud, "Not Ready for Democracy: Modernisation, Pluralism, and the Arab Spring," in *Revisiting the Arab Uprisings: The Politics of a Revolutionary Moment*, ed. Stéphane Lacroix and Jean-Pierre Filiu (London: Hurst & Co., 2018), 106.

57. Youssef, *Revolution for Dummies*, 253–256; Malsin, "Bassem Youssef Abruptly Cancels."

58. On the Arab Winter, see Stephen King, *The Arab Winter: Democratic Consolidation, Civil War, and Radical Islamists* (Cambridge: Cambridge University Press, 2020).

59. Sienkiewicz, "Out of Control," 107.

60. Amal Ibrahim and Nahed Eltantawy, "Egypt's Jon Stewart: Humorous Political Satire and Serious Culture Jamming," *International Journal of Communication* 11 (June 2017): 2807, https://ijoc.org/index.php/ijoc/article/viewFile/6359/2084.

61. *Al-Bernamig*, season 2, episode 5, 12:15.

62. Youssef, *Revolution for Dummies*, 264.

63. Youssef, *Revolution for Dummies*, 179, 189–192, 200, 203.

64. Kalin, "Here Are the Jokes."

65. Angela D. Abel and Michael Barthel, "Appropriation of Mainstream News: How *Saturday Night Live* Changed the Political Discussion," *Critical Studies in Media Communication* 30, no. 1 (2012): 5, https://doi.org/10.1080/15295036.2012.701011.

66. Day, *Satire and Dissent* 8

67. Youssef, *Revolution for Dummies*, 77, 82.

68. *Al-Bernamig*, season 2, episode 5, performed by Bassem Youssef, produced by Amr Ismail, directed by Ahmed Abbas, aired December 12, 2012, on CBC, https://www.youtube.com/watch?v=i1_ZVTN8CjE&t=1450s.

69. Youssef, *Revolution for Dummies*, 281.

70. Youssef, *Revolution for Dummies*, 96.

71. On this tendency to see fake newsmen as surrogates, see Day, *Satire and Dissent*, 44.

72. As argued by, for example, Day, *Satire and Dissent*, 58–59.

CHAPTER EIGHT

1. Helen Mann and Ramraajh Sharvendiran, "As It Happens," *CBC Radio*, August 23, 2019, https://www.cbc.ca/radio/asithappens/as-it-happens-friday-edition-1.5198581/august-23-2019-episode-transcript-1.5260143.

2. "Zimbabwe Comedian Gonyeti 'Abducted and Beaten' in Harare," *BBC*, August 22, 2019, https://www.bbc.com/news/world-africa-49433387.

3. Jason Burke, "Zimbabwean Comedian Goes into Hiding after Abduction and Beating," *Guardian*, August 23, 2019, https://www.theguardian.com/world/2019/aug/23/zimbabwean-comedian-samantha-kureya-goes-into-hiding-after-abduction-and-beating/

4. Tiseke Kasambala, "'You Will Be Thoroughly Beaten': The Brutal Suppression of Dissent in Zimbabwe," *Human Rights Watch*, November 1, 2006, 12, https://www.hrw.org/report/2006/11/01/you-will-be-thoroughly-beaten/brutal-suppression-dissent-zimbabwe; "Zimbabwe 2023," *Amnesty International*, https://www.amnesty.org/en/location/africa/southern-africa/zimbabwe/report-zimbabwe/.

5. Alexander Schmotz, "Hybrid Regimes," in *The Handbook of Political, Social, and Economic Transformation* (Oxford: Oxford University Press, 2019), 521–525, https://doi.org/10.1093/oso/9780198829911.003.0053. For the specific case

of Zimbabwe as a hybrid regime, see Itai Makone and Derica Lambrechts, "How Durable Are Hybrid Regimes? The Case of Zimbabwe as a Hybrid Regime," *Politeia* 40, no. 1 (2021): 1–20, https://www.researchgate.net/publication/363754004_How_Durable_are_Hybrid_Regimes_The_Case_of_Zimbabwe_as_a_Hybrid_Regime; Adrian Karatnycky, "The Decline of Illiberal Democracy," *Journal of Democracy* 1, no. 1 (1999), https://muse.jhu.edu/article/16935; Denisa Kostovicova, Kaldor Kostovicova, and Mary Kaldor, "Global Civil Society and Illiberal Regimes," in *Global Civil Society* 2007/8*: Communicative Power and Democracy*, ed. Martin Albrow et al. (London: Sage, 2007), 86–113.

6. Schmotz, "Hybrid Regimes," 521–522. On Zimbabwe as an "authoritarian regime," see "Political Regime," *Our World in Data*, 2023, https://ourworldindata.org/grapher/political-regime-eiu. According to both sources, nearly one third of all countries in the world are examples of "hybrid regimes."

7. Schmotz, "Hybrid Regimes," 521.

8. Schmotz, "Hybrid Regimes," 522, 521.

9. Steven Levitsky and Lucan A. Way, "The Rise of Competitive Authoritarianism," *Journal of Democracy* 13, no. 2 (2002): 52, https://scholar.harvard.edu/levitsky/files/SL_elections.pdf.

10. Amanda Källstig, "Humouring the State? Zimbabwean Stand-Up Comedians as Political Actors," PhD diss., University of Manchester, 2021, 10.

11. Simon Allison, "'You Are Too Young to Mock the Government': Zimbabwean Comedian Relives Her Abduction," *Mail & Guardian*, December 4, 2019, https://mg.co.za/article/2019-12-04-00-you-are-too-young-to-mock-the-government-zimbabwean-comedian-relives-her-abduction/.

12. Maya Oppenheim, "Zimbabwe Satirist Abducted, Stripped, and Forced to Drink Sewage amid Crackdown on Opposition," *Indepdendent*, August 23, 2019, https://www.independent.co.uk/news/world/africa/samantha-kureya-gonyeti-zimbabwe-satirist-adbucted-gonyeti-harare-a9076256.html.

13. Ryan Truscott, "Zimbabwe Comedian Abducted, Beaten as Tensions Mount," *RFI*, August 22, 2019, https://www.rfi.fr/en/africa/20190822-zimbabwe-comedian-abducted-beaten-tensions-mount.

14. "About," *Bustop TV*, https://www.youtube.com/bustoptv.

15. One exception is a three-part soap opera they produced called "MaDomestics" in 2019. The series probed themes of fiscal insolvency, marital infidelity, and government dysfunction. See, e.g., "MaDomestics Episode 1 | BUSTOP TV," *YouTube*, November 27, 2019, https://www.youtube.com/watch?v=vwDhiniWd4k&t=1s.

16. https://www.facebook.com/BUSTOPTV; https://www.youtube.com/@BUSTOPTV.

17. On the media environment in Zimbabwe and the importance of platforms such as YouTube and Facebook, see Trust Matsilele and Wishes Tendayi Mututwa, "The Aesthetics of 'Laughing at Power' in an African Cybersphere," in *The Politics of Laughter in the Social Media Age: Perspectives from the Global South*, ed. Shepherd Mpofu (New York: Palgrave Macmillan, 2021), 23–41).

18. Mbongeni Jonny Msimanga, Gibson Ncube, and Promise Mkwananzi, "Political Satire and the Mediation of the Zimbabwean Crisis in the Era of the 'New Dispensation': The Case of MAGAMBA TV," in Mpofu, ed., *Politics of Laughter*, 49. On social media dissidents, see Albert Sharra and Trust Matsilele, "This Is a Laughing Matter: Social Media as a Sphere of Trolling Power in Malawi and Zimbabwe," in Mpofu, ed., *Politics of Laughter*, 113; Daniel Hammett, Laura Martin, and Izuu Nwankwọ, *Humour and Politics in Africa: Beyond Resistance* (Bristol: Bristol University Press, 2023), 14; Florence Zivaishe Madenga, "Mimicking Power: Visualizing Satire as Journalism in Zimbabwe," *European Journal of Humour Research* 12, no. 3 (2024): 10. Also see Jacquelin Kataneksza, "Zimbabwean Twitter Is Shifting Politics," *Africa Is a Country*, October 11, 2018, https://africasacountry.com/2018/10/social-media-and-politics-in-zimbabwe.

19. For example, "Big House vs, Small House," *YouTube*, uploaded by BUSTOP TV, July 16, 2021, https://www.youtube.com/watch?v=qPfHByr2VdY&t=15s.

20. "Sadza Rababa," *YouTube*, uploaded by BUSTOP TV, March 14, 2019, https://www.youtube.com/watch?v=baiUsV2p-uQ.

21. "All Female Parliament," *YouTube*, uploaded by BUSTOP TV, October 13, 2020, https://www.youtube.com/watch?v=S6kBg-gaoCQ. Note that this video was sponsored by the Women's Academy for Leadership and Politics Excellence (WALAPE), as seen before the end-credits. "John Vuli Gate," *YouTube*, uploaded by BUSTOP TV, October 18, 2020, https://www.youtube.com/watch?v=4dxpsQ1O-ao, was sponsored by the Zimbabwe Women's Bureau. There are many other such sponsorships.

22. "Bogus Lawyer," *YouTube*, uploaded by BUSTOP TV, October 19, 2023, https://www.youtube.com/watch?v=3y8Carjw4dg.

23. "KuPassport," *YouTube*, uploaded by BUSTOP TV, August 20, 2020, https://www.youtube.com/watch?v=kGjlc8sDDyw.

24. "Order & Law:Special Unit," *YouTube*, uploaded by BUSTOP TV, July 20, 2016, https://www.youtube.com/watch?v=LZJtXQOVUKg.

25. "Order & Law:Special Unit," 0:10–0:14, 0:14–0:20, 0:38–0:42.

26. "Order & Law:Special Unit," 0:19–0:22, 0:25–0:42.

27. Allison, "'You are Too Young.'"

28. "Order & Law:Special Unit," 1:04–1:07.

29. For a discussion of the charge that Zimbabweans are politically passive see Wendy Willems, "Beyond Dramatic Revolutions and Grand Rebellions: Everyday Forms of Resistance during the 'Zimbabwe Crisis,'" *Comminicare* 29 (2010): 1–17.

30. "Order & Law:Special Unit," 1:50–2:00.

31. This criticism is made by Zimbabweans themselves. See C. Luthuli Mhlahlo, "Introduction: '(. . .) By Reflection, by Some Other Things': Tracking, Reflecting, and Taking Responsibility for the Zimbabwean Crisis," in *The Zimbabwean Crisis: Perspectives, Paradoxes, and Prospects (1997–2017)*, ed. C. Luthuli Mhlahlo and Levar Lamar Smith (New York: Peter Lang, 2020), 6.

32. Nyore Madzianike, "Has Comedienne's Case Mojo Gone Yet?" *Herald*, August 31, 2019, https://www.herald.co.zw/has-comediennes-case-mojo-gone-yet/.

33. Sabelo J. Ndlovu-Gatsheni, "Introduction: Mugabeism and Entanglements of History, Politics, and Power in the Making of Zimbabwe," in *Mugabeism? History, Politics, and Power in Zimbabwe*, ed. Sabelo J. Ndlovu-Gatsheni (New York: Palgrave Macmillan, 2015), 7. On the suppression of dissent also see Daniel Hammett, "Resistance, Power, and Geopolitics in Zimbabwe," *Area* 43, no. 2 (2011): 202–210, https://www.jstor.org/stable/41240486.

34. Nkwazi Nkuzi Mhango, "Mugabe the Hero Who Became a Villain: The Tragicomedy of the Legacy of Mugabe," in *The End of an Era? Robert Mugabe and a Conflicting Legacy*, ed. Munyaradzi Mawere, Ngonidzashe Marongwe, and Fidelis Duri (Bamenda, Cameroon: Langaa Research and Publishing, 2018), 353, https://muse.jhu.edu/book/62720-er-; Ngonidzashe Marongwe and Munyaradzi Mawere, "Robert Mugabe's Conflicted Legacy and the End of an Era?" in Mawere, Marongwe, and Duri, eds., *End of an Era?* 6.

35. Mhango, "Mugabe the Hero," 356.

36. Sabelo J. Ndlovu-Gatsheni and James Muzondidya, "Introduction: Redemptive or Grotesque Nationalism in the Postcolony," in *Redemptive or Grotesque Nationalism? Rethinking Contemporary Politics in Zimbabwe*, ed. Sabelo J. Ndlovu-Gatsheni and James Muzondidya (Oxford: Peter Lang, 2011), 10.

37. Ndlovu-Gatsheni and Muzondidya, "Introduction," 1–2. A similar decolonial line is taken by Gorden Moyo in "Mugabe's Neo-Sultanist Rule: Beyond the Veil of Pan-Africanism," in *Mugabeism? History, Politics, and Power in Zimbabwe*, ed. Sabelo J. Ndlovu-Gatsheni (New York: Palgrave Macmillan, 2015), 61.

38. This massacre is recounted in *Breaking the Silence, Building True Peace: A Report on the Disturbances in Matabeleland and the Midlands,*

1980–1988, Catholic Commission for Justice and Peace & Legal Resources Foundation, 1999, https://davidcoltart.com/wp-content/uploads/2006/10/breakingthesilence.pdf.

39. Moyo, "Mugabe's Neo-Sultanist Rule," 63.

40. Jeremy Youde, "Why Look East? Zimbabwean Foreign Policy and China," *Africa Today* 53, no. 3 (2007): 3–19, https://www.jstor.org/stable/4187790.

41. Willems, "Beyond Dramatic Revolutions," 7.

42. On the anti-West dimensions of ZANU-PF rule, see Marongwe and Mawere, "Robert Mugabe's Conflicted Legacy," 10, 25; and Eric Mazango, "Media Games and Shifting of Spaces for Political Communication in Zimbabwe," *Westminster Papers in Communication and Culture* 2 (2017): 39, 41, 43, https://doi.org/10.16997/wpcc.40. Also see Moyo, "Mugabe's Neo-Sultanist Rule," 67.

43. Ndlovu-Gatsheni and Muzondidya, "Introduction," 13.

44. Marongwe and Mawere, "Robert Mugabe's Conflicted Legacy," p12.

45. Genius Tevera and Golden Maunganidze, "From Being a Man of the People to a Senile Captive Dictator? Capturing the Different Personalities of Robert Mugabe through Play and History," in Mawere, Marongwe, and Duri, eds., *End of an Era?* 445–446.

46. Daragh Murray et al., "The Chilling Effects of Surveillance and Human Rights: Insights from Qualitative Research in Uganda and Zimbabwe," *Journal of Human Rights Practice* 16, no. 1 (2024): 409, https://academic.oup.com/jhrp/article/16/1/397/7234270#460254894.

47. See Paul Moorcraft, *Mugabe's War Machine: Saving or Savaging Zimbabwe?* (Barnsley, South Yorkshire: Pen & Sword Military, 2011); also Michael Bratton, *Power Politics in Zimbabwe* (London: Lynne Rienner, 2014).

48. Badala Tachilisa Balule, "Insult Laws: A Challenge to Media Freedom in the SADC's Fledgling Democracies?" *Comparative and International Law Journal of Southern Africa* 41, no. 3 (2008): 407. Also see Mazango, "Media Games," 38, who notes that these policies were a continuation of Rhodesian policies.

49. Jamal Jafari, "Attacks from Within: Zimbabwe's Assault on Basic Freedoms through Legislation," *Human Rights Brief* 10, no. 3 (2003): 7, https://digitalcommons.wcl.american.edu/cgi/viewcontent.cgi?article=1416&context=hrbrief; Balule, "Insult Laws," 409.

50. Jafari, "Attacks from Within," 7.

51. C. Luthuli Mhlahlo, "Operation Restore Legacy: The Coup d'État That Was but Was Not," in Mhlahlo and Smith, eds., *The Zimbabwean Crisis*, 261–284.

52. "Zimbabwe Comedian Gonyeti 'Abducted and Beaten.'"

53. Msimanga, Neube, and Mkwananzi, "Political Satire and the Mediation of the Zimbabwean Crisis"; Källstig, "Humouring the State?" 147–148.

54. Ignatius Banda, "In Zimbabwe, There Is Freedom of Speech, but No Freedom after the Speech," *InterPress Service News Agency*, January 19, 2021, https://www.ipsnews.net/2021/01/in-zimbabwe-there-is-freedom-of-speech-but-no-freedom-after-the-speech. Hammett, Martin, and Nwankwọ, *Humour and Politics in Africa*, 95. The line is attributed to various comedians; see, e.g., "Zambezi News: Brightening Up the Gloom of Zimbabwean Politics," in *Laughing Out Loud: The Politics of Satire in Africa* (Cape Town: Heinrich-Böll-Stiftung, 2016), 14, https://za.boell.org/sites/default/files/perspectives_april_2_2016_web.pdf.

55. Jeffrey Moyo, "Comedians Standing Up to 'Repression' in Zimbabwe," *Anadolu Ajansi*, February 18, 2021, https://www.aa.com.tr/en/africa/comedians-standing-up-to-repression-in-zimbabwe/2149424.

56. Källstig, "Laughing in the Face of Danger: Performativity and Resistance in Zimbabwean Stand-up Comedy," *Global Society* 35 (2021), https://pure.manchester.ac.uk/ws/files/178100550/AAM_Laughing_in_the_Face_of_Danger_Performativity_and_Resistance_in_Zimbabwean_stand_up_comedy_5.pdf; also see Hammett, Martin, and Nwankwọ, *Humour and Politics in Africa*, 39.

57. See Jenny Kuhlmann, "Zimbabwean Diaspora Politics and the Power of Laughter: Humour as a Tool for Political Communication, Criticism, and Protest," *Journal of African Media Studies* 4, no. 3 (2012): 295–314.

58. Kennedy Nyavaya, "Carl Joshua Ncube Receives Death Threats," *The Standard*, April 17, 2016, https://www.thestandard.co.zw/2016/04/17/carl-joshua-ncube-receives-death-threats.

59. https://magambatv.co.zw/; https://www.youtube.com/@magambatv.

60. Madenga, "Mimicking Power," 10.

61. Hammett, Martin, and Nwankwọ, *Humour and Politics in Africa*, 94–95; "Zambezi News: Brightening Up the Gloom of Zimbabwean Politics," 15.

62. Ashleigh Harris, "'The Diary of a Country in Crisis:' Zimbabwean Censorship and Adaptive Cultural Forms," *Journal of Southern African Studies* 47, no. 5 (2021): 787, https://www.tandfonline.com/doi/epdf/10.1080/03057070.2021.1947025.

63. Harries, "Diary," 787.

64. The fact that she was a woman, some have suggested, might have added to the incentive to punish and humiliate her; see Madenga, "Mimicking Power," 23. On women in Zimbabwean comedy, see Amanda Källstig, "Women

Stand-Up Comedians in Zimbabwe Talk about Sex—and Patriarchy," *Mail & Guardian*, May 21, 2021, https://mg.co.za/friday/2021-05-21-women-stand-up-comedians-in-zimbabwe-talk-about-sex-and-patriarchy/.

65. Jeffrey Moyo, "Politics: No Laughing Matter in Poverty-Hit Zimbabwe," *Reuters*, May 8, 2019, https://www.reuters.com/article/world/politics-no-laughing-matter-in-poverty-hit-zimbabwe-idUSKCN1SE1PV/.

66. Moyo, "Comedians Standing Up to 'Repression.'"

67. See Bhekizulu Betaphi Tshuma, Lungile Tshuma, and Nonhlanhla Ndlovu, "Humour, Politics, and Mnangagwa's Presidency: An Analysis of Readers' Comments in Online News Websites," in Mpofu, ed., *Politics of Laughter*, 94.

68. Moyo, "Comedians Standing Up to 'Repression.'"

69. Abdi Latif Dahir, "Zimbabwe's Comedians Are Ready to Deliver Satire for the Post-Mugabe Era," *Quartz*, February 8, 2018, https://qz.com/africa/1202465/zimbabwe-comedy-after-mugabe-carl-joshua-ncube-clive-chigubu-in-the-emmerson-mnangagwa-era.

70. Källstig, "Laughing in the Face of Danger," 12.

71. "Tsamba Yekuendesa Kumba," *YouTube*, 1:44, uploaded by BUSTOP TV, August 15, 2020, https://www.youtube.com/watch?v=Uiho2YLb2iQ.

72. "Ghost Worker Drax International," *YouTube*, uploaded by BUSTOP TV, June 14, 2020, https://www.youtube.com/watch?v=XfuvtFFQuDw. This video is not translated or captioned in English, so we take it on the word of Matsilele and Mututwa, "Aesthetics of 'Laughing at Power,'" 33. For more information regarding the Drax International scandal, see "Mnangagwa Links to Drax International Emerge, President Begged for $60M from Dodgy Firm," *New Zimbabwe*, June 16, 2020, https://www.newzimbabwe.com/mnangagwa-links-to-drax-international-emerge-president-begged-for-60m-from-dodgy-firm.

73. "Patriotic Porisi," *YouTube*, 1:51–2:30, uploaded by BUSTOP TV, April 14, 2021, https://www.youtube.com/watch?v=juvjpsxQSoQ. Interestingly, this video seems to advocate repeal of the Patriotic Bill, which tamps down on freedom of speech. For more on the Patriotic Bill, see "Zimbabwe: Parliament's Passing of 'Patriotic Bill' is a Grave Assault on the Human Rights," *Amnesty International*, June 9, 2023, https://www.amnesty.org/en/latest/news/2023/06/zimbabwe-parliaments-passing-of-patriotic-bill-is-a-grave-assault-on-the-human-rights/.

74. For women's advocacy groups, sponsors include Orange the World, (https://www.unwomen.org/en/what-we-do/ending-violence-against-women/unite/orange-the-world) and World Leading Schools Association (WLSA). Civic organizations and sponsors include COTRAD, Legal Resources Foundation (LRF), Zim Peace Project, and Transparency International Zimbabwe.

For videos sponsored by COTRAD, see for example "Mr Brown Chinja MaGear," *YouTube*, uploaded by BUSTOP TV, August 21, 2023, https://www.youtube.com/watch?v=REFKkR16OF0; and "BUSTOP TV—GONYETI AND MAGI—STATE OF ECONOMY—Supported by COTRAD," *YouTube*, uploaded by COTRAD Zimbabwe, June 10, 2019, https://www.youtube.com/watch?v=boc5YlkrmcU. For videos sponsored by Zim Peace Project, see "Pese pese Pfuti," *YouTube*, uploaded by BUSTOP TV, August 31, 2020, https://www.youtube.com/watch?v=HlNk79hcIGg.

75. International NGOs include She-Unity Support, International Media Support (IMS), and Actionaid. For examples of videos sponsored by these groups, see "FUSHIRAI MAKOMBA," *YouTube*, uploaded by BUSTOP TV, December 7, 2022, https://www.youtube.com/watch?v=unKFT7LKJww (Actionaid); "Madzibaba Manu," *YouTube*, uploaded by BUSTOP TV, July 26, 2021, https://www.youtube.com/watch?v=jCjcZ5bOmX8 (IMS); and "Kugara Nhaka Kuona Dzevamwe Episode 13," *YouTube*, uploaded by BUSTOP TV, December 9, 2020, https://www.youtube.com/watch?v=QIo-mozK4-s (She-Unity Support);

76. For videos sponsored by these groups, see "Madzibaba Manu," uploaded by BUSTOP TV, July 26, 2021, *YouTube*, https://www.youtube.com/watch?v=jCjcZ5bOmX8 (IMS); "Tsamba Yekufambisa Chitown neNorton," uploaded by BUSTOP TV, July 20, 2021, *YouTube*, https://www.youtube.com/watch?y=uORs_OU_Fv8 (EU); "PFEEka MASK," *YouTube*, uploaded by BUSTOP TV, July 1, 2021, https://www.youtube.com/watch?v=WZyReHfGT_M (UNDP, Oxfam); "Child Abuse," *YouTube*, uploaded by BUSTOP TV, April 20, 2021, https://www.youtube.com/watch?v=H_vlhiL1JYI (USAID, PEPFAR); "KuPassport" (IRI); "Mukadzi Anoweta Pfeka Mask," *YouTube*, uploaded by BUSTOP TV, June 4, 2020, https://www.youtube.com/watch?v=L3I9qKdzsjM (EU, UKAID, UNDP).

77. Allison, "'You Are Too Young.'"

CHAPTER NINE

1. Seth Rogen and Evan Goldberg, dirs., *The Interview* (Columbia Pictures, 2014), 58:28–58:32, 58:33, https://www.amazon.com/Interview-Seth-Rogen/dp/B00RNRD7Y4.

2. Kei Koga, "The Anatomy of North Korea's Foreign Policy Formulation," *North Korean Review* 5, no. 2 (2009): 23, http://www.jstor.org/stable/43908714.

3. Tony Shaw and Tricia Jenkins, "An Act of War? *The Interview* Affair, the Sony Hack, and the Hollywood-Washington Power Nexus Today," *Journal of American Studies* 53 (2019): 7.

4. *The Interview*, Columbia Pictures; Jeremy Helligar, "Eminem and the F-Word: Why Does Rap Still Tolerate Homophobia?" *Variety*, September 18, 2018, https://variety.com/2018/music/opinion/eminem-and-the-f-word-why-does-rap-still-tolerate-homophobia-1202947049/.

5. David Robb, "Sony Hack: A Timeline," *Deadline*, December 22, 2014, https://deadline.com/2014/12/sony-hack-timeline-any-pascal-the-interview-north-korea-1201325501/; Ben Buchanan, *The Hacker and the State: Cyber Attacks and the New Normal of Geopolitics* (Cambridge, MA: Harvard University Press, 2020), 185; Steve Kovach, "Sony Could Lose $100 Million by Pulling 'The Interview,'" *Business Insider*, December 17, 2014, https://www.businessinsider.com/sony-the-interview-loss-2014-12; "Sony's New Movies Leak Online Following Hack Attack," *NBC*, November 30, 2014, https://www.nbcnews.com/tech/tech-news/sonys-new-movies-leak-online-following-hack-attack-n258511; Jung H. Pak, "The Education of Kim Jong-un," *Brookings Institute*, February 2018, https://www.brookings.edu/articles/the-education-of-kim-jong-un/; "Sony's New Movies Leak Online Following Hack Attack," *NBC*, November 30, 2014, https://www.nbcnews.com/tech/tech-news/sonys-new-movies-leak-online-following-hack-attack-n258511;

6. Robb, "Sony Hack"; Buchanan, *Hacker and the State*, 179; Mark Seal, "An Exclusive Look at Sony's Hacking Saga," *Vanity Fair*, February 4, 2015, https://www.vanityfair.com/hollywood/2015/02/sony-hacking-seth-rogen-evan-goldberg.

7. David Robb, "The Sony Hack One Year Later: Just Who Are the Guardians of Peace?" *Deadline*, November 24, 2015, https://deadline.com/2015/11/sony-hack-guardians-of-peace-one-year-anniversary-1201636491/.

8. "North Korea Threatens War on US over Kim Jong-un Movie," *BBC*, June 26, 2014, https://www.bbc.com/news/world-asia-28014069.

9. Shaw and Jenkins, "An Act of War?" 20; Buchanan, *Hacker and the State*, 178, 181.

10. Seal, "Exclusive Look at Sony's Hacking Saga."

11. Choe Sang-Hun, "Rodman Gives Details on Trip to North Korea," *New York Times*, September 9, 2013, https://www.nytimes.com/2013/09/10/world/asia/rodman-gives-details-on-trip-to-north-korea.html.

12. Tatiana Siegel, "Seth Rogen to Direct, Star in 'The Interview' for Columbia Pictures (Exclusive)," *Hollywood Reporter*, March 21, 2013, https://www.hollywoodreporter.com/news/general-news/seth-rogen-direct-star-interview-430224/.

13. "*The Interview*—Official Teaser Trailer," *YouTube*, uploaded by Sony Pictures Entertainment, June 11, 2014, https://www.youtube.com/watch?v=Mj3uHftd5FQ.

14. For a discussion of the impact of these movies on North Korean leaders, see Victor Cha's interview with VICE News, https://www.youtube.com/watch?v=GVWyWKdhS5s; Joohee Cho, "In Koreas, Latest Bond Movie Provokes Outcry, Calls for Boycott," *Washington Post*, December 26, 2002, https://www.washingtonpost.com/archive/politics/2002/12/26/in-koreas-latest-bond-movie-provokes-outcry-calls-for-boycott/b095bdcf-b0ed-4650-9f6d-b6d414905a24/.

15. Steve Erickson, "Voyeurs in the Hermit Kingdom: *The Interview* and Other Films on North Korea," *Cinéaste*, 40, no. 2 (2015): 38, https://www.jstor.org/stable/43500785; Koga, "Anatomy of North Korea's Foreign Policy Formulation," 21.

16. Erickson, "Voyeurs in the Hermit Kingdom," 40.

17. Erickson, "Voyeurs in the Hermit Kingdom," 39.

18. "*The Interview*—Official Teaser Trailer."

19. Seal, "Exclusive Look at Sony's Hacking Saga."

20. "*The Interview*—Official Teaser Trailer," 0:16–0:19, 0:33–0:40, 0:40–0:44.

21. "*The Interview*—Official Teaser Trailer," 1:02.

22. Shaw and Jenkins, "An Act of War?" 15–16.

23. *The Interview*, Columbia Pictures, 1:41:00–1:41:14.

24. Shaw and Jenkins, "An Act of War?" 15–16.

25. Seal, "Exclusive Look at Sony's Hacking Saga."

26. Jennifer M. Wood, "Dan Sterling, *The Interview* Writer at the Center of the Sony Hack, Speaks Out," *Esquire*, December 17, 2014, https://www.esquire.com/entertainment/movies/interviews/a31646/dan-sterling-the-interview-sony-hack/.

27. Shaw and Jenkins, "An Act of War?" 2.

28. Seal, "Exclusive Look at Sony's Hacking Saga."

29. Seal, "Exclusive Look at Sony's Hacking Saga."

30. Shaw and Jenkins, "An Act of War?" 2.

31. "DPRK FM Spokesman Blasts U.S. Moves to Hurt Dignity of Supreme Leadership of DPRK," *Korean Central News Agency*, June 25, 2014, http://www.kcna.co.jp/item/2014/201406/news25/20140625-23ee.html. Around the same time, in an interview, Kim Myong-chol, executive director of the Center for North Korea–U.S. Peace, lambasted the film: Julian Ryall, "North Korea Slams US Film *The Interview* about Kim Jong-un," *Telegraph*, June 20, 2014, https://www.telegraph.co.uk/news/worldnews/asia/northkorea

/10914088/North-Korea-slams-US-film-The-Interview-about-Kim-Jong-un .html.

32. Victor Cha, "Statement before the Senate Committee on Foreign Relations Subcommittee on East Asia, the Pacific, and International Cybersecurity Policy: Assessing the North Korea Threat and U.S. Policy: Strategic Patience or Effective Deterrence?" *Center for Strategic and International Studies*, October 7, 2015, https://www.jstor.org/stable/pdf/resrep37707.pdf, 4.

33. *The Interview*, Columbia Pictures, 53:15–54:10; 57:44–57:50; 59:18–59:32.

34. *The Interview*, Columbia Pictures, 1:16–54–1:17–32. On the character of Sook see Sunny Xiang, "About Face: The Vicissitudes of Humanizing North Korea in *The Interview*," *Asian/American (Anti-)Bodies*, ed. Christopher Fan, *Post45*, December 28, 2015, https://post45.org/2015/12/about-face-the-vicissitudes-of-humanizing-north-korea-in-the-interview/.

35. *The Interview*, Columbia Pictures, 1:14:23–1:14:34, 1:14:37–1:14:42, 1:14:45–1:15:02.

36. Koga, "Anatomy of North Korea's Foreign Policy Formulation," 27.

37. Patrick Derochie, "The Driving Factor: Songun's Impact on North Korean Foreign Policy," *International Affairs Review*, George Washington University, June 15, 2020, https://www.iar-gwu.org/print-archive/the-driving-factornbspemsongunems-impact-on-north-korean-foreign-policy.

38. Siegfried Hecker, "Lessons Learned from the North Korean Nuclear Crises," *Daedalus*, Winter 2010, 53, https://nonproliferation.org/wp-content /uploads/3022/10/2009-hecker-daedalus.pdf.

39. Pak, "Education of Kim Jong-un."

40. Shaw and Jenkins, "An Act of War?" 25.

41. On North Korea developing its cyber capacities, see Daniel A. Pinkston, "North Korea's Objectives and Activities in Cyberspace," *Asia Policy* 15, no. 2 (2020): 76, https://www.jstor.org/stable/pdf/27023903.pdf; Buchanan, *Hacker and the State*, 169; Hyeong-wook Boo, "An Assessment of North Korean Cyber Threats," *Journal of East Asian Affairs* 31, no. 1 (2017): 108, https://www.jstor .org/stable/pdf/44321274.pdf.

42. Boo, "Assessment of North Korean Cyber Threats," 104–105.

43. Stephen Haggard and Jon R. Lindsay, "North Korea and the Sony Hack: Exporting Instability through Cyberspace," *East-West Center*, 2015, 3, https://www.jstor.org/stable/resrep06456.

44. Mark Shilling, "'The Interview' to Have Only Limited Release in Asia," *Variety*, December 10, 2014, https://variety.com/2014/film/news /the-interview-to-have-only-limited-release-in-asia-1201376806/.

45. Max Fisher, "Here's the Real Reason North Korea Hacked Sony. It Has Nothing To Do with *The Interview*," *VOX*, December 19, 2014, https://www.vox.com/2014/12/19/7421535/the-real-reason-north-korea-would-hack-sony-its-not-the-interview.

46. Seal, "Exclusive Look at Sony's Hacking Saga."

47. Seal, "Exclusive Look at Sony's Hacking Saga."

48. Barack Obama, "Remarks by the President in Year-End Press Conference," speech, James S. Brady Press Briefing Room, White House, Washington, DC, December 19, 2014, https://obamawhitehouse.archives.gov/the-press-office/2014/12/19/remarks-president-year-end-press-conference.

49. David E. Sanger and Michael S. Schmidt, "More Sanctions on North Korea after Sony Case," *New York Times*, January 2, 2015, https://www.nytimes.com/2015/01/03/us/in-response-to-sony-attack-us-levies-sanctions-on-10-north-koreans.html.

50. Ben Jacobs, "Trump Professes Love for Kim and Hate for Kavanaugh Torment in Freewheeling Speech," *Guardian*, September 30, 2018, https://www.theguardian.com/us-news/2018/sep/30/trump-love-kim-nasty-democrat-kavanaugh-west-virginia.

51. The episode is nicely recounted by Timothy Garton Ash in *Free Speech: Ten Principles for a Connected World* (New Haven, CT: Yale University Press, 2016), 62–72. Eyder Peralta, "What We Know about 'Sam Bacile,' the Man Behind the Muhammad Movie," *NPR*, September 12, 2012, https://www.npr.org/sections/thetwo-way/2012/09/12/161003427/what-we-know-about-sam-bacile-the-man-behind-the-muhammad-movie.

52. "Afghan Protests Continue against Qur'an Burning," *Guardian*, April 4, 2011, https://www.theguardian.com/world/2011/apr/04/quran-burning-protests-continue-afghanistan.

53. David D. Kirkpatrick and Steven Lee Meyers, "Libya Attack Brings Challenges for U.S.," *New York Times*, September 12, 2012, https://www.nytimes.com/2012/09/13/world/middleeast/us-envoy-to-libya-is-reported-killed.html.

54. Nic Robertson, Paul Cruickshank, and Tim Lister, "Pro–al Qaeda Group Seen behind Deadly Benghazi Attack," *CNN*, September 13, 2012, https://www.cnn.com/2012/09/12/world/africa/libya-attack-jihadists/index.html.

55. "Remarks by the President to the UN General Assembly," speech, United Nations Headquarters, New York, September 25, 2012, https://obamawhitehouse.archives.gov/the-press-office/2012/09/25/remarks-president-un-general-assembly.

56. Obama, "Remarks by the President in Year-End Press Conference."

57. Steven Groves and Brett D. Schaefer, "Obama's Appeasement," *Heritage Foundation*, September 19, 2012, https://www.heritage.org/global-politics/commentary/obamas-appeasement; Nick Gillespie, "Obama, Who Tried to Censor 'Innocence of Muslims' Vid, Says Sony Shouldn't Have Pulled *The Interview*," *Reason*, December 19, 2014, https://reason.com/2014/12/19/obama-who-tried-to-censor-innocence-of-m/.

58. Byron Tau, "White House Asked YouTube to 'Review' Anti-Muslim Film," *Politico*, September 14, 2012, https://www.politico.com/blogs/politico44/2012/09/white-house-asked-youtube-to-review-anti-muslim-film-135586. Critics argued that the goal of this request was in fact censorship under the guise of mitigating security risks in Benghazi: Jesse Walker, "The Obama Administration Pressures YouTube to Remove Video," *Reason*, September 14, 2012, https://reason.com/2012/09/14/the-obama-administration-pressures-youtu/; "White House Contacted YouTube about Anti-Muslim Film during Benghazi Attack, Congressman Says," *Hollywood Reporter*, May 23, 2014, https://www.hollywoodreporter.com/news/politics-news/white-house-contacted-youtube-anti-706839/.

59. Groves and Schaefer, "Obama's Appeasement."

60. "Anti-Islam Filmmaker Nakoula Basseley Nakoula Arrested on Probation Violation, Detained without Bail," *ABC News*, September 27, 2012, https://abcnews.go.com/Blotter/anti-islam-filmmaker-nakoula-basseley-nakoula-arrested-probation/story?id=17343351.

61. "First Amendment Affront," *Wall Street Journal*, October 1, 2012, https://www.wsj.com/articles/SB10000872396390444712904578024682007326890.

62. "US Anti-Islam Filmmaker Nakoula Basseley Nakoula Jailed," *BBC*, November 7, 2012, https://www.bbc.com/news/world-us-canada-20247187. On the harsh sentence, see Rich Lowry, "The Benghazi Patsy," *Politico*, May 9, 2013, https://www.politico.com/story/2013/05/the-benghazi-patsy-091101: "A violation of probation . . . doesn't typically lead to more jail time unless it involves an offense that would be worth prosecuting in its own right under federal standards."

63. Shaw and Jenkins, "An Act of War?" 6.

64. *The Interview* was the first movie written by Sterling that went to production, he revealed to *Esquire*. Wood, "Dan Sterling, *The Interview* Writer."

65. "How 'The Interview' Screenwriter Dan Sterling Became 'The Guy That Brought Down Sony'," *LAist*, December 14, 2014, https://laist.com/shows/the-frame/how-the-interview-screenwriter-dan-sterling-became-the-guy-that-brought-down-sony.

66. Wood, "Dan Sterling, *The Interview* Writer."

67. Mike Ryan, "'The Interview' Review: A Movie Not Nearly as Interesting as Its Controversy," *ScreenCrush*, December 18, 2014, https://screencrush.com/the-interview-review/; Peter Bradshaw, "*The Interview* Review—Rogen and Franco Soon Run out of Laughs," *Guardian*, February 15, 2014, https://www.theguardian.com/film/2015/feb/06/the-interview-review-franco-rogen; Geoffrey Macnab, "*The Interview*, Film Review: Misconceived, Tasteless, and Only Very Intermittently Funny," *The Interview*, February 12, 2015, https://www.the-independent.com/arts-entertainment/films/reviews/the-interview-film-review-misconceived-tasteless-and-only-very-intermittently-funny-a171781.html.

68. "Seth Rogen & Evan Goldberg Interview (Full Episode) | The Tim Ferriss Show (Podcast)," *YouTube*, 6:30–7:00, uploaded by Tim Ferriss, October 8, 2015, https://www.youtube.com/watch?app=desktop&v=7g06kP4AoyY&t=929s.

CONCLUSION

1. Tiffany May, "She Mocked Men's Bluster. Then Came the Complaints," *New York Times*, December 30, 2020, https://www.nytimes.com/2020/12/30/world/asia/male-confidence-comedian-china.html.

2. Tauqeer Abbas, "Israeli Comedian's 'Marriage Proposal' to Saudi Crown Prince Goes Viral on Arab Social Media," Pakistan Shia News Agency, 2021, https://pakistan.shafaqna.com/EN/76665.

3. Jason Zinoman, "Chiseled Cheekbones and Comic Chops: Why We Don't Like Our Stand-Ups Hunky," *New York Times*, November 15, 2023, https://www.nytimes.com/2023/11/15/arts/chiseled-cheekbones-and-comic-chops.html; Aja Romano, "What Matt Rife's Baffling Netflix Special Tells Us about Comedy," *Vox*, November 29, 2023, https://www.vox.com/culture/23980945/who-is-matt-rife-netflix-special-natural-selection-backlash-controversy-tiktok.

4. Such comedians include Britain's Frankie Boyle, the Spaniard David Suárez, the Frenchman Patrick Timsit, and America's own Shane Gillis: Peter Walker, "Frankie Boyle Meets His Match in Mother of Down's Syndrome Child," *Guardian*, April 8, 2010, https://www.theguardian.com/society/2010/apr/08/frankie-boyle-downs-syndrome; Álvaro Palazón, "David Suárez, el cómico despedido por un 'chiste' sobre el síndrome de Down: 'Ha sido una semana asquerosa,'" *ElHuffPost*, April 25, 2019, https://www.huffingtonpost.es/entry/david-suarez-el-comico-despedido-por-un-chiste-sobre-el-sindrome

-de-down-tengo-tuits-mucho-peores_es_5cc0773fe4b01b6b3efb6442.html; David Dufresne, "Dernier acte inattendu pour le sketch de Timsit sur les trisomiques," *Libération*, January 7, 1999, https://www.liberation.fr/societe/1999/01/07/dernier-acte-inattendu-pour-le-sketch-de-timsit-sur-les-trisomiques-conciliation-entre-le-comique-et_263050/; Michael Boyle, "Shane Gillis Bombs on 'SNL' with Down Syndrome and Gay Jokes," *Yahoo!*, February 25, 2024, https://www.yahoo.com/entertainment/shane-gillis-bombs-snl-down-052346849.html.

5. CD Nuckols, "10 'Canceled' Comedians Who Keep Dropping Comedy Specials," *MovieWeb*, October 11, 2024, https://movieweb.com/canceled-comedians-recent-comedy-specials/.

6. "Ken Jeong: You Complete Me, Ho," *Netflix*, February 14, 2019, https://www.netflix.com/title/80244853, 00:00–01:15.

7. Ronald Collins and David Skover, *The Trials of Lenny Bruce: The Fall and Rise of an American Icon* (Naperville, IL: Sourcebooks MediaFusion, 2002), 60, 305.

8. "Blasphemy and the Original Meaning of the First Amendment," *Harvard Law Review* 135 (2021): 690–710, https://harvardlawreview.org/print/vol-135/blasphemy-and-the-original-meaning-of-the-first-amendment.

9. See Morgan Ellithorpe, Sarah Esralew, and Robert Holbert, "Putting the Self in Self-Deprecation: When Deprecating Humor about Minorities Is Acceptable," *Humor: International Journal of Humor Research* 27, no. 3 (2014): 401–422, https://scholarshare.temple.edu/server/api/core/bitstreams/f3110fa8-1a76-4f3a-a7ab-31dd291afe5f/content.

10. Interestingly, Ken Jeong got into a mini-controversy for his use of "yellow voice" in his comedy. The coalition of the outraged were Asian Americans who found his material stereotypical and self-hating. Then again, he experienced relatively little in the way of consequences for his trespass. Predictably, he even recycled their anger into his special and worked in some jabs at his critics. See Christopher Huang, "Ken Jeong Should Know Better," *Medium*, March 3, 2019, https://christopherhuang.medium.com/ken-jeong-should-know-better-c9c85f91d3a4; "Ken Jeong and His Intentions and Impact Regarding Racial Representation in Mainstream Media," *Asian American Popular Culture: WQ17*, February 20, 2017, https://asianamericanpopularculturew17.wordpress.com/2017/02/20/ken-jeong-and-his-intentions-and-impact-regarding-racial-representation-in-mainstream-media/.

11. "'Taking Offence Has Been Elevated to a Much-Loved National Indoor Sport,'" *Times of India*, January 30, 2021, https://timesofindia.indiatimes.com

/india/taking-offence-has-been-elevated-to-a-much-loved-national-indoor-sport/articleshow/80595341.cms.

12. Zapiro, "Letter to the South African Human Rights Commission: A Response to Complaints Regarding My Cartoon," *Critical African Studies* 2 (2010): 29, https://doi.org/10.1080/20407211.2010.10530756.

13. "France's Macron: I Won't Condemn Cartoons of Prophet Mohammad," *Reuters*, September 1, 2020, https://www.reuters.com/article/world/frances-macron-i-wont-condemn-cartoons-of-prophet-mohammad-idUSKBN25ToAX/.

14. Sheryl Ross, "POTUS Stand-Up: The White House Correspondents' Dinner," in *Comedy and the Politics of Representation: Mocking the Weak*, ed. Helen Davies and Sarah Ilott (London: Palgrave Macmillain, 2018), 241.

15. Nardine Saad, "Al Sharpton: Larry Wilmore's Calling Obama the 'N-Word' Was in 'Bad Taste,'" *Los Angeles Times*, April 30, 2016, https://www.latimes.com/entertainment/envelope/cotown/la-et-ct-whcd-sharpton-larry-wilmore-20160430-story.html.

16. Tom Kludt, "Trump to Snub White House Correspondents' Dinner for Third Year in a Row," *CNN*, April 5, 2019, https://www.cnn.com/2019/04/05/media/donald-trump-skip-white-house-correspondents-dinner/index.html; Emily Stewart, "Wonder What Michelle Wolf Said to Make Everyone So Mad? Read It Here," *Vox*, April 30, 2018, https://www.vox.com/policy-and-politics/2018/4/30/17301436/michelle-wolf-speech-transcript-white-house-correspondents-dinner-sarah-huckabee-sanders.

17. Chloe Veltman, "White House Correspondents' Dinner Cancels Comedian Amber Ruffin's Appearance," *NPR*, March 29, 2025, https://www.npr.org/2025/03/29/nx-s1-5344487/white-house-correspondents-dinner-amber-ruffin.

18. Ugur Aytac, "Digital Domination: Social Media and Contestatory Democracy," *Political Studies* 72, no. 1 (2024): 7, https://journals.sagepub.com/doi/pdf/10.1177/00323217221096564.

19. "Netflix Removes Hasan Minhaj Comedy Episode after Saudi Demand," *BBC*, January 2, 2019, https://www.bbc.com/news/world-middle-east-46732786. In the compelling analysis of Joe Khalil and Mohamed Zayani, this ordeal reveals "a symbiotic relationship of mutual accommodation . . . whereby the global streaming company gains access to subscribers/audiences in exchange for loosening expectations about upholding unfettered speech and supporting artistic freedom." See Khalil and Zayani, "De-Territorialized Digital Capitalism and the Predicament of the Nation-State: Netflix in Arabia,"

Media, Culture & Society 43, no. 2 (2021): 201–218, https://doi.org/10.1177/0163443720932505.

20. "Shane Gillis: SNL Nicked by the Downs," *YouTube*, 0:00–0:08, uploaded by Zone07, February 26, 2024, https://www.youtube.com/watch?v=u31uLqxxAxo.

21. BBC, "Charlie Hebdo Receives Disputed Pen Award in New York," *BBC News*, May 6, 2015, https://www.bbc.com/news/world-us-canada-32601549.

INDEX

actively outraged, the, 17–18, 24, 45, 147, 149, 158, 169
Al-Bernamig, 118–126,
anti-Semitism, 7, 12, 39, 93–94, 96, 99, 147
apologies, 33, 42, 48, 52, 78–90, 108, 157; false, 49, 72
Arab Spring, 113, 119, 120, 123
assassin's veto, 89
audiences, 1, 10, 31, 36–38, 40–42, 47, 58, 68, 140, 158–160, 167–169; friendly, 28, 70, 72, 91; core, 32–33, 35, 126–127; majoritarian, 55, 57; volatility of, 3, 11, 18, 24, 85, 147, 164
audience participation, 17, 165, 168

Bharatiya Janata Party (BJP), 62–64, 69, 71, 73, 158, 163
blackface, 37–39, 42–43
Bollywood, 62–64, 68
BUSTOP TV, 129–131, 133–134, 136, 140, 141

cancel culture, 12, 31, 40–41, 43, 165
cancellation, 1, 12, 15, 18, 31, 41, 43, 48, 50–51, 53, 107, 119, 157, 165; effects of, 38–42, 44, 53–54, 165–166; self-, 29–31
caricatures, 75, 78, 80, 85–86, 88–89
Catholicism, 55, 81, 85, 87, 91, 96, 98, 109, 158
censorship, 5–6, 39, 74, 77, 91, 129, 136–138, 150–151
Chappelle, Dave, 12, 40, 69, 75, 158, 161, 164–166
Chappelle's Show, 17, 22, 27
Charbonnier, Stéphane (Charb), 75, 80, 83, 90–91
Charlie Hebdo (*Charlie*), 75–76, 81–94, 106, 154, 160, 168–169; caricatures of, 80, 147; cartoonists of, 82, 162, 166
Christianity, 31–33, 43, 65, 87–88, 108, 121,
Christian fundamentalists, 31, 151
CNN, 46, 48, 51, 114
coalition of the entertained, 12, 94, 109, 140, 157
coalition of the outraged, 11–12, 20, 24–25, 67, 74, 85, 157, 159
colonialism, 68, 123, 134
comedians, 3, 8–10, 12, 34, 40, 45, 50, 52, 71, 96, 107, 133, 142, 154; persecution of, 1, 13, 62–64, 126, 128–129, 137–140; provocations by, 26, 55, 69, 90, 157–158, 164–169
comedic controversy, 1–2, 7, 10, 49, 61, 75, 84, 94, 144
Consensus, The, 3–6, 8–10, 62, 144–145, 159, 161–163, 167, 169;

Consensus *(continued)*
attacks on, 12–13, 57–59, 86–87, 90–92, 116; Comedic Consensus, 5
conservative Christianity, 31–32
Cooper, Anderson, 46, 48
Coulibaly, Amedy, 84, 93, 104

Daily Show, The, 113, 115–120, 153
Das, Vir, 12, 54, 61–74, 155, 160, 162–165, 168
Demeaning Ditz, 34–35, 43
democracy, 4–6, 83, 94, 109, 114, 123, 139, 154–155
Denmark, 12, 58, 77–80, 82, 89, 166
Dieudonné M'bala M'bala, 12, 93–100, 102–107, 109, 147, 154, 155, 164–165

fake news, 13, 114–120, 123, 125–127
Far Right, 7, 81, 86, 94, 97, 109–110
Faruqi, Munwar, 62, 71, 73–74
First Amendment, 3, 47, 90–91, 152, 160, 168
free speech, 18, 57, 64, 68–69, 71, 103, 106–107, 114, 123, 129, 135–140, 150–152, 154–155, 158–159, 163, 167, 169; consensus of, 3, 6, 13, 61, 73, 88, 94, 125, 143, 163; laws on, 71, 74, 80–82, 87, 104;
fundamentalists, 1, 31, 83–84, 91, 151, 160

gay people, 9, 20–23, 25–27, 54, 95, 108, 142, 169
gender, 45, 55–57, 165
Gillis, Shane, 12, 18, 44–45, 50–55, 57, 161, 165, 167
Goldberg, Evan, 144, 150, 153–154
Gonyeti, 128–133, 136–138, 140–141, 154
Griffin, Kathy, 12, 18, 44–50, 54–58, 74, 162, 164–165
Guardians of Peace, 5, 143, 147, 150
Guild, The, 167–169

Hasmukh Complex, 62–63, 65, 72, 158, 167
hate speech, 5, 8, 103, 136, 147, 163
Hinduism, 61–62, 64–65, 73, 160
Hindutva, 62
Holocaust, 97, 99–100, 104, 106, 109
homophobia, 17, 19, 21–23, 42, 46, 56, 142
humorlessness scale, 159
hybrid regime, 129, 136, 139

illiberalism, 103, 116, 221
India, 12, 36, 58, 61–74, 116, 155, 158, 160, 161, 163
internet, 2, 13, 38, 61, 71, 89, 154, 164, 168
Interview, The, 5, 142–155, 162–163
Islam, 83, 121
Islamists, 12, 81, 91, 97, 120–124, 126, 158, 160; militant, 12, 82, 84, 89, 166
Islamophobia, 77, 83, 86, 91

#jenesuispascharlie, 85–86
#jesuischarlie, 85, 87, 93
"Jewface," 39
Jewish people, 32, 39–40, 75, 93, 95–100, 102–104, 108–110, 154
Jyllands-Posten, 76–81, 88–89, 92, 147, 160, 166

Kamra, Kunal, 62, 71–74, 161–162
Kim Jong-un, 6, 13, 142–145, 147–150, 153–155
Kureya, Samantha, 128, 130–132, 162, 165

laïcité, 104–106
Le Pen, Jean-Marie, 96, 109
Lenny Bruce, 3, 12, 63, 74, 157, 160, 164
LGBTQ community, 17–20, 28, 32, 49, 98, 107–108, 161, 166

Loi Gayssot, 104, 106
loop, the, 18–21, 157, 164, 165

MAGA, 47–48, 161, 163
Maher, Bill, 34, 56–57,
masculinity, 9, 21
meta, 12, 18, 30, 49, 53, 62, 126, 133, 157, 168; function of, 20, 36, 69, 81, 108, 164–165,
#metoo, 41, 168
minorities, 33–34, 36, 45, 56, 73, 83, 89, 106, 125
misogynism, 7, 21, 56
Mnangagwa, Emmerson, 137, 139–141
Modi, Narendra, 62–64, 71, 94, 163
moral injury, 84, 87, 88
Morsi, Mohamed, 120–122, 124–126, 158
Mubarak, Hosni, 119–121, 124
Mugabe, Robert, 134–135, 137
Muhammad, 12, 75–77, 80–84, 87, 89–90, 147

Netflix, 9, 19, 28–30, 53, 63, 69, 163
news parody, 115–116, 118, 120, 123, 125
North Korea, 5, 13, 134, 142–150, 152–154, 169

Obama, Barack, 5, 32, 47, 143, 149–152, 154–155, 162

persona drop, 18, 35, 28, 62, 157, 164
personae, 26–27, 31, 35–36, 38, 40, 42, 43, 164
political satire, 6, 115–116, 119, 123, 139, 147, 153, 162
political spectrum, 30, 86, 109
postcolonialism, 86–87, 93–94, 105–106, 109
Pre-Digital Liberal Free Speech Consensus, 3, 6, 94, 114, 143, 150, 158–159, 163, 167
propaganda, 7, 108, 138, 148
punching down, 12, 76, 86, 88–89, 158, 166–167
punching up, 12, 75–76, 88–89, 124, 158, 166

quenelles, 100, 104

racism, 21–22, 34–35, 43, 68, 82–83, 86–87, 95–96, 103, 134
rape, 30, 33, 42–43, 66, 162
religious conservatives, 4, 31, 91
right-wing comedy, 6, 7, 116
Rock, Chris, 1, 2, 40
Rose, Flemming, 77, 89, 92

satire, 1–2, 11, 35, 41, 72, 131, 141, 147, 153–154, 162
Saturday Night Live (SNL), 17, 50, 52–55, 115, 159
secularism, 4, 94, 105–106, 167
self-cancellation, 29–31, 39
self-depreciation, 46, 54, 80–81
Silverman, Sarah, 12, 18, 30–43, 49–50, 58, 161, 166
Sisi, Abdel Fattah al-, 121–122, 124–125, 158
slurs, 22–24, 33–34, 36, 50, 54, 142
social media, 2, 13, 36, 38, 44, 72, 78, 89, 166; communication with, 6, 23, 27, 56
sociology of comedy, 10, 12, 158
Stewart, Jon, 115–119
suicide, 6, 8, 20, 49, 57, 74, 77, 101, 164
Supreme Court, 5, 9, 72, 73, 161

terrorists, 1, 68, 70, 75, 82, 84, 85–85, 88, 90, 93, 104, 124
transgender people, 17, 19, 27–28
transphobia, 17–23, 19, 20–21
Trump, Donald, 44–49, 55, 57–58, 71, 150, 155, 163
Twitter, 20, 24, 32, 44, 47, 50, 56, 67

victims, 7, 42, 53, 56, 66, 89, 97, 99

Youssef, Bassem, 13, 113–115, 117–127, 154, 158, 160, 162
YouTube, 8, 53, 61, 71–73, 104, 119, 131, 151–152

Zimbabwe, 13, 63, 116, 128, 129, 130–139, 141, 165
Zimbabwe African National Union-Patriotic Front (ZANU-PF), 134–135, 137, 141
Zionism, 79, 98–101